Register Variation Online

While other books focus on special online registers, such as tweets or texting, no previous study describes the full range of everyday registers found on the searchable web. These registers are the documents that readers encounter every time they do a Google search; registers like news reports, product reviews, travel blogs, discussion forums, FAQs, etc. Based on analysis of a large, near-random corpus of web documents, this monograph provides comprehensive situational, lexical, and grammatical descriptions of those registers. Beginning with a coding of each document in the corpus, the description identifies the registers that are especially common on the searchable web versus those that are less commonly found. Multidimensional analysis is used to describe the overall patterns of linguistic variation among web registers, while the second half of the book provides an in-depth description of each individual register, including analyses of situational contexts and communicative purposes, together with the typical lexical and grammatical characteristics associated with those contexts.

Douglas Biber is Regents' Professor of English (Applied Linguistics) at Northern Arizona University. His research efforts have focused on corpus linguistics, English grammar, and register variation (in English and cross-linguistic; synchronic and diachronic). He has published over 220 research articles and twenty-three books and monographs, including primary research studies as well as textbooks.

Jesse Egbert is Assistant Professor in the Applied Linguistics program at Northern Arizona University. He specializes in corpus-based research on register variation, particularly academic writing and online language, and methodological issues in quantitative linguistic research. He has published more than thirty research articles in journals such as the *Journal of English Linguistics*, the *International Journal of Corpus Linguistics*, and *Corpus Linguistics and Linguistic Theory*.

Register Variation Online

Douglas Biber

Northern Arizona University

Jesse Egbert

Northern Arizona University

CAMBRIDGE
UNIVERSITY PRESS

CAMBRIDGE
UNIVERSITY PRESS

University Printing House, Cambridge CB2 8BS, United Kingdom

One Liberty Plaza, 20th Floor, New York, NY 10006, USA

477 Williamstown Road, Port Melbourne, VIC 3207, Australia

314–321, 3rd Floor, Plot 3, Splendor Forum, Jasola District Centre,
New Delhi – 110025, India

79 Anson Road, #06-04/06, Singapore 079906

Cambridge University Press is part of the University of Cambridge.

It furthers the University's mission by disseminating knowledge in the pursuit of
education, learning, and research at the highest international levels of excellence.

www.cambridge.org
Information on this title: www.cambridge.org/9781107122161
DOI: 10.1017/9781316388228

© Douglas Biber and Jesse Egbert 2018

First published 2018

Printed and bound in Great Britain by Clays Ltd, Elcograf S.p.A.

A catalogue record for this publication is available from the British Library.

Library of Congress Cataloging-in-Publication Data

Names: Biber, Douglas, author. | Egbert, Jesse, 1985- author.
Title: Register variation online / Douglas Biber, Jesse Egbert.
Description: Cambridge, United Kingdom ; New York, NY : Cambridge University
    Press, 2018. | Includes bibliographical references and index.
Identifiers: LCCN 2017060046 | ISBN 9781107122161 (hardback)
Subjects: LCSH: Register (Linguistics) | Context (Linguistics) | Language
    and the Internet.
Classification: LCC P302.815 .B537 2018 | DDC 306.44—dc23
LC record available at https://lccn.loc.gov/2017060046

ISBN 978-1-107-12216-1 Hardback

Contents

Contents

Figures and Screenshots

Figures

Screenshots

Tables

1 Introduction

1.1 The Expanding Web

It is obvious that computers have fundamentally changed the way we communicate. But the history of that evolution is less well-known. To a large extent, the use of computers as tools for communication can be traced back to the invention of email in the early 1970s. However, computer-mediated communication took decades to become widely available. Given the ubiquitous presence of computers in modern households and our present-day reliance on computers for obtaining information and interacting with others, it is hard to imagine a world where communication was not mediated by computers. However, even fifteen years ago, such forms of communication were relatively rare.

Email communication between two computers was invented in 1972. However, for several years, email communication was restricted to military users connected to the ARPANET. As the ARPANET morphed into the Internet in the early 1980s, it became possible for academic professionals to communicate via email. During this period, university faculty and researchers had widespread access to mainframe computers connected to the Internet, in contrast to the general public, which had much more limited access to computers. However, despite this fact, most academic professionals continued to rely mostly on surface mail for communication well into the 1980s. Instant Messaging (IM) and chatrooms were developed in the 1980s, enabling real-time interactions mediated by computers. These modes of communication were useful for users within an institution (connected to a single mainframe computer), but they had little impact on the ways in which people communicated more generally.

However, in the early 1990s, the rate of change began to accelerate. Personal computers became more widely available, and the World Wide Web became publicly accessible in 1993. At that time, it is estimated that there were only c. 130 websites on the web. But, as Table 1.1 shows, the web has exploded since then, both with respect to the number of users[1] and the number of websites.[2]

Both the number of users and the number of Websites continue to increase right up to the present day. However, the two developments are following

Table 1.1. *Growth of the World Wide Web; 2000–2017*

Year	Number of web users	Number of websites
2000	413,000,000	17,000,000
2005	1,000,000,000	65,000,000
2010	2,000,000,000	207,000,000
2015	3,200,000,000	863,000,000
2017	4,100,000,000	1,767,000,000

Table 1.2. *Growth of the World Wide Web expressed as proportional increases; 2000–2017*

Years	Percentage increase in the number of:	
	web users	websites
2000 to 2005	142%	282%
2005 to 2010	100%	218%
2010 to 2015	60%	317%
2015 to 2017	28%	105%

different trends, as shown in Table 1.2: The number of users more than doubled from 2000 to 2005 and then doubled again from 2005 to 2010. In the last seven years, the number of users continued to increase, but at a much slower rate. In contrast, the number of Websites continued to expand exponentially up until 2015, with an indication of a plateau being reached only in the last two years.

The number of documents found on the web is even more astronomical because most websites contain multiple pages (with most pages including multiple documents). For example, it has been estimated that Google has indexed over 50 billion web pages.[3]

In contrast, the two largest libraries in the world – the British Library and the American Library of Congress – each have around 170 million cataloged items (including books, manuscripts, maps, newspapers, magazines, prints and drawings, music scores, and patents).[4] To put these numbers into perspective, if each document in the British Library was about 1 foot in length, and those documents were all placed end-to-end, they would stretch around the globe once, plus the distance from London to New York. But, if each document on the indexed web was printed out and was about 1 foot in length, and those documents were all placed end-to-end, they would stretch around the globe over 3,800 times!

As a result, any end-user with a personal computer now has direct access to a mind-boggling repository of information, many times larger than the collections in the best libraries of the world. It further turns out that many of the documents collected by major libraries are copyright protected and therefore not available on the public web (see discussion below). Thus, not only is the web many times larger than collections of printed documents, it is also to a large extent nonoverlapping, as the web includes billions of documents that are not available in public libraries.

The web is only a small part of the Internet. The web consists of a system of Internet servers that support documents formatted in HTML (HyperText Markup Language). These HTML documents are linked to other documents, and thus comprise a "web." The Internet includes many additional types of communication that are not part of the public web. By 2000, Internet service providers often offered access to webmail applications as part of their standard packages, making communication through computer networks accessible to the general public. Mobile phone devices were also becoming much more popular and accessible during this same period, and the first text messages were sent in the early 1990s. Social media sites like Myspace and Facebook were first developed in the 2000s and witnessed a remarkable boom in popularity in subsequent years. For example, Facebook was developed for students at Harvard University in 2004, but only five years later (in 2009) it boasted 350 million users. By 2015, this number had increased to more than 1.5 billion users.[5] Many other innovations in online and computer-mediated communication have occurred over the last ten years, such as the development and rise in popularity of Skype and Twitter. As a result, young adults can hardly conceive of a situation where it is not possible to communicate with virtually anyone in the world through multiple channels mediated by computers and technology – and it is even becoming increasingly difficult for older generations to remember such a time.

1.2   The Kinds of Texts Found on the Web

Given these remarkable social and technological changes, it is no surprise that linguists have been intrigued by the possibility of linguistic innovation associated with these new modes of communication. As a result, there have been numerous publications devoted to the study of language on the Internet. Some of the most influential of these include Crystal's 2001 book *Language and the Internet* and Baron's 2008 book *Always On*. There have also been numerous research articles on this topic, and even entire academic journals such as *Language@Internet, The Journal of Internet and Information Systems*, and *The Journal of Computer-Mediated Communication*.

For the most part, these publications have focused on the "special" registers associated with the Internet and computer-mediated communication generally. These are registers that have emerged on the Internet, with no clear counterparts in print media. They include email messages, IM messages, chatroom interactions, interactions in online virtual worlds (MUDs, or Multi-User Dungeons), blogs, discussion forums, social-media postings, etc. These special registers emerged during the 1980s and 1990s, rapidly changing the repertoire of registers available in English (and most other languages around the world). These are the registers that we typically notice when we think of the web, and judging from the coverage of previous books and articles, it would be easy to believe that most of the web consists of these special kinds of texts.

However, even casual surfing on the web quickly indicates that this is not the case. Using a web search engine to identify documents related to almost any topic will return thousands, or even millions, of hits, but most of those documents are not instances of the "special" registers mentioned above. It is not obvious, though, what registers these other documents actually do represent.

Unfortunately, there is no simple way to determine the contents of the web. In Chapter 3, we return to this research issue, applying scientific corpus-based methods to explore the composition of the web. In the present chapter, though, we take a much simpler approach: simply illustrating the types of documents returned by web search engines.

Search engines employ massive databases with indexes of the web documents that are publicly available. It is important to note that the results returned by a search engine do not provide a random sample of web documents. Rather, a search engine employs algorithms that try to prioritize the particular documents that the end-user would most want to see. The normal end-user can employ these search engines to provide a window on the contents of the web. That window is tinted in a way that the search engine chooses: it will look at the particular landscape that the search engine chooses. But the view from that window can still be surprising and not meet our prior expectations of what we expect to see. Most surprisingly, it turns out that "special" web registers are not prevalent in most web searches. Advertisements are also not the most common type of document returned by most web searches. Rather, it appears that the most prevalent registers found on the web are various types of informational documents and news reports.

To illustrate this, we carried out a Google search on the word *horse*, which returned a total of 744 million hits. We coded the first five pages of returned hits (a total of fifty-eight documents), as shown in Table 1.3. The search results summarized in Table 1.3 are typical of many web searches: mostly informational documents, with comparatively few "special" documents and surprisingly few advertisements. Only eight of these fifty-eight documents were from websites for shopping, where the user could buy horses, horse feed, saddles, bridles, or health care services. Surprisingly, even these commercial documents were not overt advertisements. Rather, they mostly presented lists of items/services for sale, with descriptions of the items and the process for purchasing them. In addition, five other documents associated with commercial sites simply presented

Table 1.3. *Register categories for the first five pages of hits (fifty-eight documents) returned by a Google search on the word* horse

Register category	Number of documents	% of total
Information about an institution or association	19	33
Informational documents	11	19
News reports	6	10
Commercial sites	8	14
Informational documents associated with commercial sites	5	8
How-to/advice documents	2	4
Blogs	1	2
Discussion forums	1	2
Not related to the animal "horse"	5	8
TOTAL	58	100

information about horses. Three of these documents gave tips for horse breeding, training, nutrition, health care, etc. (*Horse-Journal.com*; *horsechannel.com*; *thehorse.com*), while a fourth document presented extensive information about the Chinese Zodiac Year of the Horse, sponsored by *travelchinaguide.com*.

In addition to the informational documents associated with commercial sites, the search on "horse" returned nineteen informational documents about a horse association or institution (e.g., the American Quarter Horse Association; American Horse Council; Arabian Horse Association; Kentucky Horse Council; Unwanted Horse Coalition; University of Minnesota Horse Program; Luckyorphanshorserescue.org; an association to preserve Idaho wild horses). Another eleven documents simply presented information about horses. Some of these were general encyclopedia articles or dictionary definitions, but others were more specialized (e.g., "horse facts" from National Geographic; "breeds of horses" from Oklahoma State University; research-based information about horse training and health from eXtension.org; a discussion of the origin of horses from quart.us; and information about fossil horses from the Florida Museum of Natural History). News reports can be considered as a more specialized type of informational document. In some cases, the news reports focused on current events (e.g., the outcome of a horse race). However, other news documents in the search provided in-depth discussion of a topic (e.g., the demise of wild horses, or "the ugly truth about horse racing"), making them more informational than narrative reportage. Beyond that, there were a few advice documents (relating to the care or training of horses), one blog posting relating to horses, and one discussion forum.

Of course, it is not possible to evaluate the composition of the web from a single search and only fifty-eight hits. Different words are associated with different aspects of society so we might predict very different types of documents corresponding to those words. But one surprising fact documented in the following chapters is the prevalence of information and news documents, regardless of the particular word or phrase being searched.

For example, we initially wrote this chapter during the Christmas holiday season, when the iPhone 6 was an especially hot item. It is thus reasonable to expect that a web search on "iPhone" would return mostly advertisements or documents associated with commercial sites. Surprisingly, that was not the case. Advertisements and commercial sites accounted for only 10 percent of the total hits for "iPhone." In contrast, news reports accounted for over 50 percent of the documents returned by this search. In addition, there were purely informational documents and numerous reviews, which can be regarded as a special type of informational document that provides a personal evaluation of a product. The overall predominance of informational documents in our search on "iPhone" was similar to what we saw with our search for "horse," with the primary differences being a predominance of news reports and reviews in the case of "iPhone" versus a high proportion of institutional documents and purely informational documents in the case of "horse."

Searching on other terms can result in even higher proportions of news documents and/or purely informational documents. For example, nearly 80 percent of the documents returned by a search on "Syria" (in December 2015) were news reports, including several in-depth discussions of the country or various influential groups of people in the country. Purely informational documents and editorials were also relatively common in this search. In contrast, there was only one blog posting from a university professor and no advertisements or documents related to commercial sites. At the other extreme, a search on the word "electron" returns few news reports but an extremely high proportion of informational documents.

As noted above, using this approach to explore the composition of the web is problematic, because search engines employ algorithms that prioritize documents considered important to the end user. As a result, personal documents (like opinion blogs or discussion-forum advice) might be less likely to appear in the top search results than informational or news documents from major public sources. But those documents certainly do exist on the web. For example, a Google search on "blogs about horses" returned 18.5 million hits, and a Google search on "blogs about Syria" returned fifty-five million hits! Many of these are Personal Blogs, a type of written document that has no direct counterpart in preinternet history. However, a perusal of these web pages shows that a much larger number of them are opinionated informational documents from a news agency or some other institutional site.

1.3   Situating the Searchable Web Relative to Other Discourse Domains

The present book is a description of register variation on the publicly "searchable web": the part of the Internet that all end-users can access with search engines. But there is a very large segment of the web that is not publicly accessible, sometimes referred to as the "deep web." The websites on the deep web are usually password-protected (and sometimes require a fee), associated with institutions, corporations, and publishing companies. For example, institutions, government agencies, and businesses distribute numerous memos, technical reports, and other documents internally to employees on their own networks. Publishing companies offer documents for a fee, including e-books and research articles associated with academic journals. Although it is more difficult to carry out linguistic research on documents in the deep web, personal experience with them indicates that they contain a much greater prevalence of informational documents than the searchable web generally.

In addition, the searchable web does not include the extended Internet used for private communication. Many of the new registers that have been the primary focus of recent linguistic work belong to this domain. These include recently developed registers like Facebook posts and Tweets, as well as registers with a longer history such as email messages and Instant Messages. As documented in books like Crystal (2001) and Baron (2008), these registers arose out of unique communicative circumstances, and as a result, they have developed highly distinctive linguistic characteristics.

The focus of the present book, however, is on those registers that comprise the publicly searchable web. Although they have been generally disregarded in previous linguistic research, these registers have a central place in modern society. A simple reflection of that fact is the rise of the verb *to Google*, referring to the extremely common practice of using the Google search engine to obtain information from the web. Surprisingly, though, we know little about the linguistic characteristics of the registers that result from these searches.

Part of the reason for this neglect is the perception that the informational documents found on the web are the same as informational documents found in print-media, and thus there is nothing new to be learned from a linguistic analysis of those registers. However, this perception is misleading in several respects. In the first place, we simply do not know if web registers are the "same" as print-media registers, until we actually carry out a comprehensive linguistic analysis of web documents. In fact, the descriptions in the following chapters show that this perception is far from accurate. Rather, there are numerous informational web registers that are unlike the print-media registers that we normally encounter. The case study above, on "horse," illustrates this pattern. For example, informational documents associated with a commercial site (see our full discussion in Chapters 6 and 7) are a type of text not normally encountered outside of the web. On the surface, these documents have the primary purpose of conveying information. They are not overtly persuasive, and they certainly do not fit our stereotypes for advertising. However, in many cases, these documents also have an underlying purpose of convincing the reader to make a purchase. This register is relatively pervasive on the web but has no obvious counterpart in the print-media domain.

A related problem, though, is largely methodological rather than a reflection of true differences between the print-media versus web domains. Most linguistic descriptions of print-media registers in the last 30 years have applied the analytical framework of corpus linguistics and have been based on large corpora of texts. The text categories used for the construction of those corpora have had a certain face validity, leading to the perception that linguistic analyses of those corpora fully represent the domain of print-media registers. A more careful reflection, however, quickly reveals that that is far from the case. Most written corpora to date have focused almost exclusively on published texts: novels, academic books and research articles, nonfiction books, magazine articles, and newspapers. In contrast, the population of printed texts that are not officially "published" has been almost entirely overlooked in previous corpora. Those texts include the thousands of informational brochures, reports, and documents found in businesses, medical, professional, and government offices, schools, etc. As a result, previous studies of register variation based on available corpora have described only a part of the entire population of print-media registers.

It turns out that the population of texts available on the searchable web is to a large extent complementary to the population of texts represented in current corpora. As noted above, present-day corpora mostly represent commercially published written texts. In contrast, the searchable web is largely composed of unpublished texts. That is, commercially published texts – like fictional novels, academic research articles, or even many current magazine articles – belong to the domain of the deep web and are not freely available through public web searches. As a result, the sample of written texts available in public libraries and bookstores is mostly non-overlapping with the population of texts available on the searchable web.

Thus, previous descriptions of linguistic variation among written registers, based on available corpora, differ in two major respects from an analysis of web registers: (1) they have focused on print-media registers rather than registers available in an electronic format on the web; and (2) perhaps more importantly, they have focused on traditional published registers (e.g., novels, books, or academic articles) rather than unpublished registers (e.g., informational brochures, instructional pamphlets, product reviews, or personal letters). The present book, by focusing on the full range of documents found on the searchable web, provides a first step toward filling this gap.

Finally, the study of discourse from the searchable web is theoretically important because it causes us to rethink traditional notions of "register." Since the 1960s, written corpora have been organized in terms of major textual categories, which we refer to as "registers." Those categories have been treated as if they are relatively uncontroversial: Published print-media texts usually have overt external indications of register, and thus it has not proven difficult to classify individual texts. For example, newspaper articles are published in newspapers; magazine articles are published in magazines; academic articles are published in academic research journals; novels are published as books and explicitly claim to be fictional; etc. Even specific registers often have external indicators. For example, news reportage articles are published on the front page of a newspaper (and in the "International" and "National" sections of the newspaper); sports reports are printed in the "Sports" section of the newspaper; editorials and letters to the editor are published on the editorial pages of the newspaper. These external criteria are usually sufficient for classifying written texts into register categories, and, as a result, it has not been considered to be problematic for discourse analysts (and corpus compilers) to identify the register of individual texts.

In contrast, the documents returned by a web search often have little or no indication of register category. For example, the Google search on "horses" described above returned millions of documents. Some of these documents have external indicators that help to identify their register, such as an encyclopedia article from Wikipedia, a newspaper story from the *New York Times*, or a magazine article from the *Atlantic*. However, the register category of many other documents is more nebulous, such as: an informational page about horses from the *Oklahoma State University Horse Project*; a page giving "Fun horse facts for kids" from *Sciencekids.co.nz*; a short informational text about horses from *PBS*; a guide to equine health care from *thehorse.com*; and descriptions of horse associations (e.g., the *Arabian Horse Association*, the *American Paint Horse Association*). Such web documents are familiar to any end-user of the web. But unlike most published print-media texts, the register category of these web documents is not obvious.

Observations like these lead to one of the central themes of the linguistic descriptions in the present book: that most web documents are not "pure" instances of a particular register, and that even the register categories themselves might sometimes be understood as "hybrids" that serve multiple communicative purposes (combining narrative, informational, opinionated, and how-to/advice purposes in different ways and to differing extents). By extension, these observations raise general theoretical questions about the categorizations used in previous corpus-based studies of print-media registers, raising the possibility that a hybrid perspective applied to the domain of print-media registers might also be productive. While such analyses are well beyond the scope of the present book, they do raise interesting theoretical questions regarding the notion of "register." We thus return to these issues in the concluding chapter of the book.

1.4   Overview of the Book

As noted in the sections above, the present book is innovative in three key respects:

1. It focuses on analysis of the full range of registers found on the public searchable web, rather than being restricted to a description of a few specialized Internet registers (like Tweets, Facebook posts, etc.).
2. It focuses on freely available written registers, which can be considered unpublished in the traditional sense. This focus is in marked contrast to previous corpus-based studies of written registers in the print-media domain, which have focused almost exclusively on commercially published written registers.
3. It recognizes the existence of hybrid registers, and undertakes analyses that explore different ways in which web registers are hybrid, with respect to both their situational characteristics and their linguistic characteristics.

Our linguistic descriptions are empirical, based on analysis of a large corpus of web documents: a near random sample of c. 48,000 documents from across the entire spectrum of the publicly searchable web. Chapter 2 of the book describes our methods for constructing and coding this corpus. In the initial stages of the project, the corpus consisted simply of web documents, with no indication of the register categories for those documents. In fact, we began with no preconceptions of what those register categories would be. Then, using crowdsourcing techniques, with ratings from actual end-users of the web, we developed a taxonomy of online register categories, coding each document in our corpus for its register. The taxonomy and the process of coding are described in detail in Chapter 2.

In Chapter 3, we describe the register composition of our corpus as an indication of the composition of the searchable web more generally. Eight general registers are distinguished, with numerous specific sub-registers within the general categories. We describe the relative frequency of each register category in our corpus and further introduce the possibility of hybrid registers on the web.

In Chapter 4, we move on to the overall linguistic description of the patterns of register variation, applying Multidimensional analysis. The chapter begins with an overview of the methodological framework of Multidimensional analysis, and then describes the nine linguistic "dimensions" that emerged in that analysis, coupled with descriptions of the similarities and differences among web registers with respect to each dimension.

Building on that foundation, Chapters 5–8 provide more detailed linguistic descriptions of the major registers found on the searchable web: narrative web registers (Chapter 5); opinion, advice, and persuasion web registers (Chapter 6); informational descriptions, explanations, and procedures (Chapter 7); and oral web registers (Chapter 8). These chapters document the range of specific sub-registers within each of these general categories, and describe the distinctive situational, grammatical, and lexical characteristics of those sub-registers.

Finally, Chapter 9 concludes the book with a synthesis of our research findings, a description of ongoing and future research in this area, and a discussion of the theoretical implications of this research for studies of register variation in other discourse domains. In particular, we take up the theoretical issue of how register can be investigated in a continuous space of variation. The study of registers on the searchable web forces such a perspective, but we argue in Chapter 9 that this perspective might be equally informative for the study of registers in other discourse domains. Thus, it is our hope that the present book will prove useful both for its detailed linguistic descriptions of web registers as well as its theoretical discussions of issues relating to the discourse construct of "register."

Notes

1. www.internetlivestats.com/total-number-of-websites/.
2. www.pewinternet.org/2014/03/11/world-wide-web-timeline/; https://www.internet-worldstats.com/stats.htm.
3. https://google.com/insidesearch/howsearchworks/thestory/; www.worldwidewebsize.com/.
4. https://en.wikipedia.org/wiki/List_of_largest_libraries.
5. www.statista.com/statistics/264810/number-of-monthly-active-facebook-users-worldwide/.

2 Corpus and Methods

The main goal of this book is to present a comprehensive analysis of online language that accounts for the full range of registers found on the searchable web. As we described in the first chapter, there are many methodological challenges associated with this undertaking. We begin this chapter by describing the methods we used to collect a representative corpus of documents from the searchable web. We then describe the methods we used to manually classify those documents into register categories. Finally, we describe the procedures used to identify and count a wide range of linguistic features in each text in the corpus.

2.1   Corpus Collection

As discussed in the previous chapter, the World Wide Web contains an immense collection of written documents that represents an extremely wide range of registers, including everything from well-established written registers (e.g., news articles and fiction) to novel electronic registers (e.g., question/answer forums and Personal Blogs). Despite this wealth of publicly available linguistic data, most corpora of web documents do not actually represent the types of texts typically encountered on the web. Rather, in most of these corpora the total population of web documents under investigation is artificially restricted. The web documents in these corpora are sampled from register categories that are determined on an *a priori* basis. So, for example, a sub-corpus for blogs is sampled from websites identified as blogs, FAQs are sampled from websites identified as FAQs, etc. As a result, the total population under investigation – i.e., the total range of variation represented by the corpus – is artificially restricted to samples from these few relatively well-defined register categories. This is dramatically different from the actual population of documents found on the web. A typical web search is not restricted to particular registers, search engines do not provide a way to target particular registers, and it turns out that many web documents do not fit tidily into any of the predetermined register categories. Santini (2007) refers to unconstrained web searches as explorations of the "open web" (p. 37). While the restricted approach can be justified because it is more feasible, the practical value is less clear: a normal web search is sampled from the entire "open" web, and thus documents can be instances of any register found on the web. In this section we describe the design and construction of the Corpus of Online Registers of English (CORE), a large corpus that represents the full range of web documents and register categories on the open, searchable web.

The web documents in CORE were sampled from the "General" component[1] of the Corpus of Global Web-based English (GloWbE).[2] GloWbE was designed to represent the English documents encountered in typical web searches in twenty different English-speaking countries. The GloWbE corpus contains 1.9 billion words in 1.8 million web documents, collected in November and December 2012. The web documents included in GloWbE were selected from the results of Google searches of highly frequent English 3-grams (i.e., the most common 3-grams occurring in *COCA*; e.g., *is not the, and from the*). N-grams were used to minimize the bias from the preferences built into Google searches. For each n-gram query, 800–1,000 links were saved (i.e., between eighty and a hundred Google results pages). Many previous web-as-corpus studies have used similar methods with n-grams as search engine seeds (see, e.g., Baroni & Bernardini, 2004; Baroni et al., 2009; Sharoff, 2005, 2006). It is important to acknowledge that no Google search is truly random. Thus, even searches on 3-grams consisting of only function words (e.g., *is not the*) will to some extent be processed based on choices and predictions built into the Google search engine. However, selecting hundreds of documents for each of these n-grams that consist of function words rather than content words minimizes that influence.

To create the representative sample of web pages, we randomly extracted 53,424 URLs from the GloWbE Corpus. The sample of web documents included in CORE was limited to web pages from five geographic regions: the United States, the United Kingdom, Canada, Australia, and New Zealand. Because the ultimate objective of our project is to describe the lexico-grammatical characteristics of web documents, any page with fewer than seventy-five words of text was excluded from this sample. The average length of texts in the corpus is around 1,000 words.

To create the actual corpus of documents used for our study, we downloaded the web documents associated with the URLs from our Google searches using HTTrack.[3] However, because there was a seven-month gap between the initial identification of URLs and the actual downloading of documents, c. 8 percent of the documents ($n = 3,713$) were no longer available (i.e., they were linked to websites that no longer existed). This high attrition rate reflects the extremely dynamic nature of the universe of documents on the web.

Our ultimate goal in the project is to carry out linguistic analyses of Internet texts from the range of web registers. For this reason, 1,140 URLs were excluded from subsequent analysis because they consisted mostly of photos or graphics. The final version of CORE contains 48,571 documents and nearly fifty-four million words. To prepare the corpus for grammatical tagging and linguistic analyses, non-textual material was removed from all web pages (HTML scrubbing and boilerplate removal) using JusText.[4] In the next section we describe the process of manually classifying each of these web documents into register categories.

2.2   Register Classification

As described in Chapter 1, the process of classifying web documents into register categories is difficult due to the absence of external indicators (such as publication in a printed newspaper or journal), lack of agreement about the register categories that exist on the web, and the prevalence of fuzzy register boundaries and hybrid registers. As a result, most previous attempts to reliably classify web documents into register categories have achieved only limited success (Rosso, 2008).

When we started to work on this project, we similarly assumed that end-users would be able to directly identify the register category of web texts based on their communicative purposes and other situational characteristics. We began with the seventy-eight register/genre categories identified through the wiki-based collaboration of web-as-corpus experts[5] (see the discussion in Rehm et al., 2008). We also surveyed a random sample of 200 web pages to identify additional register categories that were not represented on that list. Several of these categories were subsequently combined to produce a more manageable list of around ten to fifteen register distinctions.

We then undertook a series of pilot studies to test the extent to which end-users could reliably assign web documents to these register categories (see Egbert et al., 2015).

During this pilot research stage, we used Mechanical Turk (MTurk), an Amazon-based crowdsourcing site, to recruit and pay raters who were actual end-users of the web. This was an important innovation, which allowed us to collect massive amounts of data in a relatively quick and cost-effective way. Previous research has investigated whether results from MTurk workers are comparable to data collected using other methods, showing that there are no significant differences between MTurk workers and participants recruited from other populations (Paolacci et al., 2010; Suri & Watts, 2011). Especially for the coding tasks required for our project, we found MTurk to be an excellent means of recruiting participants and collecting data for the classification tasks.

Overall, though, the attempt to code documents directly for their register categories proved problematic, in some cases achieving agreement rates below

50 percent. As a result, we shifted to a completely different methodological approach, modifying the classification rubric into a decision tree based on the full set of relevant situational characteristics. This allowed users to focus on individual situational parameters, rather than trying to directly identify a register category. This change led to the introduction of a register hierarchy in the framework, with each situational parameter identifying a register category at a greater degree of specificity. We further added lists of specific sub-registers as an additional level of specificity, once a rater had narrowed the situational characteristics of a text down to the register level. Table 2.1 summarizes the major decisions as well as the particular register categories included in the framework.

At the top level, we asked users to make a binary decision about the mode of production:

1. Internet texts that originated in the spoken mode (e.g., transcripts of speeches or interviews);
2. Internet texts that originated in the written mode.

Then, for the written texts, we asked users to distinguish between interactive discussions (e.g., discussion forums) versus non-interactive Internet texts. Even this simple distinction is often not clear-cut on the web, because authored web documents are often followed by responses from readers in the form of comments. We thus made it clear to coders that "written interactive discussions" are distinct from written documents followed by reader comments, and that coders would be able to note the existence of reader comments for non-interactive texts later in the process.

For the first two general categories above (spoken and interactive written), we subsequently asked coders to identify a specific sub-register (e.g., spoken interview, discussion forum; see Table 2.1). Users could also select "Other" if the document did not fit clearly into one of the existing sub-register categories.

For the third general category – written non-interactive Internet texts – we asked users to distinguish among six general registers based on communicative purpose:

- to narrate or report on EVENTS (News Report/Blog, Sports Report, Personal/Diary Blog, Historical Article, Short Story, Novel, Biographical Story/History, Magazine Article, Travel Blog, etc.)
- to describe or explain INFORMATION (Description-of-a-person, Description-of-a-place/Product/Organization, FAQs about Information, Research Article, Informational Blog, Technical Report, Legal Terms and Conditions, etc.)
- to express OPINIONS (Opinion Blog, Review, Advice, Advertisement, Religious Blog, Letter-to-the Editor, Self-Help, etc.)

- to describe or explain FACTS-WITH-INTENT-TO-PERSUADE (Editorial, Description with Intent to Sell, Persuasive Article or Essay, etc.)
- to explain HOW-TO or INSTRUCTIONS (FAQ, Recipes, Technical Support, etc.)
- to express oneself through LYRICS (Song Lyrics, Poem, Prayer, etc.)

After a user had selected one of the general register categories, we asked them to identify the specific sub-register and to provide additional information about the existence of reader comments or quoted material in the document. The full list of general register and specific sub-register distinctions in our framework is listed in Table 2.1.

2.2.1 Classification of Hybrid Texts

In our later pilot studies, we began using multiple coders, and as a result, we realized that we could develop a bottom-up approach to identify hybrid register categories. In other words, user classifications of web documents that achieved low reliability were often evenly split between two categories, and some of these "hybrid" categories emerged repeatedly across a sample of texts. The existence of hybrid web texts was something we had anticipated based on the findings of previous research (see, e.g., Santini, 2007, 2008; Vidulin et al., 2009), but there had not been previously tested methods to identify the particular hybrid categories commonly found on the web. By employing four raters in our later rounds of coding, we found that we had a method to identify common hybrid categories (e.g., narrative–description), where two raters would agree on one category, and the other two raters would agree on a second category.

2.2.2 Applying the User-based Classification Approach

Given the encouraging results of our final pilot studies, which applied the hierarchical decision tree represented in Table 2.1, we proceeded to the analysis of the full CORE. MTurk was used for all steps in the coding. Before a rater could participate in the task, they were required to complete a seven-minute interactive tutorial video. They were then required to classify a practice web document with clear situational characteristics. Classification of this practice web document was checked for accuracy before raters were approved and awarded the qualification necessary to participate in the rating process. Each time the raters accepted a classification task, they were given a URL and a link to the Google Survey that required them to enter their unique MTurk Worker ID, the URL for the web document, and a unique URL identification number.

Table 2.1. *Visual representation of the key situational distinctions made in the final register framework*

Text	Text can be rated								Cannot rate*
Mode	Originally written							Originally spoken	
Participants	Single author or coauthors (non-interactive)						Multiple participants (interactive)	Spoken	
Communicative Purpose	To narrate events	To describe information	To express opinion	To use facts to persuade	To explain instructions	To express lyrically			
General Register	Narrative	Info. description/explanation	Opinion	Info. persuasion	How-to/instruct.	Lyrical	Interactive Discussion	Spoken	
Sub-registers	– News Report – Sports Report – Personal Blog – Historical Article – Travel Blog – Short Story – Novel – Biography – Magazine Article – Obituary – Memoir	– Description-of-a-thing – Informational blog – Description-of-a-person – Research article – Abstract – FAQ (informational) – Legal terms – Course materials – Encyclopedia article – Technical report	– Opinion blog – Review – Religious blog/sermon – Advice – Letter-to-editor – Self-help – Advertise	– Description-with-intent-to-sell – Persuasive article – Editorial	– How-to – Recipe – Instruction – FAQ (How-to) – Technical support	– Lyrics – Poem – Prayer	– Discussion forum – QA forum – Reader responses	– Interview – Transcript – Speech – Script	
Reader comments?									
Spoken quotes?									

*"Not enough text (mostly photos or graphics)" or "Site not found."

17

The participants then proceeded through a series of two to five screens, requesting information about the text on the web document they were to classify (see Figure 2.1 for a screenshot of the initial screen). A total of 908 raters participated in the task by rating at least one URL. Each rater was paid $0.11 for each URL that they classified. Using this process, all 48,147 web documents in CORE were coded for their register characteristics, with each text being coded by four different raters.

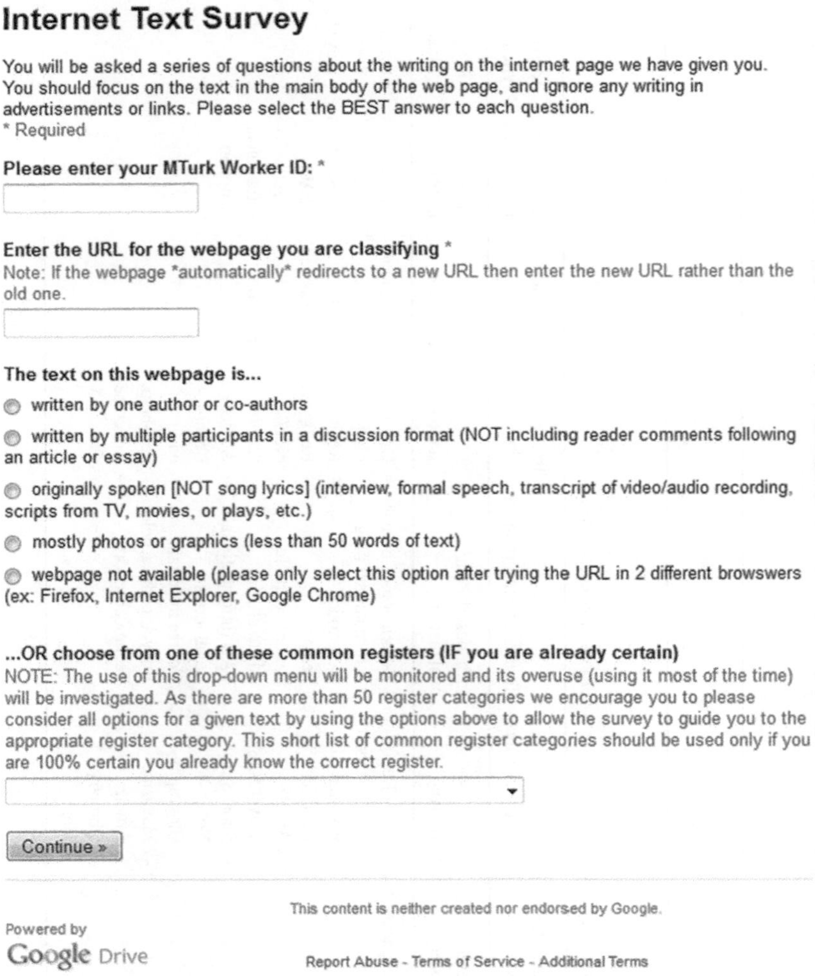

Internet Text Survey

You will be asked a series of questions about the writing on the internet page we have given you. You should focus on the text in the main body of the web page, and ignore any writing in advertisements or links. Please select the BEST answer to each question.
* Required

Please enter your MTurk Worker ID: *

[   ]

Enter the URL for the webpage you are classifying *
Note: If the webpage *automatically* redirects to a new URL then enter the new URL rather than the old one.

[   ]

The text on this webpage is...

⊙ written by one author or co-authors

⊙ written by multiple participants in a discussion format (NOT including reader comments following an article or essay)

⊙ originally spoken [NOT song lyrics] (interview, formal speech, transcript of video/audio recording, scripts from TV, movies, or plays, etc.)

⊙ mostly photos or graphics (less than 50 words of text)

⊙ webpage not available (please only select this option after trying the URL in 2 different browsers (ex: Firefox, Internet Explorer, Google Chrome)

...OR choose from one of these common registers (IF you are already certain)
NOTE: The use of this drop-down menu will be monitored and its overuse (using it most of the time) will be investigated. As there are more than 50 register categories we encourage you to please consider all options for a given text by using the options above to allow the survey to guide you to the appropriate register category. This short list of common register categories should be used only if you are 100% certain you already know the correct register.

[▼]

[Continue »]

This content is neither created nor endorsed by Google.
Powered by
Google Drive   Report Abuse - Terms of Service - Additional Terms

Figure 2.1. Screenshot of the first page of the Google Survey instrument

2.3   Searchable Online Interface for CORE

The full version of CORE, including the coded register characteristics described above, has been integrated into the suite of Brigham Young University (BYU) corpus tools made available online by Mark Davies.[6] This version of the corpus is ideal for exploring the use of particular words in each web register. In the following chapters, we rely heavily on this interface to find illustrative text examples. In the present section, we briefly describe some of the key characteristics of this online corpus interface (see Figure 2.2).

The online interface shown in Figure 2.2 allows users to search the entire CORE to investigate a wide range of linguistic patterns, including morphology, word frequencies, collocations, and syntactic patterns. The words in this online version of CORE are lemmatized, allowing users to search for individual word forms (e.g., ride) or lemmas – i.e., a word and all of its inflectional forms (e.g., ride, rides, rode, riding, ridden). This version has also been annotated for parts of speech using the CLAWS tagger, allowing users to carry out analyses of grammatical patterns. These results can be displayed in list format (see Figure 2.3) to show the most frequent words and structures that match the search query, or in bar chart format to show simple frequency distributions (see Figure 2.4).

Users can also click on the words in the List view or the bars in the Chart view to generate a list of concordance lines for the word or structure that was searched (Figure 2.5).

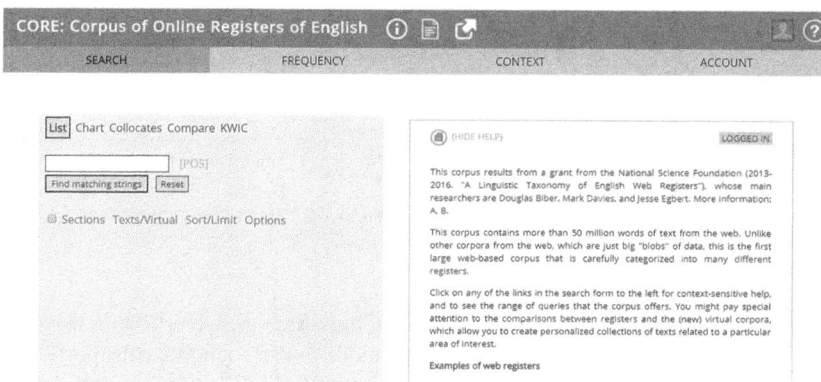

Figure 2.2. Online interface for CORE

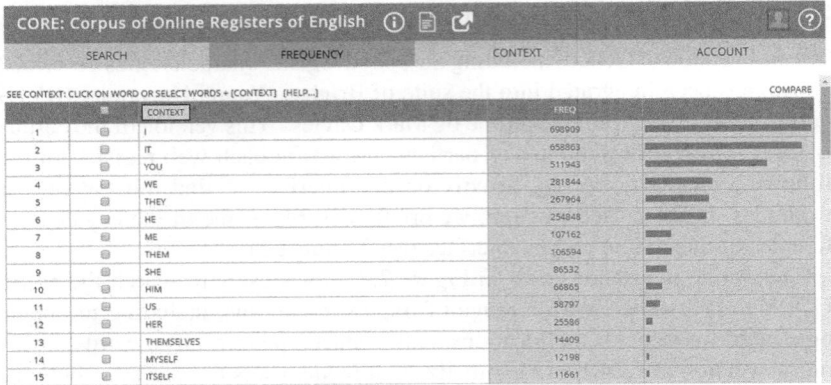

Figure 2.3. The frequency of the top fifteen most frequent pronouns in CORE

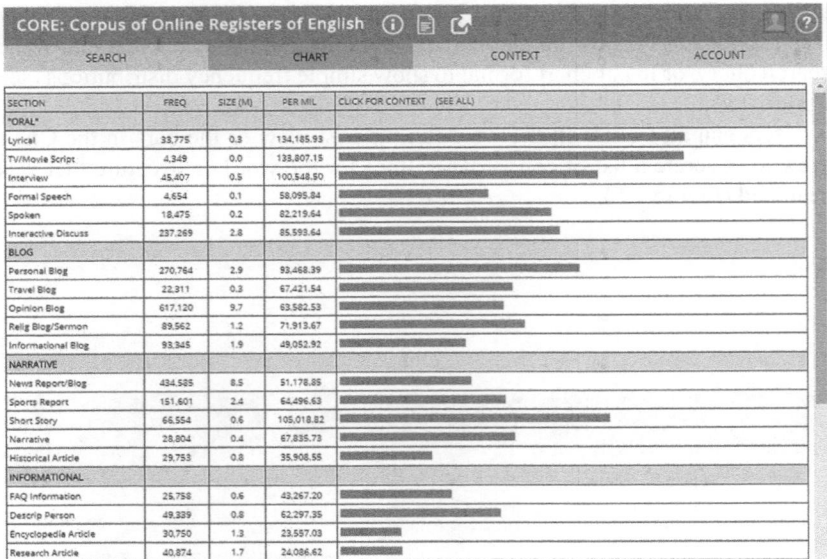

Figure 2.4. The frequency of pronouns in the first twenty registers in CORE

For the purposes of our descriptions in Chapters 5–8, we relied on this corpus interface to explore the typical patterns of use associated with particular words in more detail. This proved to be especially helpful for the interpretations of the keyword analyses in those chapters (see Section 2.4.2).

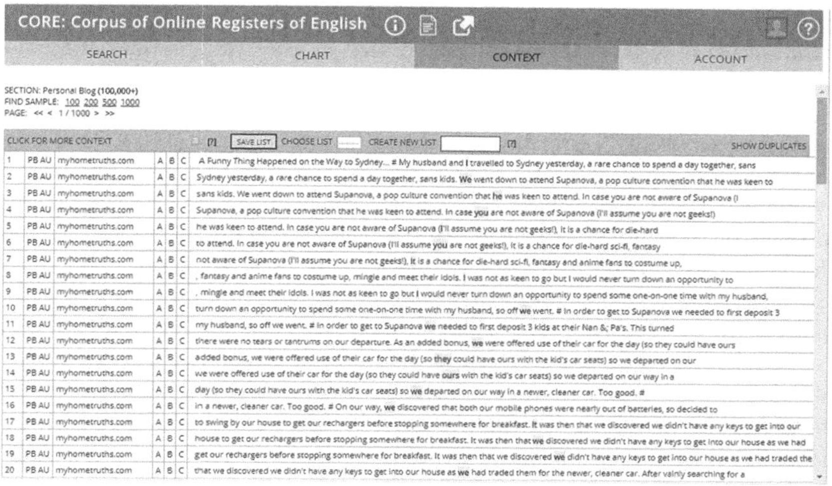

Figure 2.5. The first twenty-five concordance lines for pronouns within the Personal Blogs register

2.4   Linguistic Analysis

Chapters 4–8 of this book present linguistic descriptions of each web register based on quantitative linguistic analyses and qualitative interpretations of the discourse functions associated with those quantitative patterns. All quantitative analyses in the book use texts as the unit of observation. The choice to use texts, rather than entire corpora, as the observational unit makes it possible to calculate normed rates of occurrence and descriptive statistics for each register category. These descriptive statistics provide us with a measure of central tendency (e.g., means) and a measure of variance (e.g., standard deviation), allowing us to accurately account for linguistic variation within and between register categories. Using texts as our unit of observation also makes it possible to perform more advanced statistical procedures on the texts in the corpus, such as the Multidimensional analysis carried out in Chapter 4 and the key feature and keyword analyses in Chapters 5–8. A final benefit of using texts as the unit of analysis in this study is that our results can be interpreted at the level of the text, revealing patterns of language as it is used in actual web documents.

2.4.1   Lexico-grammatical Features

The main objective of this book is to provide a comprehensive description of linguistic variation across online registers. Therefore, the analyses in this book are based on a wide range of linguistic features, with an emphasis on features that are likely to be strongly associated with register variation in online discourse. The majority of these analyses are based on lexico-grammatical features identified by the Biber tagger. This tagger has been developed and revised over the past twenty years; the current version has both probabilistic and rule-based components, uses multiple large-scale dictionaries, and runs under Windows. This tagger achieves accuracy levels comparable to other existing taggers, but it is more robust than many taggers (achieving high accuracy rates for both spoken and written texts), and it analyzes a larger set of linguistic characteristics than most other taggers (e.g., distinguishing simple past tense, perfect aspect, passive voice, and post-nominal modifier for past-participle verbs; identifying the gap position for *WH* relative clauses; identifying several different kinds of complement clause and the existence of *that*-complementizer deletion). The Biber tagger has been used for many previous large-scale corpus investigations, including Multidimensional studies of register variation (e.g., Biber, 1988, 1995; Conrad & Biber, 2001), the *Longman Grammar of Spoken and Written English* (Biber et al., 1999), and a major study of university spoken and written registers for the Educational Testing Service (Biber et al., 2004; Biber, 2006).

After tagging each text in the corpus, we used a program called TagCount to calculate normalized rates of occurrence (per 1,000 words) for a large set of more than 150 specific linguistic features in each text. There is considerable overlap among some of these features, because lexico-grammatical characteristics can be measured at many levels of specificity. For example, the tagger includes analysis of specific lexico-grammatical characteristics (e.g., mental verbs controlling a *that*-complement clause), as well as general syntactic constructions (e.g., finite complement clauses). To the extent possible, specific lexico-grammatical features were retained in the analysis rather than more general grammatical features. In addition, redundancies were eliminated by combining some variables into a single, more general variable. Other variables were excluded from the analyses because of low overall frequencies. Appendix A lists all lexico-grammatical features that were retained for the MD analysis (discussed in Chapter 4), while Appendix B lists the lexico-grammatical features included in the key feature analysis (see Section 2.4.3).

2.4.2   Keyword Analysis

"Keyness" is the degree to which a linguistic variable – typically a word – is being used with a statistically higher (or lower) frequency in a target corpus than in a reference corpus (see, e.g., Scott, 1997; Baker, 2004). In previous studies, researchers have created keyword lists by (1) counting the total number of tokens for each word in a target and reference corpus, and (2) using a simple formula to determine which words are statistically more frequent in the target corpus. This approach has proven to be quite useful for measuring which words are strongly associated with one corpus over another. However, this method does not account for the dispersion of words across the texts of a corpus. As a result, it is possible for a word to get a high keyness score for the target corpus when it actually only occurs in a very small number of texts in the corpus.

We attempted to address this limitation in the present study by developing a new method for measuring keyness – text-dispersion keyness – which is based on a word's dispersion across texts rather than its frequency in a corpus. Specifically, we created a computer program that measures each word in terms of the number of texts where it occurs in the target corpus and the reference corpus. The two counts for each word are then compared using a log-likelihood test to determine whether the word is used in significantly more texts in the target corpus than in the reference corpus.

Egbert and Biber (in press) compare this new text-dispersion keyness method with four other keyness methods using the Travel Blogs corpus as the target and the rest of the CORE as the reference corpus. Based on a comparison of the top hundred words identified as key by these five methods, they find that the text-dispersion keyness method excludes many words that are questionable in their distinctiveness to Travel Blogs (e.g., *we, that, was, not*) and in their generalizability to travel blog web documents (e.g., *contiki, hrp, thai*). This data offers strong support in favor of using the text-dispersion keyness method for our purposes in this study.

For each of the keyword analyses in Chapters 5–8, we treat the register being investigated as the target corpus and use all of the other texts in the CORE as the reference corpus. Thus, the keyword lists represent the words that are used in many more web documents in the register of interest than in documents from other register categories. In every case, these analyses produced a large set of words that were statistically key for the target corpus. However, we focused only on the first hundred words from those lists. To aid in our interpretation of discourse function, each of these hundred words was assigned to a semantic category based on the authors' judgments. In some cases, words were assigned to an "Other" category because they did not fit naturally into one of the other categories.

2.4.3   Key Feature Analysis

As mentioned above, keyness has traditionally been applied only to words. In this study, we apply keyness to lexico-grammatical features to measure key features. However, our method for measuring key features is quite different, mostly because grammatical structures are generally much more frequent than individual word types. Thus, for the lexico-grammatical features we measure keyness using Cohen's d formula:

$$d = \frac{M_1 - M_2}{SD_{pooled}}$$

where:

$$SD_{pooled} = \sqrt{\frac{SD_1^2 + SD_2^2}{2}}$$

In this formula, the mean rate of occurrence for a linguistic feature in the target corpus (M_2) is subtracted from the mean rate of occurrence for the same feature in the reference corpus (M_1). The result is then divided by the pooled standard deviation (SD_{pooled}), which places the result on a standardized scale. This approach allows us to assign higher rankings to lexico-grammatical features that are used much more in the target (large positive d values) and much less in the target (large negative d values).

According to Cohen (1977), d values can be cautiously interpreted as follows:

d	Size
> ±0.80	Large
> ±0.50	Medium
> ±0.20	Small

To use an example from Chapter 5, place nouns occurred more than twice as frequently, on average, in the Travel Blogs sub-corpus (M_1 = 13.35 per thousand words, SD_1 = 8.07) than in the rest of the CORE (M_2 = 5.65 per thousand words, SD_2 = 6.53). We can compute SD_{pooled} using the formula above to get $\sqrt{8.07^2 + 6.53^2 /2} = 7.34$. Using these values in the Cohen's d formula, we get 13.35 − 5.65/7.34 = 1.05. Using Cohen's (1977) benchmarks, we can interpret this as a large effect size, showing that, on average, place nouns are used much more in Travel Blogs than in the rest of the CORE.

We used the same set of lexico-grammatical features for all of the key feature analysis in Chapters 5–8. This set of forty-four features was selected from the list of features identified by the Biber Tagger and counted by the TagCount program. Each of these features was chosen because we expected it to reveal meaningful differences between one or more of the individual registers and the rest of the CORE. This list represents a wide range of lexico-grammatical structures and grammatical classes (see Appendix B). Unlike the keyword analysis, in the key feature analysis we report features that are key in the positive and negative direction. In other words, we include features that are much more frequent in the target as well as those that are much less frequent. For the purposes of the key feature analysis in Chapters 5–8, we report all features with d values of ± .20. However, our interpretations focus on the strongest key features, with a special emphasis on the strong positive key features. The key feature results are summarized in figures throughout Chapters 5–8. In addition, descriptive statistics for the d-values, including both mean scores and standard deviations for each sub-register, are given in Appendix C.

Note

1. Approximately 31 percent of GloWbE is sampled exclusively from websites labeled as blogs by Google, whereas the other 69 percent is sampled from across the full open web. This "General" component includes blogs as well, in addition to the vast array of other registers available on the searchable web.
2. http://corpus2.byu.edu/glowbe/
3. www.httrack.com
4. http://code.google.com/p/justext
5. www.webgenrewiki.org/
6. http://corpus.byu.edu/core/

3   A Survey of the Registers on the Publicly Searchable Web

3.1   Contrasting Online Registers with Registers in Other Discourse Domains

Corpus-based studies of register variation in a discourse domain generally follow three major methodological stages: (1) observational research is carried out to identify the major registers that exist in the discourse domain; (2) sampling procedures are applied to collect a representative sub-corpus for each of those registers; (3) corpus-analysis techniques are applied to describe the patterns of linguistic variation within and across those registers. Researchers have been especially concerned about the validity of the third stage; for example, assessing the precision and recall for the automatic analysis of targeted linguistic features. Researchers also usually acknowledge the importance of the second stage, providing some discussion of how the corpus was collected and some evaluation of the extent to which the corpus represents the targeted registers. In contrast, the first stage is rarely acknowledged. Researchers obviously spend time thinking about the registers that exist in the discourse domain (and therefore the registers to include in the corpus), but they generally do not document the methods used for that process. As a result, this stage of research is usually evaluated with a kind of face validity, based on our assumptions that we have successfully included the major registers that exist in the target domain.

Corpus-based research on the web has usually proceeded in the same way, first identifying important registers based on their perceptual salience, and then building a corpus to represent those registers. For example, blogs are strongly associated with the web, and most corpus-based studies of web registers have included consideration of that register (e.g., Herring & Paolillo, 2006; Grieve et al., 2010; Titak & Roberson, 2013). Emails and Twitter – even though they are not part of the searchable web – are strongly associated with the Internet and also often included in such studies. Newspaper reportage – a register transferred from print media – is also very salient on the web and therefore frequently studied.

In the domain of non-Internet language, there is really no alternative methodology for constructing a corpus for the study of register variation. There is no way to itemize and bound the total spoken and written language produced in any given day or even the total written discourse in existence at any point in time. Thus, there is no way to empirically determine the set of registers that exist in a language, and certainly no way to construct a random sample that accurately represents the proportion of each register in the entire language.

The searchable web is fundamentally different in this regard: the population of searchable web documents is finite, itemized, and indexed, so, at least in theory, it is possible to obtain a random sample from the entire web that provides an accurate proportional representation of the full range of registers found on the web at a given point in time. This is exactly what we attempted to accomplish in the present project, as described in Chapter 2 (see also Egbert et al., 2015). By using Google searches of highly frequent English 3-grams (e.g., *is not the, and from the*), we were able to exploit Google's indexed sampling frame of the web while minimizing the content biases built into Google searches. The result was a corpus of c. 48,000 web documents sampled randomly from across the full spectrum of the searchable web.

However, this methodology for constructing a representative corpus does not in itself identify the register category of each document. And it turns out that that task is far from trivial (see Kilgarriff & Grefenstette, 2003; Santini & Sharoff, 2009; Crowston et al., 2010; Rosso & Haas, 2010; Sharoff et al., 2010; Fletcher, 2012).

In Chapter 2, we described how we tackled these problems through an innovative approach. First, we based our investigation on a much more representative corpus than most previous studies. This corpus is larger (48,571 web documents) and was changed through random sampling from across the full range of documents that are publicly available on the web. Second, instead of relying on individual expert coders, we recruited end-users of the web for our register coding, with each document coded by four different raters, so that we could assess the degree of agreement among users. Finally, we did not require that coders try to choose directly from a predefined set of specific register categories. Rather, we asked coders to identify basic situational characteristics of each web document, coded in a hierarchical manner. Those situational characteristics led to general register categories, which eventually led to lists of specific sub-registers. In the present chapter, we explore the composition of the searchable web based on the results of this coding.

3.2   Exploring the Distribution of Registers on the Searchable Web

As described in Chapter 2, the present project analyzed the register category of web documents by relying on the judgments of non-expert users of the web. That is, we asked users to code basic situational characteristics of each web document, building on the situational framework for register description developed in Biber and Conrad (2009, see especially chapter 2). These situational characteristics were organized in a hierarchical framework (see Table 2.1). Raters were first asked to code general characteristics like the mode (spoken or written) and interactivity. Then, for written non-interactive documents, raters were asked to identify the major communicative purpose (see page 15).

Finally, after a user had identified these general register characteristics, we asked them to select a specific sub-register under the general category. For example, Interviews and TV scripts were possible choices under the Spoken general category, while News Reports and Travel Blogs were possible choices of specific registers under the Written, Non-interactive, Narrative general category.

Overall, raters were able to achieve "moderate agreement" for their coding of general register categories for the 48,571 documents in our corpus (Fleiss' Kappa = 0.47).[1] A more detailed consideration of the agreement results, however, shows stronger results. This allows us to offer an interpretation of the register category for most documents in our corpus. Thus, Table 3.1 shows that raters were able to achieve majority agreement (at least three of the four raters) on the general register category for nearly 70 percent of the web documents in the corpus. All four raters agreed on the classification of c. 37 percent of the texts, and three of the four raters agreed on the classification of an additional c. 32 percent of the texts. For 29.2 percent of the documents, the ratings resulted in a split involving a combination of two or three registers. It turns out, though, that a few of the specific combinations in these splits occurred repeatedly in the corpus. As a result, we explore the possibility that these common 2-2 and 2-1-1 splits represent interpretable "hybrid registers" in Chapter 9.

Table 3.1. *Agreement results for the general register classification of 48,571 web documents*

4 agree	3 agree	2-2 split	2-1-1 split	No agreement
17,935	15,684	5,682	8,515	755
36.9%	32.3%	11.7%	17.5%	1.6%

Table 3.2. *Agreement results for the specific sub-register classification 48,571 web documents*

4 agree	3 agree	2-2 split	2-1-1 split	No agreement
11,769	13,220	3,526	14,576	5,480
24.2%	27.2%	7.3%	30.0%	11.3%

The levels of agreement were lower for the coding of specific sub-register categories (Fleiss' Kappa = 0.40). Table 3.2 shows that raters were able to agree on the sub-register for c. 51 percent of the web pages (with three or all four raters in agreement), but there was no agreement at all on the specific sub-register for 11.3 percent of the documents.

These results reflect the difficulty of identifying specific sub-register categories for web documents (see discussion in Section 2.2), and the usefulness of our hierarchical approach based on basic situational characteristics and communicative purposes. In general, raters were able to agree on those situational characteristics and the associated general register categories, but they experienced considerable difficulty determining the specific sub-register. For example, many documents were classified as "non-interactive written informational description/explanation" by all four raters. But those same raters were often not able to agree on specific sub-registers, so that the same document might be classified as an Informational Blog, a description of a person, Informational FAQs, Legal Terms and Conditions, or an Encyclopedia Article. As we show below, this difficulty does not apply uniformly to all sub-registers. Rather, some documents are readily categorized, while there is almost no agreement on the specific categories of other documents.

The data obtained from the end-user coding process allows us to explore the composition of the web, asking which registers are especially prevalent and which ones are relatively rare. Thus, Table 3.3 shows the breakdown of general register categories (presented in order of frequency) for the 33,619 documents that raters agreed on (i.e., the documents where three or four raters were in agreement; see Table 3.1).

Our perceptions regarding the composition of the web are colored by the searches that we typically do, and by the pages that search engines direct us to. As a result, few of us have accurate intuitions concerning the actual composition of the web. For example, based on most users' experiences, we might predict that advertisements are the most frequently found type of document on the web. Table 3.3 shows, however, that this is not the case. Informational

Table 3.3. *Frequency information for general register categories*

General register	Documents	Majority agreement (%)
Narrative	15,171	31.2
Informational Description/Explanation	7,042	14.5
Opinion	5,452	11.2
Interactive Discussion	3,104	6.4
How-to/Instructional	1,126	2.3
Informational Persuasion	794	1.6
Lyrical	605	1.2
Spoken	325	0.7
Hybrid (see below)	14,197	29.2
No agreement	755	1.6
TOTAL	48,571	100

persuasion documents are usually a kind of indirect advertisement, presenting descriptive information about a place or product with the goal of persuading the reader to purchase something. However, those documents are not prevalent in our random sample of web pages (only c. 1.6 percent of the total), and otherwise there are few web documents that were classified as overt advertisements in our corpus.

The scarcity of advertisements in our corpus can be attributed to several factors. First, typical usage of the Internet can lead a user to believe that advertisements are more prevalent than they actually are. Many users commonly shop online and regularly encounter advertisements on commercial sites, and search engines are structured to direct users to commercial sites, even when users are not shopping online. A second major factor, though, is that many advertisements on the web are not primarily textual and thus not represented in our corpus. For example, pop-up web pages are not part of the searchable web (and so not included in our sample), and advertisements found on the sides of a web page were removed in the "scrubbing" process of our corpus creation. In addition, our corpus includes only pages with at least seventy-five words of prose, and thus excludes all advertisement pages consisting mostly of photos with little prose. However, even considering all of these factors, the results presented in Table 3.3 show that our perceptions of the web can be dramatically different from its actual composition, and in particular, advertisements do not dominate the textual content of the searchable web.

Instead, our findings show that narrative texts are by far the most common register on the web: 31.2 percent of all documents in our corpus. In addition, a large proportion of the "hybrid" documents include narrative purposes (see discussion in Chapter 9). As a result, over 50 percent of all documents on the web have a narrative purpose. Informational description/explanation documents (c. 14 percent of the corpus) and opinion documents (c. 11 percent of the corpus) are also both prevalent on the web.

Thus, taken together, the three general register categories of Narrative, Informational description/Explanation, and Opinion, account for well over 80 percent of the documents on the web. In contrast, the other five categories (Interactive discussion, How-to/Instructional, Informational persuasion, Lyrical, and Spoken) are considerably less common. In the following sections, we provide more detailed descriptions of each of these general registers. Then, in Chapters 5–8, we provide detailed descriptions of the main sub-registers found within each general category.

3.3 Communicative and Textual Characteristics of General Web Registers

3.3.1   Narrative

Table 3.4 shows that half (52.5 percent) of the narrative texts in our corpus are general news reports, while an additional 16 percent are sports news reports. Many of these texts were originally published in print media and have simply been transferred to the web. Others are news reports incorporated into a regular blog. At first, we planned to distinguish news blogs from regular news reports (which have their origins in print media). In practice, though, it proved nearly impossible to determine whether a news/sports report was originally published in a print newspaper, or whether it had been written specifically for a blog. As a result, we combined reports and blogs into a single category. We did, however, distinguish Sports Reports/Blogs as a specialized sub-category of general News Reports/Blogs.

Taken together, news reports and sports reports comprise 21.4 percent of the entire corpus (i.e., 10,411 of the 48,571 documents in the corpus). This percentage is higher when we include "hybrid" documents that can be treated as news reports combined with some other purpose (e.g., News Blogs that report on events with an opinionated bias – see Chapter 9). As a result, well over 25 percent of the searchable web consists of news reports with a narrative focus, packaged in many different ways, from a bewildering array of sources, focused on an incredible range of topics (past events involving nations, sports teams, celebrities, entertaining stories, etc.).

The Personal Narrative Blog – recounts of past personal events – is also an important sub-register in this category, comprising 11.3 percent of all narrative web documents, or c. 3.5 percent of all documents in our corpus. From a

Table 3.4. *Frequency information for narrative sub-register categories*

Register	#	%
Narrative		
News Report/Blog	7,967	52.5
Sports Report/Blog	2,444	16.1
Personal Narrative Blog	1,718	11.3
Historical article	206	1.4
Travel Blog	128	0.8
Short story	117	0.8
Novel	32	0.2
Biographical story/history	33	0.2
Magazine article	18	0.1
Obituary	5	0.03
Memoir	1	0
Other	0	0
No majority agreement on sub-register	2,502	16.5
Total	15,171	100

technical perspective, it is difficult to formulate a precise operational definition for blogs. However, end-users of the web have little trouble identifying many web documents as clear instances of blogs (because they are often explicitly labeled as blogs). There are many specific sub-types of blogs (see Herring et al., 2005; Sindoni, 2013, chapter 3); in our framework, we included Blog sub-registers under the general register categories of narrative (News Reports/ Blogs, Sports Reports/Blogs, Personal Narrative Blogs, Travel Blogs), informational description (Informational Blogs), and opinion (Opinion Blogs).

The blogs grouped into the category of Personal Narratives are recounts of past events that the blogger participated in; for example daily experiences while learning how to weave, events that occurred with a new baby, experiences at a fashion week, experiences being outdoors during the winter. Although we treat them as a separate category in our analysis, Travel Blogs can also be considered a special sub-type of Personal Narrative Blog. It is not clear who the intended audience is for many blogs or how widely read they are. But one thing is clear: there is no shortage of people who are eager to share their own personal experiences and opinions with a public audience (see Guadagno et al., 2008; Sindoni, 2013, chapter 3). The high rate of occurrence for these Personal Narrative Blogs is especially remarkable given that our corpus is sampled from the searchable public web, and thus excludes private social media messages, where there is presumably much more of this type of communication (see Sindoni, 2013: 120–3).

All other sub-registers of narrative are considerably less frequent on the web, including many registers that are widely recognized in print media (e.g., Historical Articles, Short Stories, Novels, Biographies). This illustrates a general trend emerging from our study: that the most common registers found on the web are not those typically analyzed in corpora of published written texts. Conversely, although the most widely analyzed registers from published writing can be found on the web, they are typically rare in comparison to other web registers.

3.3.2   *Informational Description/Explanation*

The second most frequent general register on the web is Informational description/Explanation (14.5 percent of the total documents in our corpus – see Table 3.3). This category includes the informational registers typically analyzed in corpora of published written texts, such as Research Articles, Abstracts, Encyclopedia Articles, and Technical Reports. However, similar to the pattern observed for narratives, these sub-registers from print media are generally rare on the web in comparison to other types of texts. For example, academic research articles – the focus of an extensive body of corpus-based research – comprise less than 3 percent of the general Informational register.

Encyclopedia articles are a special case here: they are not especially prevalent or important in published media, but they are prominent on the web, with links to encyclopedia articles being returned by many searches. In the everyday experience of a typical college student or teacher, Internet encyclopedia sites are hugely important, having become the go-to source of information on many topics. For this reason, it would be easy to assume that a large part of the web is composed of encyclopedia articles. However, Table 3.5 shows that this is not the case: encyclopedia articles comprise only 6.6 percent of the general informational register category, which corresponds to less than 1 percent of our total corpus.

Table 3.5 shows that most of the documents in the general informational register are not instances of specific well-defined sub-registers/genres. When we were developing the register classification framework, we had difficulty identifying other named sub-registers in this category, and as a result, we included categories associated with communicative purposes (Simple Description, Description-of-a-person) and specific format (Informational Blog). The most important of these sub-registers is Simple Description, which is specified as including descriptions of a place, product, organization, program, job, etc. Descriptions-of-a-person is a related sub-register of this category.

Table 3.5. *Frequency information for informational sub-register categories*

Register	#	%
Informational description/explanation		
General description	1,584	22.5
Encyclopedia article	465	6.6
Informational Blog	337	4.8
Description of a person	236	3.4
Research article	197	2.8
Abstract	147	2.1
FAQ about information	108	1.5
Legal terms and conditions	103	1.5
Course materials	44	0.6
Technical report	6	0.1
Other	18	0.3
No majority agreement on sub-register	3797	53.9
Total	7,042	100

Informational Blogs are very similar in purpose, but are distinguished primarily by their format. Taken together, these three sub-registers comprise c. 30 percent of the documents in the Informational category. These are mostly non-institutional documents presenting descriptive information about almost any conceivable object or topic. Many of these are descriptions of tangible objects or places, such as hotels, restaurants, towns, national parks, types of gems and minerals, types of bolts and screws, useful tools for gardening, etc. Some other documents in these categories provide information about more abstract processes or concepts, such as statistics about different countries around the world, a description of the Office of the Director of Public Prosecutions, and a description of the Sideloader Delivery method.

Most of the documents in this general register did not fit tidily into any of these specific sub-registers. That is, although raters had no difficulty agreeing that these documents were instances of the general category Informational Description/Explanation, they were unable to agree on a specific sub-register for 53.9 percent of the documents. These are mostly informational documents prepared by various organizations, government entities, and other institutions, describing and explaining information related to almost any conceivable topic. They tend to be more technical, abstract, and conceptual than the documents that raters classified as simple description, but the framework failed to provide specific sub-register categories that clearly fit the purposes of these documents. Some examples include documents about:

- The advantage of parallel circuits over series circuits
- Food safety following floods
- Stress can become a serious illness
- Attention Hunters: "It's Time to Get the Lead Out" (an announcement prohibiting lead bullets)
- The Major Planets in October 2011
- Middle schooling – Rationale
- What is a trustee?

These documents are all clearly informational – some more descriptive, and others more explanatory. On the whole, they tend to be technical in content, although they are often packaged for a general readership. Raters had no trouble identifying these as instances of a general "Informational description/ Explanation" register. As such, documents like these illustrate the utility of our hierarchical approach, where it is easy for raters to identify basic situational parameters but nearly impossible to agree on specific sub-register categories.

3.3.3   Opinion

Opinion web pages are nearly as common as informational pages (see Table 3.3). As Table 3.6 shows, more than a third of these were classified as Opinion Blogs (37.9 percent), while another 21 percent were classified as

Table 3.6. *Frequency information for opinion sub-register categories*

Register	#	%
Opinion		
Opinion Blog	2,064	37.9
Review	1,145	21.0
Religious Blog/Sermon	461	8.5
Advice	246	4.5
Letter-to-the-editor	18	0.3
Self-help	3	0.06
Advertisement	2	0.04
No majority agreement on sub-register	1,513	27.8
Total	5,452	100

reviews. Similar to Personal Narrative Blogs, it is not always clear who writes Opinion Blogs and how many people read these blogs. But it is clear how popular these forms of expression are. The difference between the two types of blogs concerns the primary communicative purpose: narrating past events versus expressing opinions about topics including government, society, etc.

Reviews differ from Opinion Blogs in that they have a specific focus for their evaluations, providing assessments of specific products, services, art, performances, etc. Beyond that, the rest of this category consists of Religious Blogs/ Sermons (8.5 percent) and Advice Documents (4.5 percent). Here again, we see the rarity of a register considered to be important in corpora of published written texts: letters to the editor comprise only 0.3 percent of the Opinion general category, while overt Advertisements (with more than seventy-five words of prose – see Section 3.2) are extremely rare.

3.3.4   Other General Registers

The other five general register categories – Interactive Discussion, How-to/ Instructional, Informational Persuasion, Lyrical, and Spoken – occurred much less frequently than the three major categories of Narration, Informational Description/Explanation, and Opinion. However, it is clear from Table 3.7 that these registers each comprise one or two especially important sub-register categories. For example, Discussion Forums and Question/Answer forums are especially important, making up a combined 87.6 percent of the Interactive Discussion category. Similar to Blogs, these are specialized web registers not found in print media.

Most documents in the Lyrical category consist of song lyrics, while interviews are especially prevalent in the Spoken category. Not surprisingly, how-to explanations, recipes (i.e., a special category of How-to specifically for cooking), and more formal instructions for other processes dominate the How-to/ Instructional category.

The Informational Persuasion register consists mostly of the sub-register Description-with-intent-to-sell. These are similar to infomercials, in that the primary content is information about a place or product, while the underlying motivation is to persuade the reader to visit a place or purchase a product or service. Although this is the dominant sub-register of Informational Persuasion, these documents are not especially prevalent on the web generally (accounting for only c. 1.6 percent of the entire corpus). These documents can be considered as a kind of hybrid register, combining the communicative purposes of informing/describing/explaining with a persuasive goal. As a result, users actually had difficulty agreeing on this register categorization. As we show in the following section, there were other important differences in the extent to which these categories were perceptually well-defined for users.

Table 3.7. *Frequency information for other sub-register categories*

Register	#	%
Interactive discussion		
Discussion forum	1,810	58.3
Question/answer forum	911	29.3
Reader/viewer responses	7	0.2
Other	2	0.06
No majority agreement on sub-register	374	12.0
TOTAL	**3,104**	**100**
How-to/Instructional		
How-to	544	48.3
Recipe	126	11.2
Instructions	70	6.2
FAQ	17	1.5
Technical support	9	0.8
Other	0	0
No majority agreement on sub-register	360	32.0
TOTAL	**1,126**	**100**
Informational persuasion		
Description-with-intent-to-sell	691	87.0
Persuasive article or essay	14	1.8
Editorial	8	1.0
No majority agreement on sub-register	81	10.2
TOTAL	**794**	**100**
Lyrical		
Song Lyrics	527	87.1
Poem	54	8.9
Other	4	0.7
No majority agreement on sub-register	20	3.3
TOTAL	**605**	**100**
Spoken		
Interview	250	76.9
Transcript of video/audio	28	8.6
Formal speech	22	6.8
TV/movie script	12	3.7
Other	5	1.5
No majority agreement on sub-register	8	2.5
TOTAL	**325**	**100**

3.3.5   Extent to Which General Web Registers Are Perceptually Well-Defined

The preceding sections focus on the large number of documents that users were able to agree on. An alternative perspective is to consider the perception of the registers themselves, investigating the extent to which these categories are perceptually well-defined for users. That is, if one user codes a document as an instance of a register, what is the likelihood that the other three users will perceive this same register?

Table 3.8 presents Fleiss' Kappa agreement coefficients for each register, showing that there are large differences in the extent to which the categories are perceptually well-defined. At one extreme, there is high agreement for Interactive Discussion and Lyrical documents: if one rater perceived a document as belonging to these categories, it is likely that other raters would agree.

At the other extreme, we see a low rate of agreement for Informational Persuasion. In fact, it turns out that there were 4,506 documents that were coded by only one rater as an instance of Informational Persuasion, versus only 216 documents where all four raters agreed on a coding of Informational Persuasion. Thus, this register category was especially nebulous for most raters (often coded instead as Informational Description/Explanation and/or Opinion).

In part, the results summarized in Table 3.8 indicate that these general register categories are not equally well-defined for end-users. But these results also reflect the fact that many documents are not pure instances of a single register. So, for example, Table 3.3 shows that the registers of Informational Description/Explanation and Opinion are perceptually well-defined: these are two of the three most common register categories in our corpus, and thousands of documents in our corpus were coded with complete agreement as belonging to these categories. At the same time, Table 3.8 shows low levels of agreement

Table 3.8. *Fleiss' Kappa coefficients indicating the extent to which raters agreed in their perceptions of each register category*

Register category	Fleiss' Kappa
Narrative	0.51
Informational Description/Explanation	0.37
Opinion	0.36
Interactive Discussion	0.86
How-to/Instructional	0.47
Informational Persuasion	0.26
Lyrical	0.82
Spoken	0.46

Table 3.9. *Frequency information for texts containing reader comments, by register (excluding interactive discussions)*

	Total	# with reader comments	% with reader comments
Narrative	15,171	5,055	33.3
Informational Description/ Explanation	7,042	510	7.2
Opinion	5,452	2,034	37.3
How-to/Instructional	1,126	307	27.3
Informational Persuasion	794	236	29.7
Lyrical	605	74	12.2
Spoken	325	61	18.8

for the overall coding of these two categories (Fleiss' Kappa = 0.37 and 0.36). This apparently contradictory finding suggests the need for an alternative perspective on register variation, recognizing the existence of a continuous space of variation, as a way to complement the traditional perspective based on discrete clear-cut register categories. We return to this alternative perspective in Chapter 9.

3.3.6 Reader Comments in Web Documents

Many web documents could be analyzed as discourse from two different registers, because they include the main text followed by reader comments. Table 3.9 shows that this type of blended document can occur with any of the non-interactive written registers.[2] However, it is interesting to note that reader comments are much more likely with some registers than others. In particular, Narrative, Opinion, How-to, and Informational persuasion documents are commonly followed by reader comments (27–37 percent of the time), while comments are much less likely in response to Informational, Lyrical, or Spoken documents (7–19 percent of the time). (Interactive Discussions are excluded from consideration, because they include reader participation by definition.) Blogs are especially likely to include reader comments: 55 percent of narrative Personal Blogs, 49 percent of Opinion Blogs, and 22 percent of Informational Blogs include comments from readers.

3.4 Register Categorization Used in the Following Chapters

It will be clear from the preceding sections that there is no single "correct" way to divide up the discourse domain of the web into register categories. In our corpus, each document has been coded for both its general register category (e.g., Narrative, Informational Description, Opinion) as well as its more specific sub-register (e.g., Opinion Blog or Product Review). In addition, because each document was coded by four different raters, we know the extent to which end-users agree on these register categories.

Our goals in the present chapter were to survey the kinds of registers found on the web, and to investigate the extent to which each of those document types was more or less prevalent in this discourse domain. We have thus presented the results of our register coding with no attempt to minimize its messiness, reflecting the actual complexities of language use on the web.

However, for the linguistic descriptions in Chapters 4–8, we have reorganized the corpus to focus on the major register distinctions that emerge from the analyses in the present chapter. The results presented here show that three general register categories are dominant on the web: Narrative, Opinion, and Informational Description/Explanation (see Table 3.3). Other categories that were treated as general registers in our coding framework are considerably less common, and can be regarded as sub-registers under one of those three general categories. Thus, Informational-Persuasion documents can be treated as a special sub-register under the general Opinion category, and How-to/Procedural documents can be treated as a special sub-register under the general Informational Description/Explanation register. Thus, Chapters 5–7 focus on these three general registers and the major sub-registers within each category. The remaining three general registers – Spoken, Interactive discussions, and Lyrical – are all "oral" in nature in that they are relatively interactive, interpersonal, subjective, and/or produced in real time. Thus, these registers are all discussed together in Chapter 8.

We focus primarily on the linguistic characteristics of specific sub-registers for the linguistic descriptions in Chapters 4–8. For the quantitative analyses in those chapters, we assigned each document in the corpus to a single category. Preference was given to the more specific sub-registers (e.g., Advice Pages, Travel Blogs, Sports News Reports), as these are more informative for applied purposes and better defined linguistically (see Biber & Egbert, 2016). Thus, if two or more coders agreed on a specific sub-register for a document, the text was assigned to that category. The remaining documents were coded as "Other" sub-registers in their general register category (e.g., Other Narrative, Other Opinion, or Other Informational Description) in cases where at least three of the four raters agreed on the category. And finally, c. 10 percent of the documents in the corpus were simply excluded from the descriptions in Chapters 5–8 because raters did not agree on their register categorization. We return to the description of those documents in Chapter 9, when we discuss registers on the web in a continuous space of situational variation.

Table 3.10 lists the general register categories used for the following chapters, together with the sub-registers grouped under each of those categories.

The specific distribution of documents across categories is presented at the beginning of each chapter. This categorization is also used as the basis for the register distinctions found on the online version of the corpus.[3]

3.5   Chapter Summary

The approach for register classification adopted here – a bottom-up hierarchical framework based on underlying situational characteristics – allows us to account for the register characteristics of most web pages. Raters generally agree on the general register category of c. 69 percent of the web pages included in our corpus (see Table 3.2). Approximately another 29 percent of the documents in our corpus can be regarded as "hybrid" registers belonging to a few combinations that occur commonly on the web (e.g., Narration + Information Description; Narration + Opinion; see the discussion in Chapter 9). Taken together, these results indicate that 80–90 percent of web pages can be meaningfully described for their register characteristics.

The general register categories that we ended up with are mostly associated with different general communicative purposes (e.g., narrating, informing, giving opinions). These are quite different in nature from the tidy register categories usually employed in written corpus designs (e.g., academic research articles or newspaper editorials). As discussed in previous chapters, this difference reflects a fundamental difference between the discourse domains of published written texts versus searchable web documents. One consequence of this difference is that register distinctions are considerably more difficult to determine for web documents than for published written texts. However, it also turns out that the register distinctions defined in terms of basic communicative purposes are not necessarily simple, because many texts combine multiple purposes. For this reason, it is not surprising that the classification of web registers proves to be quite messy and complicated – a topic we return to in Chapter 9.

One interesting finding, though, is that only a few general registers dominate the documents found on the searchable web. These are not necessarily the most salient registers or the ones that most users would predict to be especially common. For example, news/sports reports/blogs are especially prevalent on the searchable web, making up c. 21 percent of the total documents in our corpus. Various kinds of informational descriptions/explanations are also common (c. 14 percent of the total), as well as opinionated texts (c. 11 percent of the total). In contrast, interactive discussions and forums, how-to/procedural documents, lyrical, and spoken transcriptions are all much less frequent.

It is perhaps not surprising that our research findings show that Blogs are probably the quintessential register of the searchable web, comprising 20–25 percent of our corpus. Blogs can vary widely in their situational characteristics and

Table 3.10. *Register categorization used for the linguistic descriptions in Chapters 4–8*

Narrative
- News Report
- Personal Blog
- Sports Report
- Historical Article
- Travel Blog
- Fictional Short Story/Novel
- Other Narrative

Opinion/advice/persuasion
- Opinion Blog
- Review
- Description-with-intent-to-sell
- Advice
- Religious Blog/Sermon
- Other Opinion/Persuasion

Informational descriptions, explanations, and procedures
- How-to/Instructional documents or blogs
- Recipes
- Academic Research Articles/Abstracts
- Encyclopedia Articles
- Descriptions-of-a-person
- Informational FAQs
- Informational Blogs
- Other Information

Oral
- Interactive Discussion
- Lyrical
- Interview
- Other Spoken

communicative purposes, and as a result, specific blog sub-registers ended up being categorized under several of our general registers. At one extreme are the Personal Blogs that are not associated with any institution; these can serve narrative, informational, or opinionated purposes, with an incredible array of specific communicative purposes. At the other extreme are institutional News/ Sports Blogs, which are in some cases virtually indistinguishable from published news reports. Taken together, blogs provide a microcosm of the incredible range of variation found on the web.

Our prediction is that these register distinctions, defined in terms of basic situational characteristics, will correspond to systematic patterns of linguistic variation. In the following chapters, we explore the lexico-grammatical characteristics of these categories, to document systematic linguistic patterns of register variation on the web. In Chapter 4, we first present the results of a Multidimensional analysis to identify the underlying parameters of linguistic co-occurrence and document the overall patterns of register variation on the searchable web. Then, in Chapters 5–8, we present detailed linguistic descriptions of each major web register and the important sub-registers within each of those categories.

Notes

1. Fleiss' Kappa is a measure of interrater agreement that is well-suited to the design of our study. Unlike related measures of interrater agreement (e.g., Cohen's Kappa), Fleiss' Kappa does not require that the same raters code each of the documents in the dataset. However, like Cohen's Kappa, Fleiss' Kappa accounts for chance agreement among raters, making it more robust than simple percent agreement. Kappa values in the range of 0.41– 0.60 can be interpreted as "moderate agreement" (Landis & Koch, 1977).
2. This option is not applicable to written interactive discussions, which incorporate reader comments by definition. We are not sure why transcribed texts of spoken events are not followed by reader comments in our sub-corpus.
3. http://corpus.byu.edu/core/.

4 Overall Patterns of Register Variation on the Searchable Web: A Multidimensional Analysis

4.1 Introduction

We begin our linguistic description of web registers by taking a wide perspective, applying Multidimensional (MD) analysis to study the overall patterns of register variation among web documents. In MD analysis, the distribution of a large set of linguistic features is analyzed in a multi-register corpus of texts. Specifically, factor analysis is used to identify the systematic co-occurrence patterns among these linguistic features, or the "dimensions," – and then texts and registers along each dimension.

MD analysis provides a complementary linguistic/quantitative perspective to the keyness measures developed in the following chapters. That is, in Chapters 5–8, we focus on particular registers and consider in detail the distinctive linguistic and functional characteristics of each one. In contrast, the present chapter includes consideration of the full range of web registers, analyzed with respect to the full set of lexico-grammatical characteristics. Detailed analysis of particular web registers permits more in-depth descriptions of the distinctive linguistic characteristics used to fulfill the communicative functions of those texts. However, as a foundation for such descriptions, it is useful to document the overall patterns of register variation in this discourse domain. This is the primary goal of the present chapter.

For this research purpose, we need an analytical approach designed to capture the ways in which linguistic features work together as a system. The approach employed throughout the present book is comparative and relies on quantitative methods to determine the relative distribution of individual linguistic features. By using quantitative comparisons to the range of other web registers, the descriptions are able to determine whether a given frequency of occurrence is notably common or rare in a target register. This quantitative comparative approach treats register as a continuous construct: texts are situated within a continuous space of linguistic variation, enabling analysis of the ways in which registers are more or less different with respect to the full range of core linguistic features.

The descriptions in the present chapter have an additional analytical characteristic: they are based on statistical analysis of linguistic co-occurrence. The relative distribution of common linguistic features, considered individually, cannot reliably distinguish among registers. There are simply too many different linguistic characteristics to consider, and individual features often have idiosyncratic distributions. That is, although the distributions of individual features are interpretable in functional terms, these individual patterns cannot be used to determine the extent to which any two registers are holistically similar or different. Rather, overall patterns of register variation are describable with respect to sets of co-occurring linguistic features.

The importance of linguistic co-occurrence has been emphasized by several linguists in the past. Brown and Fraser (1979: 38–9) observe that it can be "misleading to concentrate on specific, isolated [linguistic] markers without taking into account systematic variations which involve the co-occurrence of sets of markers." Ervin-Tripp (1972) and Hymes (1974) identify "speech styles" as varieties that are defined by a shared set of co-occurring linguistic features. Halliday (1988: 162) defines a register as "a cluster of associated features having a greater-than-random [...] tendency to co-occur."

Although this general theoretical perspective has been widely accepted, linguists lacked the methodological tools required for such analysis before the availability of corpus-based techniques. The MD approach was developed to analyze the linguistic co-occurrence patterns associated with register variation in empirical/quantitative terms. Early MD studies investigated the patterns of variation among general spoken and written registers in English (Biber, 1985, 1986, 1988), while subsequent studies documented the patterns of register variation in other languages (see, e.g., Biber, 1995), or in more specialized discourse domains (see, e.g., Conrad & Biber, 2001). Biber (2014) introduces the MD analytical approach and surveys the studies of register variation carried out to date, with a focus on the possibility of universal patterns of register variation. (We return to this possibility in the concluding section of Chapter 4.)

MD analysis uses the power of multivariate statistical techniques to investigate the quantitative distribution of linguistic features across texts and registers. Linguistic co-occurrence is analyzed in terms of underlying "dimensions" of variation which are identified quantitatively, by a statistical factor analysis, rather than on an a priori functional basis. The dimensions resulting from MD analysis have both linguistic and functional content. The linguistic content of a dimension is a group of features (such as nouns, attributive adjectives, or prepositional phrases) that co-occur regularly in texts. On the assumption that co-occurrence reflects shared functions, these co-occurrence patterns are interpreted to assess the situational, social, and cognitive functions most widely shared by the linguistic features.

4.2   Overview of Methods for MD Analysis

The MD approach uses statistical factor analysis to reduce a large number of linguistic variables to a few basic parameters of linguistic variation: the "dimensions." First, the distribution of each individual linguistic feature is analyzed in a corpus of texts. Factor analysis is then used to identify the systematic co-occurrence patterns among those linguistic features – the "dimensions" – and then texts and registers are compared along each dimension. Each dimension comprises a group of linguistic features that usually co-occur in texts (e.g., nouns, attributive adjectives, prepositional phrases); the dimensions are then interpreted to assess their underlying functional associations. (Technical details of factor analysis as applied in MD analysis are discussed in Biber (1988), chapters 4–5; Biber (1995), chapter 5.)

After the statistical analysis is completed, dimensions are interpreted functionally, based on the assumption that linguistic co-occurrence reflects underlying communicative functions. That is, linguistic features occur together in texts because they serve related communicative functions. In the 1988 analysis, the dimensions were interpreted in relation to underlying functional parameters like "Involved versus Informational Production" and "Narrative versus Non-narrative Discourse."

Each dimension can have "positive" and "negative" features. Rather than reflecting importance, positive and negative signs identify two groupings of features that occur in a complementary pattern as part of the same dimension. That is, when the positive features occur together frequently in a text, the negative features are markedly less frequent in that text, and vice versa.

A second major step in interpreting a dimension is to consider the similarities and differences among registers with respect to the set of co-occurring linguistic features. To achieve this, *dimension scores* are computed for each text, by summing the individual scores of the features that co-occur on a dimension (see Biber, 1988: 93–7). Once a dimension score is computed for each text, the mean dimension score for each register can be computed. Plots of these mean dimension scores allow linguistic characterization of any given register, comparison of the relations between any two registers, and a fuller functional interpretation of the underlying dimension.

4.3   Statistical Details for the Multidimensional Analysis of Web Registers

For the present study, we began with the more than 150 specific lexico-grammatical features identified by the Biber tagger (see, e.g., Biber et al., 1999). There is considerable overlap among some of these features, because lexico-grammatical characteristics can be measured at many different levels of specificity. For example, the tagger includes analysis of specific lexico-grammatical characteristics (e.g., mental verbs controlling a *that*-complement clause), as well as general syntactic constructions (e.g., finite complement clauses). To the extent possible, specific lexico-grammatical features were retained in the analysis rather than more general grammatical features. In addition, redundancies were eliminated by combining some variables, and dropping other variables that had low overall frequencies. Variables with low communalities in the preliminary factor analysis runs (reflecting low shared variance with the overall factor structure) were eliminated.

Fifty-seven linguistic variables were retained for the final analysis (see Appendix A). Readers are referred to Biber et al. (1999) and Biber (2006) for descriptions of these individual linguistic features. Principal component analysis (using the FACTOR Procedure in SAS, with METHOD=PRIN) was used to extract the factors.[1] The ten-factor solution was selected as optimal. This decision was based on inspection of the scree plot and eigenvalues (retaining most factors with eigenvalues >1.0), and the interpretability of the factors extracted in different solutions. However, one of those factors was not readily interpretable, so the discussion below focuses on the remaining nine factors.[2] The factor solution accounted for 42.7 percent of the cumulative shared variance.[3] Factors were rotated using a Promax rotation, which resulted in generally small correlations among the dimensions (Dimensions 1 and 2: $r = 0.32$; Dimensions 2 and 3: $r = -0.39$; Dimensions 1 and 5: $r = 0.42$; Dimensions 2 and 5: $r = 0.36$; all other correlations between dimensions <0.25).

The FACTOR procedure in SAS (specifying the option "Score") was used to compute standardized factor scores for each document. We then computed mean factor scores (referred to as "dimension scores") and standard deviations for each register. Tables 4.1 and 4.2 present the results of ANOVAs (from the GLM procedure in SAS), showing that all nine dimensions are significant predictors of register variation. The values for R^2 in these tables provide a direct measure of importance, indicating the percentage of the variance among dimension scores that can be predicted by knowing the register categories.

Table 4.1 presents the results for the comparison of mean scores across the eight general register categories distinguished in our study, with all other documents in the corpus grouped into an additional "other" category. Table 4.2, then, presents the results for the comparison of mean scores across the 25 specific sub-register categories distinguished in our study (see the detailed discussions in Chapters 5–8).

The first five dimensions are moderately strong predictors, while dimensions 6–9 have weaker R^2 values. In addition, a comparison of Tables 4.1 and 4.2 shows that the dimensions are relatively strong predictors of

Table 4.1. *Dimensions as predictors of general register variation (eight general register categories + "other")*

Dimension	F-score	*p* value	Variance explained (R^2)
1	767.5	<0.0001	12.3%
2	630.8	<0.0001	10.4%
3	1027.6	<0.0001	15.8%
4	1612.5	<0.0001	22.8%
5	883.7	<0.0001	13.9%
6	306.5	<0.0001	5.3%
7	194.2	<0.0001	3.4%
8	134.4	<0.0001	2.4%
9	240.5	<0.0001	4.2%

Table 4.2. *Dimensions as predictors of specific sub-register variation (twenty-five specific sub-registers)*

Dimension	F-score	*p* value	Variance explained (R^2)
1	574.8	<0.0001	26.4%
2	302.0	<0.0001	15.9%
3	618.9	<0.0001	27.9%
4	736.0	<0.0001	31.5%
5	520.8	<0.0001	24.5%
6	263.2	<0.0001	14.1%
7	150.6	<0.0001	8.9%
8	112.9	<0.0001	6.9%
9	191.9	<0.0001	10.7%

variation among specific sub-registers (Table 4.2), but they are only weak predictors of variation among the general registers (Table 4.1). These results reflect the fact that the specific sub-register categories are better defined – both situationally and linguistically – than the general register categories. The MD analysis in the present chapter thus includes discussion of the relations among both general registers and specific sub-registers. However, in the following chapters we focus on detailed descriptions of specific sub-registers.

Table 4.3 below summarizes all of the major results from the MD analysis. Table 4.3 is organized into four columns:

- Column 1 briefly summarizes the functional interpretation of the dimension.
- Column 2 lists the important co-occurring linguistic features that comprise the dimension (i.e., all features with loadings > ±0.3; features with loadings > ±0.2 are listed in parentheses).
- Column 3 lists specific sub-registers that have distinctive characterizations with respect to the dimension.
- Column 4 gives + or – symbols to signify the dimension score level for the sub-registers in column 3. Seven levels are distinguished for the dimension scores:

> ±1.5 shown by + + + + + + / –––––––
> ±1.2 shown by + + + + + / ––––––
> ±0.9 shown by + + + + / –––––
> ±0.6 shown by + + + / –––
> ±0.3 shown by + + / ––
> ±0.15 shown by + / –

Unmarked registers (with scores near 0.0) shown by 0.

The linguistic features with important positive and negative loadings on each dimension are listed in Column 2. Each dimension can have 'positive' and 'negative' features. Rather than reflecting importance, positive and negative signs identify two groupings of features that occur in a complementary pattern as part of the same dimension. That is, when the positive features occur together frequently in a text, the negative features are markedly less frequent in that text, and vice versa. To aid in the interpretation of each dimension, the presentation in Column 2 groups together features that are structurally/semantically/functionally similar. However, it is important to emphasize that these are post-hoc groupings that had no influence on the identification of linguistic co-occurrence patterns by the factor analysis.

Column 3 gives a semi-graphical display of specific registers, reflecting the dimension score for each one. Registers with large positive dimension scores are listed at the top; registers with large negative dimension scores are listed at the bottom. These dimension scores correspond to the use of the linguistic features listed in Column 2. For example, Table 4.3 shows that Lyrical documents have a large positive score for Dimension 1, and that score corresponds to the frequent use of positive Dimension 1 features (e.g., verbs, pronouns, stance features) coupled with an infrequent use of negative Dimension 1 features (e.g., definite articles, prepositional phrases). Encyclopedia Articles have a large negative score for Dimension 1, corresponding to the opposite linguistic

Table 4.3. *Summary of results from the MD analysis*

Key to the dimension score levels:
> ±1.5 shown by + + + + + + / ——————
> ±1.2 shown by + + + + + / —————
> ±0.9 shown by + + + + / ————
> ±0.6 shown by + + + / ———
> ±0.3 shown by + + / ——
> ±0.15 shown by + / –
Unmarked registers (with scores near 0.0) shown by 0

Dimension interpretation	Co-occurring linguistic features on the dimension	Summary of the dimension scores for selected sub-registers	Dimension score level
DIMENSION 1			
Oral-involved versus literate	Positive Features (+) Verbs: progressive aspect, non-past tense, activity verbs Pronouns: first-person pronouns, second-person pronouns Stance features: desire verb + *to* clause, mental verbs, attitudinal adjectives not controlling a complement clause, (stance adverbs) (type-token ratio, verb + *WH* clause)	Lyrical TV Dialogue Advice Interviews Personal Blogs Interactive Discussion	+ +
		Short Stories	0
VERSUS	Negative Features (–) definite articles, prepositional phrases, passive non-finite relative clauses, (concrete nouns)	Religious Blogs/Sermons Other Information Research Articles Historical Articles Encyclopedia Articles	– – – – – – – – – – – – – – – – – –

DIMENSION 2

Oral elaboration	Positive Features (+)	
	Verbs: existence verbs, mental verbs, epistemic verbs (not controlling a complement clause)	
	Verb + complement clause: likelihood verb + *that* clause, certainty verb + *that* clause, (verb + *to*-clause (excl. desire verbs), verb + *WH* clause)	
	That complementizer deletion (first-person pronouns)	
	Lyrical	+ + + + + +
	TV Dialogue	+ + + +
	Interactive Discussion	+ + +
	Interviews	+ + +
	Other Spoken	+ +
	Short Stories	+ +
	Description-with-intent-to-sell	0
VERSUS	Negative Features (−)	
	(Activity verbs, proper nouns, type–token ratio)	
	Formal Speeches	− −
	News Reports	− −
	Descriptions-of-a-person	− −
	Historical Articles	− −
	Recipes	− −

(*cont.*)

51

Table 4.3. (cont.)

DIMENSION 3

Oral clausal narrative versus literate nominal information

Positive Features (+)
- Verbs: past tense verbs, perfect aspect verbs, activity verbs
- Adverbs: time adverbs, place adverbs, (total other adverbs)
- Adverbial clauses (excl. conditional)
- Pronouns: first-person pronouns, (*it*, third-person pronouns)
- (Noun phrase features: definite articles, concrete nouns)

Short Stories	+ + + + + +
Lyrical	+ + + + + +
TV Dialogue	+ + + +
Personal Blogs	+ + +
Interactive Discussion	+ + +
Interviews	+ + +
Sports Reports	+ + +
How-to/Instructional	0

VERSUS

Negative Features (−)
- Long words
- Nouns: common nouns, process nouns
- Nominal modifiers:
  attributive adjectives
  premodifying nouns
  (finite relative clauses)

Formal Speeches	− −
Informational Blogs	− −
FAQs about Information	− − −
Other Informational	− − −
Research Articles	− − − − −

DIMENSION 4

Reported communication

Positive Features (+)
- Communication verb + *that* clause, communication verbs not controlling a complement clause
- Complementizer *that* deletion
- Likelihood verb + *that* clause
- (perfect-aspect verbs, past-tense verbs, prediction modals, common nouns)

News Reports	+ + +
Sports Reports	+ +
Spoken	+
Opinion Blogs	+
Interviews	+

VERSUS

Negative Features (−)
- Nominalizations
- (second-person pronouns)

Recipes	0
Research Articles	− −
Encyclopedia Articles	− − −
Other Informational	− − −
How-to/Instructional	− − −
Description-with-Intent-to-Sell	− − −

DIMENSION 5

Irrealis versus informational narration

Positive Features (+) Modal verbs: prediction, necessity, possibility modals Conditional adverbial clauses Verbs: copula *BE*, non-past tense Second-person pronouns, epistemic adjectives (not controlling a complement clause), demonstrative pronouns, clausal coordination	Lyrical TV Dialogue Advice How-to/Instructional FAQs about Information Interactive Discussion	+ +
	Recipes	0

VERSUS

Negative Features (−) Past tense verbs Prepositional phrases (progressive-aspect verbs, proper nouns, attributive adjectives, type–token ratio, long words)	Encyclopedia Articles Research Articles Descriptions-of-a-person Historical Articles	− − − − − − − − − − − − − − −

DIMENSION 6

Procedural / explanatory discourse

Positive Features (+) Causative/facilitation verbs, progressive aspect verbs, verb + *to-*clause (excl. desire verbs) Process nouns (activity verbs, possibility modals, long words, linking adverbials, communication verbs not controlling a complement clause)	FAQs about Information Research Articles How-to/Instructional Advice Informational Blogs	+ + + + + + + + + + + + + + + + +
	Description-with-intent-to-sell	0

VERSUS

Negative Features (−) Proper nouns (indefinite articles, contractions)	Spoken Sports Reports Travel Blogs Lyrical Interviews TV Dialogue	− − − − − − − − − − − − − − − − − − −

(cont.)

Table 4.3. (cont.)

DIMENSION 7

Nominal/literate stance	Positive Features (+) Stance noun phrase features: cognitive nouns, stance noun + prepositional phrase, stance noun + complement clause, other stance nouns (epistemic verbs not controlling a complement clause, process nouns, communication verbs not controlling a complement clause)		
	Research Articles	+ + + +
	Formal Speeches	+ + +
	Religious Blogs/Sermons	+ +
	Opinion Blogs	+ +
VERSUS	Other Spoken	0
	Sports Reports	– –
	Recipes	– – –
	TV Dialogue	– – – –
	Lyrical	– – – – –

DIMENSION 8

Description of humans	Positive Features (+) Human nouns Third-person pronouns Finite relative clauses Indefinite articles (Communication verb + *that* clause, communication verbs not controlling a complement clause, past-tense verbs)		
	Short Stories	+ + + + +
	Descriptions-of-a-person	+ + +
	Religious Blogs/Sermons	+ + +
	Encyclopedia Articles	+ +
VERSUS	Advice	0
	Lyrical	– –
	How-to/Instructional	– –
	Formal Speeches	– –
	Travel Blogs	– –
	Recipes	– – – –

DIMENSION 9

Non-technical explanation or description	**Positive Features (+)**	
	Concrete nouns, common nouns	
	Indefinite articles	
	(premodifying nouns)	
		Recipes	+ + + + + +
		How-to/Instructional	+ + + +
		FAQs about Information	+ + +
		Advice	+ +
		Reviews	+ +
		Informational Blogs	+ +
		Short Stories	0
VERSUS			
	Negative Features (−)	Other Spoken	− −
	Nominalizations	Encyclopedia Articles	− −
		TV Dialogue	− −
		Formal Speeches	− − −
		Religious Blogs/Sermons	− − −

characteristics: few positive Dimension 1 features but frequent use of negative Dimension 1 features.

Finally, Column 4 provides a semi-graphical indication of the magnitude of the dimension score for each of the registers listed in Column 3. The display is semi-graphical because the registers in Column 3 line up vertically with the Dimension Score Level in Column 4. Positive dimension scores reflect frequent use of the 'positive' features on a dimension, coupled with rare use of the 'negative' features on that dimension. Negative dimension scores reflect the opposite characteristics. However, it is possible for a register to have a negative dimension score even when there are no 'negative' features on a dimension – i.e., in the case where a register rarely uses the 'positive' features on that dimension. For example, lyrical documents and TV dialogues have large negative scores on Dimension 7, because the 'positive' features defining this dimension (stance noun phrase features) are extremely rare in those registers.

4.4   Multidimensional Patterns of Register Variation Online

4.4.1   Oral-Literate Dimensions

Consideration of the dimension score levels for registers (Column 4 in Table 4.3) indicates that Dimensions 1–3 are similar in distinguishing among oral versus literate web registers. Lyrical documents are marked on all three dimensions, while TV Dialogue and Interactive Discussions also have large positive scores on the three dimensions. Written informational registers have negative scores on all three dimensions.

Beyond those similarities, there are some less noticeable differences in the register patterns. Encyclopedia Articles and Research Articles have a large negative score on Dimension 1, reflecting the absence of the positive features on this dimension, combined with high frequencies for the negative Dimension 1 features. Religious Blogs/Sermons have a small negative score on Dimension 1, while TV Dialogue has a small to moderate positive Dimension 1 score.

One major difference between the first two dimensions is that Dimension 1 defines a clear opposition between two discourse styles – Oral-involved versus literate – whereas Dimension 2 primarily identifies a single discourse style: the style of elaboration found in oral discourse. Finally, Dimension 3 combines three major functional influences: an oral versus literate contrast; a narrative versus non-narrative/informational contrast; and a clausal versus phrasal/nominal contrast. Apparently, all of the oral registers in our corpus tend to have narrative communicative purposes, as do written narrative registers (e.g., Fictional Short Stories/Novels, Personal Blogs, Sports Reports). At the other extreme, registers like Research Articles, FAQs about Information, and Informational Blogs are marked by the absence of positive/narrative Dimension 3 features, together with high frequencies of the negative informational-nominal-phrasal features on this dimension.

Despite the similarities in register patterns, these three dimensions are clearly distinct in their linguistic composition. The positive features on Dimension 1 include dynamic activity verbs, progressive aspect verb phrases, and present tense, combined with pronouns and stance features. The positive features on Dimension 2 include stative verb classes and complement clause constructions. The positive features on Dimension 3 include past tense verbs and perfect aspect verb phrases, combined with adverbs and pronouns (opposed to long words and features associated with complex noun phrases).

These linguistic differences reflect the different functional underpinnings of the dimensions. Thus, the positive features on Dimension 1 include dynamic verbs and verb tenses (progressive aspect, non-past tense, and activity verbs), first- and second-person pronouns, and some stance features. These are stereotypically "oral" features, but they also reflect a high degree of interactivity and personal involvement. Such features are common not only in Lyrical documents and TV Dialogue; they are also common in written Advice documents and Personal Blogs, which reflect high personal involvement.

Table 4.3 shows that these Dimension 1 personal involvement features are rare in Encyclopedia and Research Articles (which have a large negative score on Dimension 1). Instead, we find a frequent use of the negative Dimension 1 features in these registers: noun phrases with definite articles, prepositional phrases, and passive non-finite relative clauses. These are features used to convey information, but they also reflect a kind of impersonal "detachment," in opposition to the dynamic, "involved" functions of the positive features.

The Dimension 1 pattern of variation for general registers shows that it defines a fundamental opposition between spoken/oral-involved versus written/literate/informational registers. For example, [1], [2], and [3] illustrate the dense use of positive Dimension 1 "oral" features in a song [1], a TV Transcript [2], and an Interactive Discussion, which is written but interactive [3]. In each of the text samples below, we have marked important linguistic features from the dimension in italics, bold, and underline.

[1] Lyrical
Bold marks non-past-tense verbs;
Italics mark progressive-aspect verbs;
<u>Underline marks first- and second-person pronouns</u>
Neither of <u>us</u> ever thought, back on the first day that <u>we</u> met
<u>We</u> were both so convinced that the dream would never **end**
Nobody saw the signs man, it'**s** funny how love **is** blind man
'Cause it **can be** over just as fast as it **begins**

So now I be *sitting* here, I'm alone trying to **stuff** my fear
Checkin' out one of the pictures there up on the shelf
The story behind my song, **is** that you never **know** what you **got** 'til it's gone

http://lyrics.wikia.com/Scatman_John:Sorry_Seems_To_Be_The_Hardest_Word

[2] TV Dialogue
Bold marks non-past-tense verbs;
Italics mark stance verbs;
Underline marks first- and second-person pronouns
V : Fortunately, I got to you before they did.
Evey Hammond : You got to me? You did this to me? You cut my hair? You tortured me?
   You tortured me! Why?
V : You *said* you *wanted* to **live** without fear. I *wish* there'd been an easier way, but there
   wasn't. I *know* you may never **forgive** me ... but nor will you **understand** how hard it
   was for me to **do** what I did. Every day I saw in myself everything you see in me now.
   Every day I *wanted* to end it, but each time you *refused* to give in, I *knew* I couldn't.
   [...] See, at first I *thought* it was hate, too. Hate was all I *knew*, it built my world, it
   imprisoned me, taught me how to **eat**, how to **drink**, how to **breathe**
[...]
V: So if you've seen nothing, if the crimes of this government **remain** unknown to you
   then I would *suggest* you *allow* the fifth of November to **pass** unmarked. But if you
   see what I **see**, if you *feel* as I *feel*, and if you would *seek* as I *seek*, then I *ask* you to
   stand beside me one year from tonight, outside the gates of Parliament, and together
   we shall **give** them a fifth of November that shall never, ever be *forgot*

www.imdb.com/character/ch0002908/quotes

[3] Interactive Discussion
Bold marks non-past-tense verbs;
Italics mark progressive aspect verbs;
Underline marks first- and second-person pronouns
It also **depends** where your (*sic*) *downloading* from. sometimes its not VM's fault. Also
   maybe you *getting* traffic **managed**, have you considered this?
If you signed up for a 12 month contract with virgin media broadband and your out of
   the initial 30 day period I dont think you can simply "**cancel**". You can still **get** BT
   installed but you will be **required** to keep *paying* for VM.
If someone's helped you out **say** thanks by *clicking* on the Kudos Star. If someone's
   solved your problem, why not **mark** their message as an Accepted Solution
I was only *trying* to **make** you aware that if you signed up for BT and a 12 month contract that if you **are** still under a 12 month contract with virgin media it would not **be**
   that easy to **cancel**. But if you **want** to **act** like an immature child then **be** my guest.

http://community.virginmedia.com/t5/Up-to-30Mb-Setup-
Equipment/729kbps-im-supposed-to-be-getting-10mb/
td-p/884921

In contrast, [4] illustrates the use of negative Dimension 1 "literate"
features (and the relative absence of positive Dimension 1 features) in a
research article.

[4] Research Article
Bold marks prepositions;
Italics mark definite articles;
Underline marks passive, non-finite relative clauses

Follow up experiments used macrophage isolated **from** *the* bone marrow (BM) **of** wildtype (WT) mice. *The* data **from** WB mushroom extracts is shown **since** *the* highest TNF secretion **from** RAW 264.7 cells was found **in** *the* WB stimulated cultures (Fig. 1-α). *The* BMDM cells are untransformed mouse macrophage that produce a variety **of** cytokines. Three cytokines produced **by** macrophage were picked **for** analysis: TNF-α, interleukin (IL)-10 and IL-1-α (Fig. 2-β). BMDM cells plus DMSO (control) cultures did not produce TNF-α, IL-10 or IL-1-β (data not shown). Like *the* results **from** *the* RAW 264.7 cell line, WB extracts alone stimulated TNF-α production.

www.biomedcentral.com/1471-2172/10/12

The Dimension 1 scores for other registers further help with the functional interpretation. For example, Table 4.3 shows that there are important differences among opinion sub-registers with respect to these linguistic features: Advice documents are extremely "involved," while News-Opinion Blogs (and editorials) and Religious Blogs/Sermons are detached and "informational" rather than "involved." [5] and [6] illustrate these differences:

[5] Advice
Bold marks non-past-tense verbs;
Italics mark progressive-aspect verbs;
Underline marks first- and second-person pronouns

You will **stop** *pulling* on others to **make** you special only when you **accept** the full responsibility of *making* yourself **feel** special. This means *learning* to **give** yourself all that you may be *trying* to **get** from others. [...] Instead of *trying* to **get** others to **give** you what you want, you can:

- **Attend** to your feelings throughout the day and **explore** what you may be *doing* that is *causing* painful feelings, rather than *making* others responsible for your feelings.
- **Attend** to your own needs rather than *expecting* others to **meet** your needs.
- [...]

www.streetdirectory.com/travel_guide/7814/self_improvement_and_motivation/
the_need_to_feel_special.html

[6] Religious Blog
Bold marks prepositions;
Italics mark definite articles

It is a snare **to** a man to utter a vow (**of** consecration) rashly, and **after** vows to inquire whether he can fulfill them. Both clauses are a protest **against** *the* besetting sin **of** rash and hasty vows. Compare *the* marginal reference.

Who devoureth that which is holy - It is a sin to take that which belongs **to** God, his worship, or his work, and devote it **to** one's own use.

And **after** vows to make inquiry - That is, if a man be inwardly making a rash vow, *the* fitness or unfitness, *the* necessity, expediency, and propriety **of** *the* thing should be first carefully considered.

http://bible.cc/proverbs/20-25.htm

Similarly, there is a large range of variation among narrative registers with respect to Dimension 1 scores. For example, Personal Blogs are highly "involved" on this dimension (see [7]); Short Stories are intermediate; while Historical Articles are extremely "informational" in their Dimension 1 characteristics ([8]).

[7] Personal Blog
Bold marks stance verbs;
Italics mark progressive aspect verbs;
Underline marks first- and second-person pronouns
Like last year (2011 event recaps here and here), I've come home with my head *spinning* and full of ideas that I can't wait to implement over the coming months.
The event was brilliant. On the networking front (although I **prefer** "connecting" or, let's face it, *chatting* up a storm) I had a ball *catching* up with the women I met last year, as well as *meeting* some of my beautiful readers in person – and let's not **forget** the B-School babes. There were fabulous ladies at every turn.
[...]
Other highlights of the weekend were having a good ol' chat to Sarah Wilson at the post-event drinks on Friday night (yes, she is beyond amazing).
[...]
<Comments to the post>
What a great wrap up Rach! Can't **believe** we didn't get a chance to chat. I **promised** myself we would on Saturday but by Saturday my dear sinuses were *tormenting* me so I wasn't in the right shape to **talk** to anyone.
[...]
I'm very much looking forward to *having* a bit of extra time over my holidays where I can spend some time on my blog... I miss it so much but life is just *getting* in the way at the moment.

http://inspacesbetween.com/blogging-business/
problogger-event-2012-the-full-wrap-up-pt-1/

[8] Historical Article
Bold marks prepositions;
Italics mark definite articles;
Underline marks passive non-finite relative clauses
In 1851, **during** *the* time that there was a gold rush **in** California, a gold rush began **in** Australia. *The* gold **in** California was mainly **in** *the* form **of** very fine grains, called gold dust.

However, **in** Australia, it was not unusual **for** gold nuggets, some very large, to be found.

The Largest Australian Nuggets

In October 1872 Holtermann's Nugget was found. **At** that time it was *the* world's largest specimen **of** reef gold. It weighed 286 kg and measured 150cm **by** 66cm. Also famous are: *The* Hand **of** Faith (27.2 kg), *the* Welcome Stranger (73.4 kg) and *the* Welcome (69.9 kg) nuggets.

www.kidcyber.com.au/topics/gold.htm

Even spoken sub-registers and informational-written sub-registers vary to some extent along this dimension: Within the general register of spoken discourse, TV Dialogue is extremely "involved" (see [2] above), while Formal Speeches have an intermediate Dimension 1 score. And within the general register of informational description, sub-registers like Research Articles and Encyclopedia Articles have some of the largest negative Dimension 1 scores (see [4] above).

Dimension 2 can similarly be interpreted as relating to a general oral–literate opposition, but the linguistic basis of that contrast relates to structural elaboration rather than personal involvement. That is, the co-occurring linguistic features on Dimension 2 include stative verbs (existence verbs and mental verbs) and three types of dependent clauses (complement clause constructions: *that*-clauses, *to*-clauses, and *WH* clauses). Lyrical discourse – especially songs – are extremely marked for the use of these elaborated features, but they are common in all spoken sub-registers of our corpus (see [1] and [2] above, repeated here with complement clause constructions marked in bold).

[9] Lyrical
Neither of us ever thought, back on the first day that we met
We were both so convinced that the dream would never end
Nobody saw the signs man, it's funny **how love is blind** man
'Cause it can be over just as fast as it begins
So now I be sitting here, I'm alone trying **to stuff my fear**
Checkin' out one of the pictures there up on the shelf
The story behind my song, is that you never know what you got 'til it's gone

http://lyrics.wikia.com/Scatman_John:Sorry_Seems_To_Be_The_Hardest_Word

[10] TV Dialogue
V : Fortunately, I got to you before they did.
Evey Hammond : You got to me? You did this to me? You cut my hair? You tortured me? You tortured me! Why?
V : You said **you wanted to live without fear**. I wish **there'd been an easier way**, but there wasn't. I know **you may never forgive me**... but nor will you understand **how hard it was for me to do what I did**. Every day I saw in myself everything you see in me now. Every day I wanted **to end it**, but each time you refused **to give in**, I knew

I couldn't. [...] See, at first I thought **it was hate, too**. Hate was all **I knew**, it built my world, it imprisoned me, taught me **how to eat, how to drink, how to breathe**. [...]

V: So if you've seen nothing, if the crimes of this government remain unknown to you then I would suggest **you allow the fifth of November to pass unmarked**. But if you see **what I see**, if you feel as I feel, and if you would seek as I seek, then I ask you **to stand beside me one year from tonight**, outside the gates of Parliament, and together we shall give them a fifth of November that shall never, ever be forgot.

www.imdb.com/character/ch0002908/quotes

These features are also quite common in "oral" written registers, such as Interactive Discussions (Discussion Forums or Question-Answer forums – see [3] above) as well as Short Stories (see [11]) and Personal Blog narratives (see [7] above).

Finally, Dimension 3 comprises stereotypically narrative linguistic features, such as past-tense verbs, perfect-aspect verbs, activity verbs, place and time adverbs and most types of adverbial clauses (except conditional clauses). The narrative style captured by Dimension 3 is mostly first-person (shown by the high loading for first-person pronouns), although third-person pronouns also co-occur with these features. The most marked web registers with respect to Dimension 3 are Lyrical texts (especially songs – see [1] above) and Interactive Discussions (see [3] above). However, Table 4.3 shows that Short Stories are actually the most extreme in their reliance on these features:

[11] Short Stories
Italics mark activity verbs;
Bold marks past tense verbs;
Underline marks first- and third-person pronouns

My mother ***returned*** to her content state and promptly ***bustled*** into the house. While she ***showered*** and ***changed*** I ***went*** into her kitchen and ***washed*** a mound of dirty dishes. This **was** just how I **imagined** being a detective would be, me in my mother's house, *washing* her dishes. I ***finished*** as my mother ***stepped*** out of her bedroom. She **wore** an ivory blouse, pearl necklace, black pants, and heeled shoes. Her hair **was** fully done and all her make-up **was** applied. She **looked** like she **was** *going* to an art gallery, not a crime scene.

www.fictionontheweb.co.uk/2012/11/the-poisoned-dancer-by-alex-artukovich.html

Personal Blogs are also extremely marked for the use of these features (see [7] above). Interestingly, though, Historical Articles have only an intermediate "narrative" score on Dimension 3 (see [8] above), while News Reports are actually "informational" rather than "narrative" in their Dimension 3 score:

[12] News Report
Italics mark nouns;
Bold marks premodifying nouns;
Underline marks attributive adjectives

There are now *reports* that at least 12 *people* have been killed in *today's crackdown.* *Reuters* reports that the *number* killed in *Hama* has risen to six, and *Avaaz* claims a further *six* were killed in *Homs.* Some of the latest **YouTube** *videos* to emerge from *Syria* are too gruesome to even link to.

The European *Union* has agreed to impose *sanctions* on 14 Syrian *officials* for their *part* in a violent **government** *crackdown* against *protesters,* but **President** Bashar *al-Assad* was not among those targeted.

After a *meeting* of **EU** *ambassadors,* the 27 **country** *bloc* said it would impose **travel** *restrictions* and **asset** *freezes* on the 14 *individuals,* with the *measures* to be formally approved early next *week* if no **member** *state* objects.

While *Assad* is not on the *list,* there is the *possibility* that he will be added in *time,* the *official* said.

www.guardian.co.uk/news/blog/2011/may/06/syria-libya-middle-east-unrest-live

Somewhat surprisingly, spoken TV Dialogue is also extremely narrative with respect to Dimension 3 features (see [2] above), while spoken Formal Speeches are actually marked for the absence of these narrative features.

Linguistically, the negative pole of Dimension 3 is composed of long words and several features related to complex noun phrases: common nouns; process nouns; and three types of nominal modifiers (attributive adjectives, premodifying nouns, and finite relative clauses). These features are especially prevalent in informational registers. At the same time, Dimension 3 shows that these informational registers tend to be linguistically non-narrative. However, there is some variation among informational sub-registers. For example, Descriptions-of-a-person (including biographies) and Encyclopedia Articles are intermediate along Dimension 3, employing both "narrative" and the "informational" linguistic features. In contrast, Research Articles are extremely marked on Dimension 3, making a dense use of the negative noun phrase features coupled with rare use of the positive "narrative" features (see [4] above).

Dimensions 1–3 distinguish among registers in similar ways. Lyrical texts (especially songs) are noteworthy for their frequent use of positive features from all three dimensions. Interactive Discussions and Spoken Discourse (especially TV Dialogue) are also highly marked for their frequent use of the linguistic features defining all three dimensions. At the other extreme, informational written documents have negative scores on all three dimensions.

From a statistical perspective, the dimensions are defined in terms of linguistic co-occurrence patterns. That is, each factor is extracted as a set of linguistic features that tend to co-occur frequently in texts, with no consideration of the register category of those texts. Similarities in the patterns of register variation across dimensions reflect the fact that linguistic co-occurrence is functional. In particular, the opposition between "oral" and "literate" discourse has been identified in previous MD studies as the single most important parameter of register variation (see Biber, 2014). However, that functional parameter has multiple grammatical/structural correlates, and those have been separated into multiple dimensions of variation in the present analysis. In particular, Dimension 1 features are primarily those associated with personal involvement and interactivity (e.g., progressive aspect, first- and second-person pronouns, stance verbs, stance adjectives, stance adverbs), while Dimension 2 features are those associated with the typical syntactic structure of oral discourse, especially verb + complement clause constructions. Dimension 3 is similarly defined as an opposition between verbs (and adverbs) versus noun-phrase features, but it has the added specialized element of past-tense/perfect-aspect/ activity verbs.

In general, stereotypically "oral" registers use both the personal involvement features associated with Dimension 1 as well as the finite complement clause features associated with Dimension 2. However, there are exceptions to this generalization. For example, opinion-advice documents are extremely marked for their frequent use of positive Dimension 1 features (associated with personal involvement), but they make only moderate use of the complement clause structures associated with Dimension 2. Conversely, "oral" dependent clause structures are frequently employed in fictional narrative, resulting in a large positive Dimension 2 score, but Short Stories are not especially marked for the personal involvement features defining Dimension 1. Dimension 3 shows somewhat different patterns of register variation. For example, Short Stories is the most marked register with respect to the positive "oral narrative" features defining this dimension. However, other more informational registers, like Sports Reports and Travel Blogs, are also noteworthy for their frequent use of positive Dimension 3 features, while they are not especially marked for frequent use of the positive features associated with Dimensions 1 and 2.

In summary, the first three dimensions in the present study can all be regarded as oral–literate oppositions. However, they are each defined by different sets of co-occurring linguistic features. The patterns of register variation along these three dimensions are similar, distinguishing between stereotypically oral registers such as Spoken Discourse, Interactive Discussions, and Lyrical Texts, versus stereotypically written registers like Academic Research Articles and Encyclopedia Articles. At the same time, though, each dimension is associated with its own unique pattern of register variation, reflecting the particular set of co-occurring linguistic features.

4.4.2   Narrative Dimensions

Dimensions 3, 4, and 5 all have some relation to narrative communicative purposes. Dimension 3, discussed above, contrasts the stereotypical narrative styles found in Short Stories and other "narrative" registers with the informational styles found in registers like Academic Research Articles.

Dimension 4, interpreted as "Reported Communication," also contrasts narrative with informational registers, but there are two major differences from Dimension 3:

(1) oral registers (Spoken discourse, Interactive Discussions, and Lyrical discourse) are unmarked with respect to Dimension 4; and
(2) the relations among specific narrative sub-registers are strikingly different from Dimension 3: News Reports are especially marked with respect to Dimension 4 features, while Short Stories and Historical Articles are both unmarked.

Linguistically, Dimension 4 has a completely different basis from Dimension 3. As discussed in the last section, Dimension 3 consists of stereotypical narrative features, including past-tense and perfect-aspect verbs, time and place adverbials, and pronouns. In contrast, Dimension 4 is composed of communication verbs co-occurring with likelihood verbs controlling *that*-clauses. This dimension is interpreted as reflecting reported communication, a function that is especially prevalent in News Reports (see [12] above). In contrast, Short Stories are more likely to include direct reports of speech (see [11] above), while informational narrative registers like Historical Articles include comparatively few reports of past communication (see [8] above).

The primary function of Dimension 5 is to identify irrealis discourse (see discussion in Section 4.4.3). In this case, narrative discourse is the opposing (negative) pole. Linguistically, the negative pole of Dimension 5 is defined by few co-occurring features: past tense verbs, prepositional phrases, and other features with smaller factor loadings. As a result, the most important linguistic characteristic of "negative" Dimension 5 registers is the absence of irrealis features, rather than the presence of narrative features. We turn to a discussion of those irrealis features in the following section.

4.4.3   Dimensions with More Specialized Discourse Functions

4.4.3.1   Irrealis Discourse

Dimension 5 is interpreted as signaling irrealis discourse versus informational/ narrative discourse. The primary function associated with irrealis discourse is the comparison and contrast of various conditions, possibilities, obligations, and eventualities. Linguistically, these functions are served by a frequent use of modal verbs (possibility, obligation, prediction), conditional clauses, second-person pronouns, epistemic adjectives, and copula *BE*. Several of the text samples given above illustrate this irrealis style, including the samples from Lyrical documents (see [1] above) and Interactive Discussions (see [3]).

How-to/Instructional documents also generally employ this constellation of linguistic features; for example:

[13] How-to/Instructional
Italics mark modal verbs;
Bold marks conditional IF-clauses;
<u>Underline marks second-person pronouns (including possessive determiners)</u>
To register for ANZ Internet Banking <u>you</u> need a Customer Registration Number (CRN) and Telecode.
ANZ Phone Banking customers
If <u>you</u> have already registered for ANZ Phone Banking use this CRN and Telecode to register for ANZ Internet Banking.
What's a CRN and how *can* I get one?
This *will* be either a nine digit number provided to <u>you</u> by an ANZ Customer Service Consultant or <u>your</u> 15 or 16 digit card number.
Enter <u>your</u> password. It *should* be 8-16 characters long and a combination of numbers and letters. <u>You</u> *will* need at least one number and one letter in <u>your</u> password. <u>Your</u> password *should* have no spaces or symbols.
How do I register for ANZ Internet Banking?
To register for ANZ Internet Banking <u>you</u> need a CRN and a Telecode . **If** <u>you</u> have not already been supplied with a valid CRN [...], please call the ANZ Internet Banking team [...]
If <u>you</u> have already registered for ANZ Phone Banking use the same CRN and Telecode to register for ANZ Internet Banking.
If <u>you</u> do not have a valid CRN or have forgotten <u>your</u> CRN, please call the ANZ Internet Banking team [...]

www.anz.com/internet-banking/help/getting-started/register/

The general registers of spoken discourse, opinion, and informational description do not usually adopt this irrealis style. However, specific sub-registers within these general categories do often employ irrealis discourse, including TV Dialogue (a sub-register of spoken discourse; see [2] above) and Advice (see [5]). Similarly, FAQs about Information are an example of a register that frequently employs irrealis features; for example:

[14] FAQ about Information
Italics mark modal verbs;
Bold marks conditional IF-clauses;
<u>Underline marks second-person pronouns (including possessive determiners)</u>
Q: I am having trouble losing the extra pounds from the turkey I ate over the holidays and I entered a lightweight category. Will I be able to race?
A: **If** <u>you</u> are over the 135lb max for women or 165lb for men, <u>you</u> *will* not be allowed to race in that category. NO EXCEPTIONS . However, <u>you</u> *will* be able to race in an open weight category for <u>your</u> age group and the registration team *will* give priority to accommodate <u>you</u> in a heavier category closest to <u>your</u> age and eligibility. There is no additional cost or penalty for changing weight categories. **If** <u>you</u> are unsure, please consult <u>your</u> coach for advice on <u>your</u> weight. Ideally, <u>you</u> *should* be at <u>your</u> category weight two weeks prior to February 5, 2012.

Q: *Can* I pick which ergometer I get to race on?

A: No, lane assignments are done randomly by computer. It is very important to sit in the correct lane matched by your name on the screen. Lane officials *will* be able to help you find your lane **if** you are unsure and each erg is labelled.

Q: **If** I have to scratch my race *can* I get my entry fee refunded?

A: It depends when you scratch. **If** you do not scratch before February 1, 2012 by 5:00 p.m. your race fees are non-refundable for any reason. **If** you reported your withdrawal and scratch to the Entries Co-ordinator and received a reply email that it was received before Feb 1 deadline you are eligible for a refund. However, you *will* have to wait. Refunds *will* only be processed starting 14 days after the event and mailed out to you.

www.cdnindoorrowing.org/faqs.html

4.4.3.2   Procedural/Explanatory Discourse

The constellation of co-occurring linguistic features associated with Dimension 6 function to tell readers what to do and how to do it – "Procedural/explanatory discourse." These features include causative/facilitation verbs (e.g., cause, result in) and process nouns (e.g., procedure, process), together with progressive aspect and activity verbs. There are several web registers – including How-to documents (and other instructions), FAQs, and Advice Blogs – that frequently employ these features to describe procedures or offer other explanations.

[15] Examples from How-to/Instructional documents

Bold marks causative/facilitation verbs;

Underline marks activity verbs;

Italics mark process nouns

That extra step can **cause** the *process* to drag on three times as long as a normal home.

Basically, since this *procedure* **resulted in** lost visitor paths, I switched to automatic tagging.

Find out how TrinityP3's range of services can **help** you make more informed decisions on your advertising costs.

[16] FAQ about Information

Bold marks causative/facilitation verbs;

Italics mark process nouns

Among other unforeseen problems, indiscriminate *use* of joint ownership can **cause** an increase in estate taxes over the joint lives of married persons, **force** double probates in the event of simultaneous *deaths*, create unfairness as to who pays for funeral expenses and *claims* against the decedent, raise undesired exposure during life to the debts of co-owners, and **cause** a shortage of funds for payment of estate taxes which can **cause** litigation with the taxing authorities.

www.floridabar.org/tfb/tfbconsum.nsf/48e76203493b82ad852567090070c9b9/
a0091ab18d4875d085256b2f006c5b75?OpenDocument

[17] Advice
Bold marks causative/facilitation verbs;
Underline marks activity verbs
The run might **elevate** heart rate and get a nice boost of serotonin, but a longer brisk
    walk will actually **facilitate** fat burning and weight loss.

> http://lajollamom.com/2011/01/drink-warm-lemon-water-in-the-morning/

Interestingly, these features (especially process nouns) are also common in
informational Research Articles, which include descriptions of the procedures
used for empirical research, together with the results of those procedures; for
example:

[18] Research Article
Italics mark process nouns
The ENCODE project aims at characterising the entire human hereditary information
    in more detail in order to identify functions for the large, non-protein-coding part
    of the human genome and to place it in context with the *regulation* of gene *activity*.
    One prerequisite was the *development* of novel *methods* for large-scale experi-
    mental *approaches* as well as for data handling and analysis. Using biochemical
    and bioinformatics *approaches*, it was possible to identify "candidates" of DNA
    elements that co-determine when and where in the human body a gene is active.

> www.alphagalileo.org/ViewItem.aspx?ItemId=123846&CultureCode=en

4.4.3.3   Nominal/Literate Stance

Research Articles is the register that is most marked for Dimension 7 features,
which is interpreted as "nominal/literate stance." These features are almost
entirely stance nouns that occur in a range of different grammatical environ-
ments (controlling complement clauses and prepositional phrases, as well as
other contexts). These stance nouns can express various epistemic meanings,
such as certainty (e.g., fact, knowledge), likelihood, possibility, doubt, or a person's claim or assertion. Stance nouns can also express other meanings related
to future plans or proposals. Stance nouns are generally quite rare in most web
registers. However, they are comparatively common in Research Articles. For
example:

[19] Examples from Research Articles
Bold marks stance nouns;
Italics mark stance nouns + to clause;
Underline marks stance nouns + *that* clause (including predicative *that* clauses)
The **need** *to consider different genetic materials* is also highlighted by the **fact** that
    varieties of many crops [...] show great production variation
One **possibility** is that females may find the questions more sensitive than males.
A recurrent **claim** is that the criminal justice system does not place value on the per-
    spectives of victims

4.4.3.4   Description of Humans

Dimension 8 is a highly specialized dimension, interpreted as relating to the description of humans. There are few linguistic features grouped on to this dimension, including human nouns (e.g., boy, girl, guy, gal, father, wife, adult, scholar, advisor, attorney, supervisor), third-person pronouns, and finite relative clauses (which often serve to identify the reference of a person). Not surprisingly, these features are common in documents that raters had classified as Descriptions-of-a-person; for example:

[20] Descriptions-of-a-person
Bold marks human nouns;
Italics mark indefinite articles
Priscilla Beaulieu Presley (born Priscilla Ann Wagner on May 24, 1945, in Brooklyn, New York) is *an* American **model**, **author** and **actress** and the only **wife** of Elvis Presley. Her biological **father**, James Wagner, was *a* **pilot** who was killed in *a* plane crash when Priscilla was just *an* **infant**.

http://priscilla.elvispresley.com.au/

However, these linguistic characteristics are even more common in Short Stories (see [11] above), as well as in other registers like Religious Blogs and Encyclopedia Articles (which often focus on the lives of important persons).

4.4.3.5   Non-technical Description

Finally, Dimension 9 opposes two nominal styles: positive Dimension 9 scores reflect a dense use of concrete nouns and other common nouns; negative Dimension 9 scores reflect a dense use of nominalizations. The two registers that are especially marked with respect to these features are How-to/Instructional documents and Recipes. Both of these registers are especially marked for the dense use of concrete nouns and other common nouns. In fact, we often find lists of noun phrases in these texts, with comparatively little need for full clauses. [21] illustrates this style of discourse:

[21] Recipe
Bold marks concrete nouns;
Italics mark indefinite articles;
<u>Underline marks other common nouns</u>

- 1/2 <u>cup</u> **sugar**
- 1.75 <u>cups</u> plain **flour**
- 1 tbsp baking **powder**
- 2 **eggs**, slightly whisked already
- 1/2 cup **milk**
- *A* little under half *a* **stick** of **butter** (110g) – melted
- lots of **vanilla** <u>essence</u> (3-5 **spoons**)

- lots of **blueberries** (fresh/frozen...doesn't matter)
- **Oven**: 200°C

Spray *a* 12-hole **muffin pan** with cooking **spray**. Mix dry ingredients (**sugar**, **flour**, baking **powder**) together in *a* **bowl**. Whisk wet ingredients (**eggs**, **milk**, **butter**, essence) together for about *a* minute or two, then add to dry ingredients. [...]

http://crissybakes.wordpress.com/2012/03/09/blue-muffins-for-a-long-weekend/

4.5   Dimensions of Variation on the Web in Comparison to Other Discourse Domains

The results of the present MD analysis provide strong confirmation for the proposed universals of register variation that have emerged from previous MD studies (see discussions in Biber (1995), chapters 7 and 10; Biber (2014)). Those universals include:

- Linguistic dimensions reflecting the fundamental opposition between clausal/"oral" discourse versus phrasal/"literate" discourse
- Linguistic dimensions reflecting different aspects of narrative versus non-narrative discourse
- Linguistic dimensions reflecting the expression of stance

All three of these functional considerations are strongly reflected in the present MD analysis of web registers. At the same time, there are notable differences between our MD analysis of web registers and previous MD analyses of other discourse domains. The present analysis identifies more dimensions of variation than in most previous analyses. These dimensions are each represented by a relatively large number of co-occurring linguistic features, and they are readily interpretable in functional terms by reference to the shared functions of those features together with the distribution of registers along the dimension. However, the overall analysis results in finer-grained distinctions than in most previous studies. These distinctions reflect the comprehensive nature of the corpus (as well as the large number of lexico-grammatical features included in the analysis). Thus, the corpus is based on a large random sample of the complete searchable web, incorporating a considerably more diverse set of registers than in most previous MD studies; these include Lyrical texts, TV Dialogue, spoken Interviews, Advice columns, Personal Blogs, How-to/Instructional documents, FAQs, Short Stories, News Reports, Opinion Blogs, Encyclopedia Articles, Research Articles, etc.

Although our corpus represents a comprehensive near-random sample of documents from the public searchable web, it is important to keep in mind the kinds of texts that are not included. Most obviously, our study does not include private Internet registers (e.g., email messages, tweets, and other social-media postings). At the other extreme, though, our corpus also does not include any documents from the "deep web." These are the millions of password-protected informational documents stored on the Internet, including research articles published in academic journals and technical documents found on corporate or institutional sites. Our results here show that informational documents comprise <15 percent of the documents found on the publicly searchable web. However, if it were possible to sample documents from the private "deep" web, that proportion would be much higher, including a much greater number of highly technical texts.

The discourse domain of the searchable web further differs from the domain analyzed in most previous MD studies by its absence of true spoken discourse. Our web corpus includes TV Dialogue, transcribed Interviews, and transcribed Formal Speeches. The corpus also includes Lyrical texts, including Song Lyrics. However, those texts are limited in number, and there are no examples of genuine face-to-face conversation. Despite these differences, three of the dimensions in the present analysis relate to a fundamental oral–literate opposition, incorporating the same "oral" lexico-grammatical features as in previous analyses (e.g., verbs, adverbs, pronouns, finite adverbial clauses, finite complement clauses).

The findings from the present chapter strongly support the conclusion that language use on the web is distinct in many ways from other discourse domains. While certain web registers are similar or identical to their traditional, non-web counterparts (e.g., Encyclopedia Articles, Editorials, News Reports, Song Lyrics, Recipes), there are many other non-web registers of English that are not readily available on the public searchable web (e.g., textbooks, contemporary fiction novels, refereed academic journal articles, corporate technical reports – as well as conversation and most other genuinely spoken registers). And at the same time, there are other web registers that do not exist outside of the web (e.g., Travel Blogs, Personal Blogs, and Interactive Discussion forums). In the following chapters, we provide further linguistic descriptions of each of the major registers found on the web, exploring the similarities and differences to non-web registers in more detail.

Notes

1. Principal Components Analysis and Exploratory Factor Analysis are related statistical procedures (both options under the FACTOR Procedure in SAS). We chose a Principal Components Analysis in the present case, because it is more appropriate for large studies, reducing a set of highly correlated variables to a small number of underlying parameters, explaining the maximal amount of variance in the data. Readers are referred to the online documentation for the FACTOR procedure in SAS at https://support.sas .com/documentation/cdl/en/statug/63347/HTML/default/viewer.htm#factor_toc.htm.
2. For the sake of convenience, "exact" factor scores were computed directly in SAS. This method differs from the procedure used in most previous MD studies, which instead computed factor scores by summing the standardized values of variables with high

loadings on a factor and ignoring variables with low loadings. In actual practice, there is little difference between the two methods, especially when they are applied to identify the relative differences among registers as in the present case.

In our discussion here (and in Table 4.3), we have reordered the factors to group together dimensions that have related functional interpretations. Thus, Dimensions 1, 2, and 3 in Table 4.3 relate to the oral–literate distinction; Dimensions 3, 4, and 5 all have some relation to narrative registers; and Dimensions 6–9 reflect more specific discourse functions.

We dropped the original Factor 5 from the discussion here because it is not readily

New dimension number (used in the present paper)	Original factor number
1	1
2	4
3 (inverted)	3
4	7
5	2
6	9
7	6
8	8
9	10
— drop —	5

interpretable. The primary linguistic features loading on the original Factor 5 are general adverbs, linking adverbials, stance adverbials, type–token ratio, clausal co-ordination, and demonstrative pronouns. Spoken discourse and opinion documents are marked for the presence of these co-occurring features; informational documents and lyrical documents are marked for the absence of these features.

3. This percentage is similar to the rates for other factor analyses of registers; for example, the seven-factor solution in Biber (1988) accounted for 51.9 percent of the shared variance, while the four-factor solution in Biber et al. (2015) accounted for 44 percent of the shared variance.

5   Narrative Registers

5.1   Introduction

The Narrative register contains 17,692 texts, or about 36 percent of the documents in the CORE, making it the largest register category in the corpus. Table 5.1 contains a breakdown of the distribution of texts across the seven sub-registers within the Narrative category. News reports are by far the most common of the Narrative sub-registers, and the most common sub-register category in the CORE. News reports comprise nearly 59 percent of the Narrative category and about 21 percent of the CORE. Personal Blogs and Sports Reports each contain nearly 3,000 texts, or about 17 percent of the Narrative sub-corpus. The other four categories were less frequent, each containing fewer than 500 texts.

As mentioned previously, although research on online language focuses on the web's novel, non-traditional register categories, most online texts actually belong to register categories that are the same, or at least quite similar, to a traditional print register category. The texts in the Narrative register category are prime examples of this. Most of these texts have situational characteristics that are not unique to the web. News Reports and Sports Reports have long

Table 5.1. *Sub-register categories in the Narrative category with text counts*

Sub-register	Count
News Report	10,399
Personal Blog	2,957
Sports Report	2,938
Historical Article	497
Travel Blog	371
Short Story	272
Other Narrative	258
TOTAL	17,692

been printed in newspapers. Historical Articles have been published in various forms in magazines and books. Likewise, Short Stories have a long history of publication in periodicals and book collections. While blogs as a publication outlet did not exist before the Internet, Travel Blogs share many characteristics with travel columns in newspapers and magazines. Personal Blogs are similar in many ways to personal journals and diaries. The key difference is that Personal Blogs are public rather than private.

The large number of Narrative documents on the web shows that recounting and describing past events are important functions in online discourse. In this chapter we attempt to present a comprehensive description of the situational and linguistic characteristics of Narrative registers online. In Section 5.2, the situational characteristics of the Narrative register will be briefly summarized, followed by a detailed comparison of situational characteristics of the six sub-registers. Section 5.3 and 5.4 present results from three linguistic analyses of these narrative sub-registers, including a review of the MD analysis dimension scores for the sub-registers and detailed analyses of each sub-register category using key grammatical analysis and keyword analysis. These sections also include detailed functional interpretations of the linguistic findings, which are aimed at connecting the linguistic results with the situational characteristics established in Section 5.2. Finally, in Section 5.5 we summarize and discuss the major findings from this chapter.

5.2   Survey of Narrative Sub-registers

All of the texts in the Narrative register category share certain characteristics. In our corpus, all of the Narrative texts are written rather than spoken. In addition, all of the texts in the Narrative register category are produced by a single author or set of coauthors, rather than being coconstructed by multiple participants in an interactive format. The audience for these registers is general, with relatively little specialist background knowledge required for understanding. Finally, all of the texts in this register category share the purpose of narrating past events. Beyond these shared attributes, the sub-register categories within the Narrative register vary along at least four situational parameters: author, audience, production circumstances, and purpose. These differences are summarized in Table 5.2.

News Reports and Sports Reports share many of the same characteristics. Both are typically written by authors who specialize in news or sports journalism, respectively, to audiences interested in reading about recent events in those areas. In terms of production circumstances, Sports and News Reports are professionally revised and edited. However, these two categories also include Sports Blogs and News Blogs, which in some cases are written by amateurs. In contrast with all of the other sub-registers in the Narrative category, News and

Table 5.2. *Situational characteristics of Narrative sub-registers*

Sub-register	Author	Audience	Production circumstances	Purpose
News Report	News writer	Readers interested in news	Usually preplanned, professionally edited, and time-sensitive	Report on recent events
Sports Report	Sports writer, specialist	Readers interested in sports	Usually preplanned, professionally edited, and time-sensitive	Commentary on athletes and athletic events
Personal Blog	Blogger	Readers interested in the subject and/or the author of the blog	Usually preplanned and edited by the author. Can be interactive	Report and/or commentary on personal events
Historical Article	Historian	Readers interested in a historical topic	Usually preplanned. May be professionally edited	Description of noteworthy people and events from the past
Travel Blog	Traveler	Readers interested in a location or the traveler	Usually preplanned and edited by the author. Can be interactive	Description and commentary on travel destinations
Short Story	Fiction author	Fiction readers	Usually preplanned and professionally edited	Entertainment

Sports Reports are the only ones that are usually time-sensitive. In other words, publishers of News and Sports Reports are usually highly motivated to publish and update their articles as quickly as possible.

Personal Blogs and Travel Blogs share many characteristics. Both can be written by non-professional writers to readers who are interested in either the topic of the blog or the writer of the blog (e.g., family, friends, fans). Both are typically edited by the author rather than by professional editors. Personal Blogs tend to be somewhat interactive in nature, as there is typically a comments section at the end of these blogs, and it is not uncommon for authors to use their blog posts or the comments section to interact with their readers.

Personal Blogs are written about a wide range of topics. Examples of topics included in the corpus are parenting, quilting, video games, and style (see Screenshot 5.1). Examples of titles in parenting blogs include: "When Your Toddler Grabs from the Baby," "How Children Develop Toxic Shame," and "What if your Child DOES Know Right from Wrong and Chooses to Do Wrong?" Titles of Personal Blogs on style include: "What is Navy and

THE SEVEN YEARS OF BLOGGING CHRISTMAS

When you've been blogging as long as me (8 years next year), you've accumulated a lot of photos of Christmases past. In the interests of nostalgia and laziness, I thought I'd take you back in time to my many and varied (and not-so-varied) vintage Christmas outfits of the past! In a vaguely chronological order...

ABOUT Lorem ipsum dolor sit amet, consectetur adipisicing elit, sed do eiusmod tempor incididunt ut labore et dolore magna aliqua. Ut enim ad minim veniam, quis nostrud exercitation ullamco laboris nisi ut aliquip ex ea commodo consequat. Duis aute irure dolor in reprehenderit in voluptate velit esse cillum dolore eu fugiat nulla pariatur.

Back in 2008, I loved swing dancing. I wore this two-piece candy-cane striped set to a Christmas swing dance, complete with holly in my hair! Can't remember the brand, but I do know it is long gone.

CATEGORIES

UNCATEGORISED

Screenshot 5.1. A Personal Blog post
www.diaryofavintagegirl.com/

What Colours Work Well with It?," "How to Make a Monochromatic Outfit Interesting," and "How to Put Together a Corporate Wardrobe on a Budget."

As mentioned above, the blog (derived from a web log) is one of the few publication types that is exclusively found online. Blogs do not constitute a single register category. Rather, a blog is simply a mode of web publishing that allows virtually anyone with a computer and an Internet connection to publish their writing online. Due to this absence of restrictions on who can publish with a blog, it is often difficult to determine their specific situational characteristics. For example, a Travel Blog could be written by a travel enthusiast to describe her recent vacation (e.g., Screenshot 5.2), or it could be written by a professional travel writer to describe a travel destination. Examples of Travel

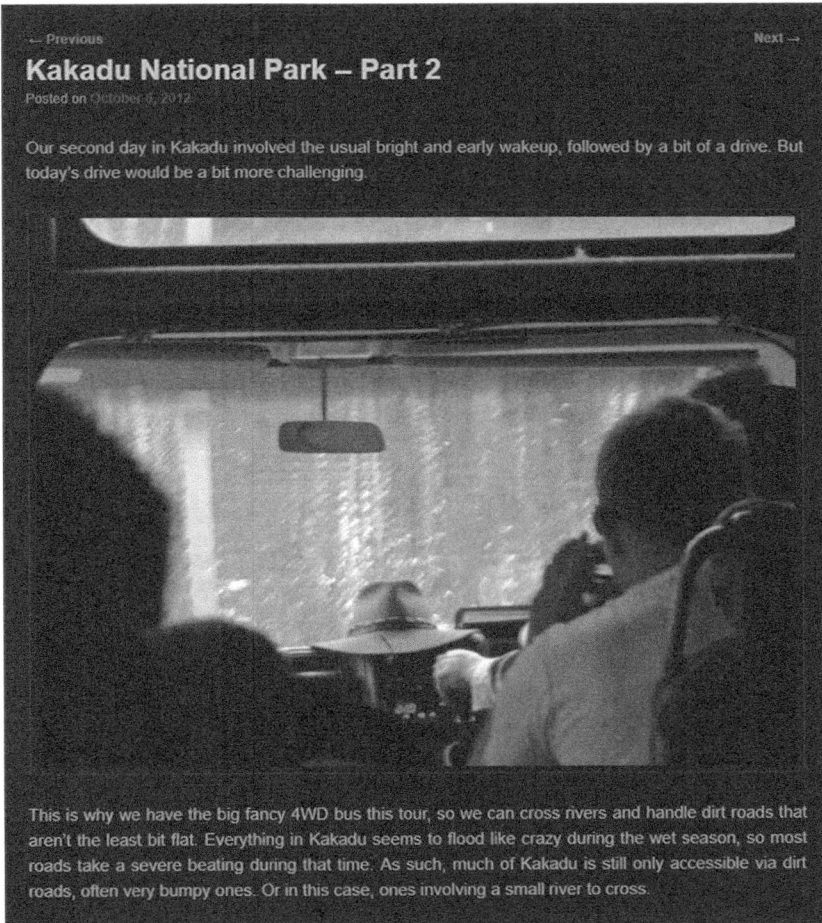

← Previous   Next →

Kakadu National Park – Part 2
Posted on October 9, 2012

Our second day in Kakadu involved the usual bright and early wakeup, followed by a bit of a drive. But today's drive would be a bit more challenging.

This is why we have the big fancy 4WD bus this tour, so we can cross rivers and handle dirt roads that aren't the least bit flat. Everything in Kakadu seems to flood like crazy during the wet season, so most roads take a severe beating during that time. As such, much of Kakadu is still only accessible via dirt roads, often very bumpy ones. Or in this case, ones involving a small river to cross.

Screenshot 5.2. Travel Blog
www.themissingyear.com/archives/4448

Blog titles include: "The Art of the Chilled Out Trip to Paris," "Miami is Nice, So I'll Say It Twice," and "Where to Go in Eastern Sicily."

Historical Articles give narrative accounts of noteworthy people or events from the past. These articles come from a wide variety of sources, including websites of government entities and historical societies and blogs by history buffs. The Historical Articles published by large organizations are typically edited professionally, while the independent articles are simply published by

FUGUES FICTION RECOMMENDATIONS
SHERLOCK HOLMES

ABOUT   ALL STORIES   **NEW ADDITIONS**   SEARCH
SEARCH BY CATEGORY   SEARCH BY TAGS

back to Fugues in the Key of X

TAG: **RATING: PG**

December 19, 2010

mad_mauldlin, "A City on the Head of a Pin"

When John first woke up, he could that he was on powerful narcotics. Thus he was not at all bothered that the technician recording his vital signs was sporting a large pair of glossy white wings. "Oh, hello," she said when she noticed him staring at her. "How are you feeling?"

"Pretty," was about all John was able to get out, before he slipped under again.

It was harder to ignore the second time, when consciousness was there to stay. The doctor explaining his injuries to him was very clever and very patient, and optimistic about a full recovery; he felt rather bad that he couldn't pay attention. "Dr. Watson?" she asked eventually. "Are you all right?"

"Fine," John said, staring at her wings.

Screenshot 5.3. Short Story
http://keyofx.org/fiction_sherlockholmes/tag/rating-pg/page/4/

individuals through blogs or personal websites. Titles of Historical Articles include: "Napoleon Bonaparte – Notable Australian Connections," "Uncovering Secrets of the Sphinx," and "Senkaku/Diaoyu: Islands of Conflict."

In contrast with the other sub-registers in the Narrative category, the Short Stories sub-register includes fiction writing in the form of entire short stories or segments of longer fictional works. Many of the texts in this category are written and posted on the web by amateur fiction writers, including fan fiction written based on original works such as Sherlock Holmes (see Screenshot 5.3). This category also contains some chapters or other sections of previously published fiction written by well-known fiction authors. The texts in this category are written for the primary purpose of entertainment.

5.3   Summary of MD Analysis Results for Narrative Sub-registers

The MD analysis we reported on in Chapter 4 revealed linguistic variation across the Narrative sub-register categories. In this section we briefly summarize those patterns across each of the nine dimensions.

The only sub-register with a strong positive score along Dimension 1 – Oral-involved versus literate-informational – was Personal Blogs, showing that the texts in this sub-register use the most features related to audience involvement and oral discourse. This is related to the interactive nature of many Personal Blogs which was mentioned in the previous section. Travel Blogs were the only other sub-register with a positive Dimension 1 score, although the mean score was close to zero. On the negative end of Dimension 1, Historical Articles had the lowest mean score, demonstrating their descriptive, informational purpose. News Reports and Sports Reports also had negative Dimension 1 scores.

Dimension 2 – Oral elaboration – resulted in positive scores for Personal *Blogs* and Short Stories, revealing a higher use of features associated with mental states (e.g., mental verbs, epistemic verbs) and colloquial discourse (e.g., *that* deletion, first-person pronouns). In Personal Blogs these features are used to express the authors' thoughts and feelings in an informal, colloquial manner. In Short Stories these features are often used by the author to represent the thought processes of and dialogue among fictional characters. Historical Articles, News Reports, and Sports Reports had relatively strong negative loadings on Dimension 2, showing a stronger emphasis on facts and events than on the thoughts and words of people.

Most of the sub-registers had positive mean scores on Dimension 3 – Oral narrative versus written information. Personal Blogs, Travel Blogs, and Sports Reports used the most features associated with oral narrative (e.g., past-tense verbs, time and place adverbs, first- and third-person pronouns) while News Reports used more features related to written information (e.g., premodifying nouns and attributive adjectives). This shows that News Reports are the most informationally dense of all the Narrative sub-registers, whereas the majority of the other registers are more elaborated.

News Reports had the strongest positive score on Dimension 4 – Reported Communication – followed by Sports Reports. This is unsurprising when we consider that journalists, whether of news or sports, often rely heavily on direct quotes to represent events or people's reactions to them. The only sub-register to receive a negative score on this dimension was Travel Blogs. This is probably because these texts tend to be the least human-focused of all the sub-registers, focusing primarily on facts related to a geographic location.

Every Narrative sub-register received a negative score on Dimension 5 – Irrealis versus Informational Narration. Clearly, Narrative texts are less focused on hypotheticals and possibilities and more focused on recounting information about past events. Unsurprisingly, Historical Articles have the highest negative score along this dimension due to their focus on objective, factual content.

All but one of the sub-registers received a negative mean score on Dimension 6 – Procedural/explanatory discourse, demonstrating fundamental differences between Narrative texts and other registers in the corpus (e.g., How-to, Informational Description). The Narrative sub-registers are not only characterized by limited use of language features related to procedures and explanation, but they also tend to use higher frequencies of the negative-loading features (e.g., proper nouns, indefinite articles).

Similar to the previous dimension, all sub-registers had negative scores on Dimension 7 – Literate stance, except for News Reports, which had a very low positive score. Like the previous dimension, Dimension 7 reveals a clear distinction between Narrative registers and Informational registers in the corpus. The authors of Narrative texts are typically more concerned with recounting events than they are with establishing their stance or position in relation to a given subject.

Dimension 8 shows that Short Stories strongly prefer features related to "Description of Humans." This is probably because readers of fiction lack the contextual information necessary to visualize and understand fictional characters unless the author explicitly provides it. This type of human description is also used in other sub-registers (e.g., Historical Articles, News Reports), although to a much lesser extent. Travel Blogs received a strong negative score on this dimension, once again demonstrating their heavy focus on locations rather than people.

The only sub-register with a notable positive score on Dimension 9 – Non-technical description – was Travel Blogs. While Travel Blogs often contain narrative about travel, they also contain descriptions of the characteristics of travel destinations. The other Narrative sub-registers, especially Sports Reports and Historical Articles, lack this heavy focus on description.

The plots in Figure 5.1 show the mean dimension scores for the Narrative sub-registers. However, it is also important to consider the range of variation

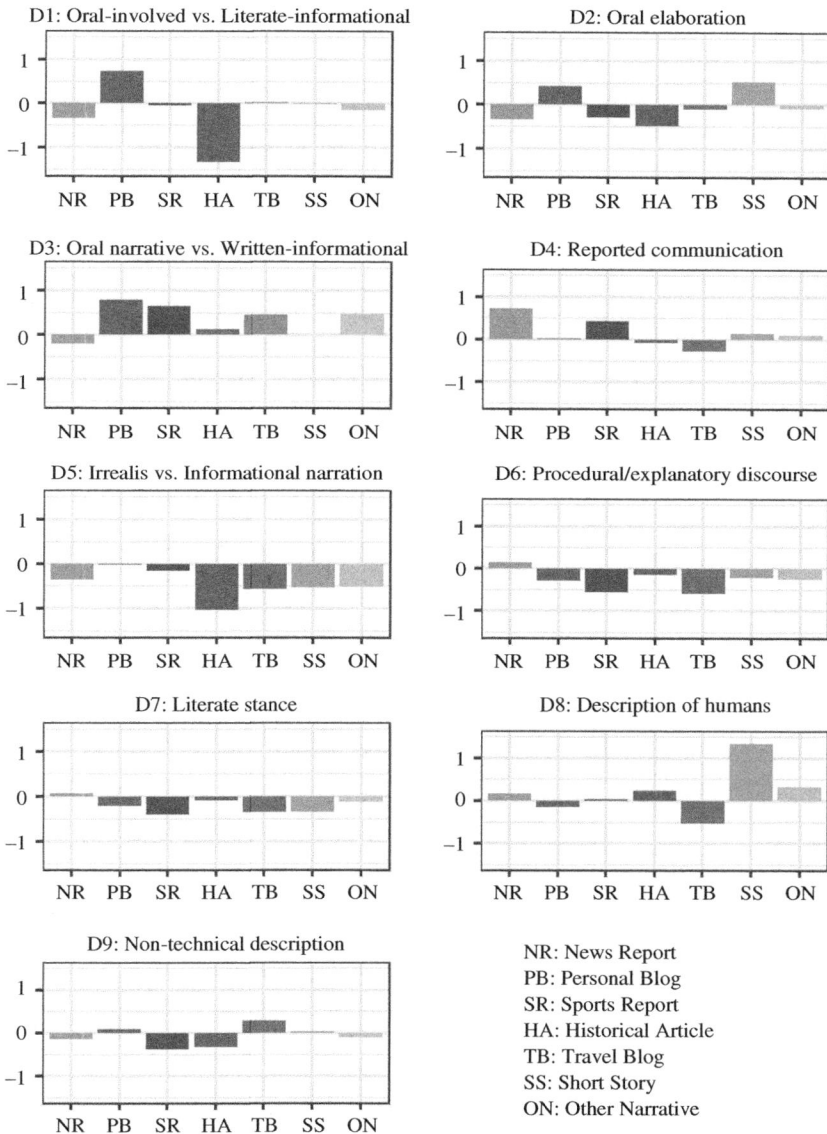

Figure 5.1. Dimension scores across the seven Narrative sub-register categories

Table 5.3. *Dimension score means and standard deviations for Narrative sub-registers*

Register	D1		D2		D3		D4		D5		D6		D7		D8		D9	
	M	SD	M	SD	M	SD	M	SD	M	SD	M	SD	M	SD	M	SD	M	SD
News Reports	-0.34	0.79	-0.34	0.86	-0.20	0.88	0.72	0.90	-0.36	0.78	0.14	0.94	0.07	0.90	0.17	1.09	-0.14	0.87
Personal Blog	0.73	0.87	0.43	0.94	0.79	0.83	0.02	0.70	-0.11	0.79	-0.29	0.78	-0.21	0.81	-0.15	0.89	0.10	0.82
Sports Report	-0.05	0.82	-0.28	0.89	0.64	0.69	0.44	0.76	-0.16	0.85	-0.57	0.75	-0.40	0.72	0.04	0.74	-0.39	0.78
Hist. Article	-1.3	0.61	-0.47	0.66	0.13	0.77	-0.09	0.52	-1.0	0.55	-0.15	0.70	-0.09	0.74	0.24	0.91	-0.32	0.84
Travel Blog	0.02	0.73	-0.10	0.75	0.46	0.90	-0.28	0.53	-0.56	0.65	-0.60	0.65	-0.35	0.67	-0.52	0.61	0.30	0.77
Short Story	0.00	0.75	0.52	0.73	1.72	0.86	0.15	0.59	-0.53	0.66	-0.21	0.52	-0.34	0.60	1.35	1.08	0.04	0.77

within each sub-register to measure the extent to which the register is well-defined linguistically. This in turn is an indication of the extent to which the register is well-defined situationally.

Table 5.3 presents the standard deviations (in addition to mean dimension scores) for each sub-register. Sub-registers like Historical Articles, Travel Blogs, and Short Stories have generally small standard deviations across the dimensions. These sub-registers are relatively constrained for their situational characteristics and communicative purposes, and as a result, the documents within each sub-register tend to be quite similar linguistically. In contrast, sub-registers like News Reports and Personal Blogs tend to have larger standard deviations across dimension scores, indicating that there is a considerably greater range of linguistic variability among documents within those categories. This finding reflects the fact that News Reports and Personal Blogs are less sharply delimited situationally, especially with respect to the range of communicative purposes included within those categories.

5.4   Detailed Grammatical and Lexical Analyses of Narrative Sub-registers

5.4.1   News Reports

The results of the key feature analysis revealed that News Reports are marked by numerous grammatical structures and semantic classes of words. There were eight positive key features that met our inclusion criteria of $d \geq 0.30$ (Figure 5.2).

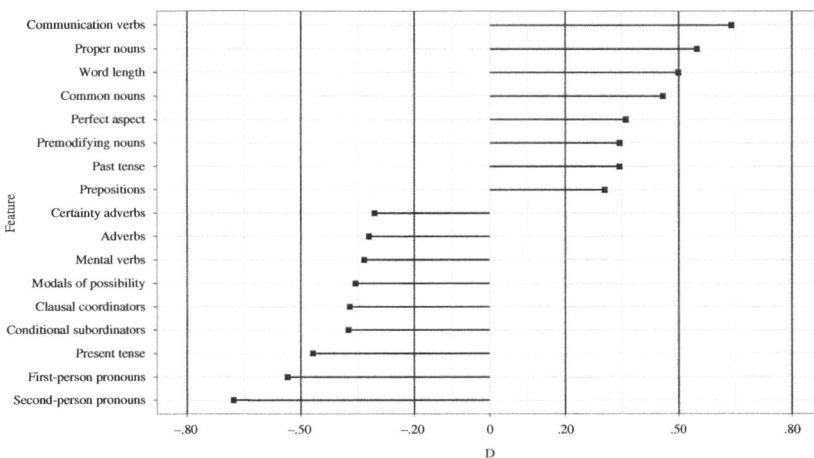

Figure 5.2. Key grammatical features for the News Reports sub-register

News reporting relies heavily on communication verbs (e.g., say, announce, reply, inform, question). Communication verbs in news facilitate direct speech reporting, which is extremely common in News Reports (see [1]).

[1] "Stealing from the organization's one thing," Steele **said**. "Stealing from the kids, that really gets my goat, so to speak." The supervisor, Matthew, who also did not want his name printed, **called** the claims "outrageous" and **said** he received a flood of angry calls within a day of leaving YESS WFM.

www.edmontonexaminer.com/2010/09/28/fundraiser-may-not-be-what-it-seems

Communication verbs are also common in news due to its frequent reporting of statements from public figures and organizations (see [2]).

[2] Egypt's higher military council **said** it would **announce** measures for a transitional phase after President Hosni Mubarak stepped down.

www.msnbc.msn.com/id/41506482/ns/world_news-mideast_n_africa/t/
egypt-protesters-vow-massive-demonstrations/

Proper nouns are also extremely common in news. Proper nouns identify names of people, places, and organizations, all of which are common topics in News Reports. Together, [1] and [2] contain proper nouns in all three of those categories: people (*Steele, Matthew, President Hosni Mubarak*), organizations (*YESS WFM*), and places (*Egypt*).

The key feature analysis also revealed that News Reports tend to have longer words than the rest of the corpus. This could be related to a heavy reliance on nominalizations and other specialized terms, which are often longer words. Examples of these types of longer words can be seen in [3].

[3] The findings I presented today change it from impractical to plausible and worth further investigation. "The additional energy reduction realized by oscillating the bubble intensity is an interesting conjecture that we will enjoy looking at in the lab." www.dailymail.co.uk/sciencetech/article-2204913/Nasa-breakthrough-suggests-Star-Treks-warp-drives-possible-practical.html

Nine negative key features met our criteria. The strongest of these features are first- and second-person pronouns. The relatively low frequencies of these pronouns relates to the lack of interaction and involvement in News Reports.

The keyword analysis for News Reports (Table 5.4) reveals many words that are strongly associated with News Reports. The first hundred words on the list were classified into seven semantic categories, with a few words left over in an "Other" category. The most common keyword category, "People – names and titles," contains some proper names (*Barack Obama, Mitt Romney*). This corpus was collected in 2012 during the presidential election cycle in the United States, hence the relatively high frequency of the names Barack

Table 5.4. *Keywords for the News Report sub-register*

People – names and titles	Government	Reporting	Figures/ details	Politics	Places	News features	Other
analyst	arrested	according	2011	campaign	britain's	guardian	advising
analysts	coalition	accused	billion	democrat	cameron	news	funding
authorities	committee	added	cent	democrats	dal	reuters	investigation
barack	council	allegations	million	election	india's		launched
ceo	country's	announced	nov	political	jammu		released
chairman	county	confirmed	percent	presidential	kashmir		
chief	court	report	thursday	republican	srinagar		
deputy	cuts	reported	tuesday	republicans	uk		
director	economic	reporters	wednesday	vote			
executive	economy	reports	year				
former	federal	said					
he	foreign	says					
leader	global	statement					
mayor	gov	told					
minister	government	warned					
mitt	government's						
mr	national						
obama	plans						
obama's	police						
officer	public						
officials	sector						
president	security						
residents							
romney							
secretary							
senior							
spokesman							
spokeswoman							

Obama and Mitt Romney, the two general election candidates in that election. This category also contains many titles for government and corporate officials (*president*, *minister*, *mayor*, *director*, *chairman*). Within News Reports, these titles are frequently included in appositive noun phrases to provide additional information about people who are mentioned in the news by name (see [4]).

[4] Jack Kamrad, chief psychologist for the Peel District School Board in Ontario, said his staff receive a lot of referrals for students born late in the school year, especially in the youngest grades.

www.theglobeandmail.com/life/health-and-fitness/adhd-diagnosis-more-likely-for-kids-born-later-in-the-year-study/article551676/

The second largest category, "Government," contains words related to government bodies (*police*, *council*, *committee*), law enforcement (*police*, *arrested, court*), and taxes (*cuts, plans*). This category makes sense considering that government is one of the aspects of life that all news readers share in common. News readers within a particular country may differ in gender, age, race, education, political orientation, religion, and personal hobbies, but they all share a common system of government and laws. This makes these topics of high relevance and interest to a large number of news readers.

Reporting words are the third most common keyword category. These words share functions related to communication verbs that were described above. News reports are replete with reported speech and commentary on statements made by public figures.

Figures and details is the fourth category. Words in this category function as vehicles for the description of facts and figures, a common purpose of News Reports.

[5] By the close of 2011, that had fallen to 25 per cent. Three-quarters of the way through 2012 that figure may well have fallen even further.

www.edge-online.com/features/the-state-of-facebook-
gaming-according-to-king-com/

As mentioned above, political commentary is one important purpose for many News Reports, especially during a presidential election. Some of the words in the places category were initially quite surprising (*Srinagar, Kashmir, Dal*). It turns out, however, that there was a link to an article related to a breaking news story in Srinagar, Jammu, India, that was included in many of the news articles that were downloaded for our corpus, thus skewing the counts for a few of the low frequency content words that were contained in that headline. Finally, there are three words that were classified as news features (*news, Reuters, Guardian*). While the words in the "Other" category did not fit tidily into any of the other categories, they are easily interpretable as news-related words.

Overall, the results of the linguistic analyses reported here characterize online News Reports as an informationally dense written register focused on the reporting of high-interest current events in a narrative style. This is done through a heavy reliance on facts, public information, and reported speech from experts or other high-profile public figures.

5.4.2   Personal Blogs

Personal Blogs are the second most common narrative sub-register. Of all the registers in the narrative category, Personal Blogs are the most distinct from traditional print registers. While Personal Blogs are similar in some ways to personal journals or diaries, they are fundamentally different in that they are intended to be publicly available and read by an audience. The linguistic results

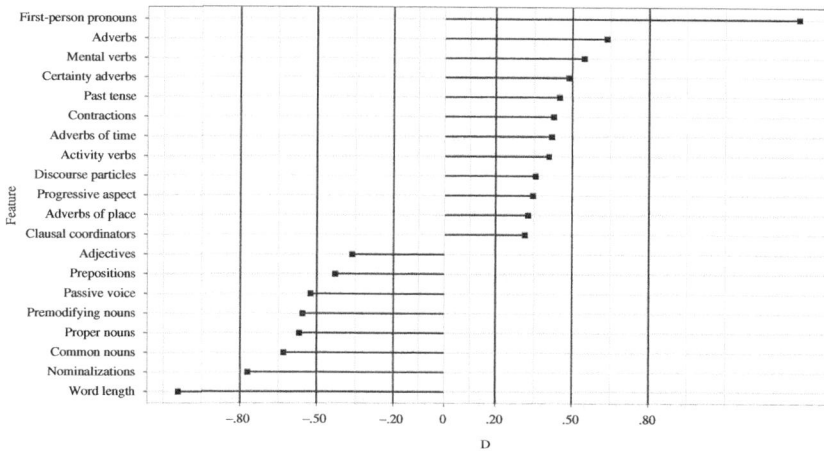

Figure 5.3. Key grammatical features for the Personal Blogs sub-register

in this section characterize Personal Blogs as a distinctive text variety that definitely deserves to be studied in its own right.

The three strongest positive key features for the Personal Blogs register are 1st person pronouns, adverbs, and mental verbs (Figure 5.3).

On average, Personal Blogs use first-person pronouns more than twice as frequently as the other texts in CORE. By definition, Personal Blog posts are written by a single person and, in most cases, the topics of the blog posts are focused on the writer's personal life. Selection [6] demonstrates this focus on the writer's personal life. It is interesting to note that the only other person mentioned in this sentence (husband) is referred to in relation to the writer. Rather than using her spouse's first name, or another title, the writer refers to him as *my husband*.

[6] **I** was not as keen to go but **I** would never turn down an opportunity to spend some one-on-one time with **my** husband, so off **we** went.
   http://myhometruths.com/2011/06/a-funny-thing-happened-on-the-way-to-sydney/

Adverbs are used more frequently on average in Personal Blogs than in the other registers in the corpus. Adverbs are often used as emphatics (*a lot, really*) and amplifiers (*completely, extremely*) in this register. The use of adverbs for these purposes is illustrated in [7].

[7] I was feeling **fully – completely** and **utterly** – resentful about having to set the alarm.
                                          http://miserablebliss.ca/blog/2007/04/14/its-okay/

Stance adverbs are particularly frequent in Personal Blogs. The expression of personal stance is a common function in Personal Blogs. [8] and [9] illustrate how stance adverbs are used in Personal Blogs.

[8] The point of the whole exercise was, **obviously**, to try and promote the company a bit more informally.

www.diaryofavintagegirl.com/

[9] When I back my quilts, I LOVE to piece together all the fabric left-overs because, **frankly** I hate to look at the fabric ever again. So **essentially** there are two quilts in one.
http://booilley.blogspot.com/2012/11/quilting-along-with-dogs.html

The negative key features for Personal Blogs reveal that this sub-register tends to use shorter words and fewer nouns (nominalizations, common, proper, and premodifying), as well as fewer passive voice constructions (see Figure 5.3). These features are associated with informationally dense written registers and a more literate discourse style.

The top hundred keywords were manually classified into seven major categories, with an additional "Other" category (see Table 5.5). The most frequent category is labeled "Stance." This adds additional evidence in support of our conclusion that stance is an important characteristic of Personal Blogs, especially considering that only three of the words on the "Stance" list are adverbs.

Table 5.5. *Keywords for the Personal Blogs sub-register*

Stance	Time/measurement	Description	Personal pronouns	Topics	Blogging	Family/friends	Other
couldn't	birthday	amazing	her	bed	blog	couple	am
decided	bit	awesome	i	chocolate	blogging	dad	anyway
excited	day	beautiful	i'd	coffee	busy	friend	back
favourite	days	cute	i'll	dinner	photos	friends	didn't
feel	hour	fun	i'm	girl	post	husband	going
feeling	life	gorgeous	i've	hugs	posts	kids	got
felt	little	lovely	me	lunch	thank	mom	hadn't
glad	lots	nice	mine	sleep	thanks	mum	haven't
happy	morning	pretty	my	trip	write		oh
hope	night	stuff	myself	walk			sat
knew	started	sweet	she	woke			wasn't
know	tomorrow	things					went
love	week	wonderful					xx
loved	weekend						
maybe	weeks						
really	yesterday						
thought							
too							
wanted							

Most of these words are used to express personal stance. An example of this type of stance can be seen in [10].

[10] Sometimes though I do **feel** older. This **feeling** does loose the luster. Not often but at times the experience **feel** less fresh. I **think** this is why at times I loose sight or sense of perspective.
                          http://drewginn.blogspot.com/2012/03/in-middle-of-trials.html

The second largest keyword category was given the label of "Time/measure-ment." Most of the words in this category are nouns or adverbs used to express a time reference. Personal Blogs tend to be heavily narrative, so they rely on references to past events. In addition, they typically reflect the style and tone of an entry in a personal diary/journal, where details regarding the timing of events are known, valued, and documented (see [11]).

[11] I've dozed off on every train journey this **week** and **yesterday** felt so ill I thought I might throw up in a meeting. **Tonight** I nearly cried because hubby's lamb stew with dumplings was just so beautiful.
                          http://ifnarky.com/2012/09/26/3-that-there-is-a-brain-fart/

The third keyword category is "Description." Teasing apart the words in this category from those in the "Stance" category was difficult in some cases. The main distinction we made was based on whether the word was focused on describing an object or event, or the stance of the blogger regarding that object or event. It should be noted, however, that in both cases the blogger is making qualitative judgments about things, events, or people. Examples of this type of descriptive word are bolded in [12].

[12] They were just **exquisite**! The work that goes into each mat is **phenomenal**, they're **gorgeous**. The colours are so **vibrant** and the **wonderful** textures from all the materials would make it a joy to play on.
                          http://littlepieceofpie.com/

Eleven different variations of personal pronouns combine to form the fourth category. Examples of these pronouns can be seen in [10] and [11]. The fifth category, labeled "Topics," contains content words that offer some insight into the topics that personal bloggers write about. The sixth category includes words related to the actual process of writing blog posts and maintaining blogs. One of the most common functions for these words is to apologize for not posting blogs more often or not writing more interesting blog posts (see, e.g., [13] and [14]).

[13] I go through phases every now and then of wanting to give up **blogging**. I **write** a load of rubbish really, and when I see some of the more profound **blogs** written I want to delete this **blog** of brain fart.
                          http://ifnarky.com/2012/09/26/3-that-there-is-a-brain-fart/

[14] Sorry I didn't write a **blog** a few weeks ago. Life in the Pritchard house has been a little crazy.

http://10fourdesign.com/studio-dogs/

Finally, there were several words related to the topic of family and friends. The Personal Blogs in the CORE are public, but it seems that the primary audience typically comprises family and friends with whom the blogger shares a social "offline" relationship. Thus, there is a heavy focus on friends, family members, and relationships with these people. Examples of this can be seen in [6], [11], and [14].

In summary, the results of the key linguistic feature analyses reveal that Personal Blogs are generally narrative and highly involved. They are also author-focused with a high use of personal stance markers. The keyword analysis showed that stance, time reference, and detailed descriptions were the most common semantic categories.

5.4.3   Sports Reports

Sports Reports are a relatively frequent register category in the CORE. As discussed previously, there are many situational similarities between Sports Reports and News Reports. However, there are also important distinctions, including topic and purpose. The three strongest positive key features for Sports Reports include proper nouns, third-person pronouns, and activity verbs (Figure 5.4).

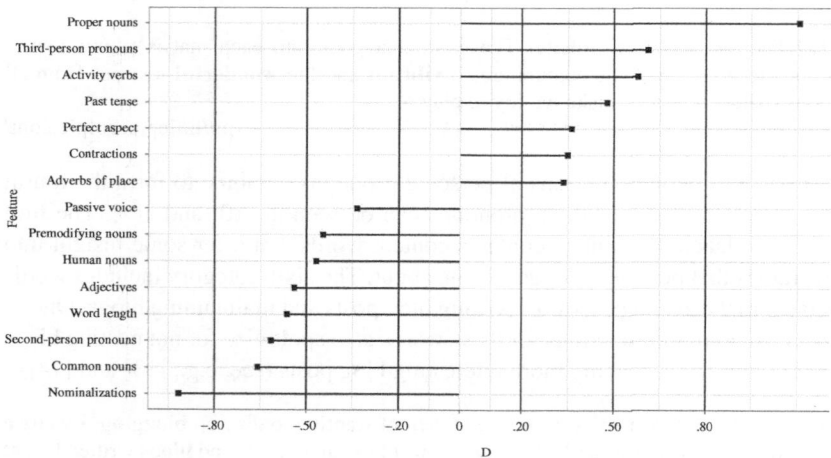

Figure 5.4. Key grammatical features for the Sports Reports sub-register

Proper nouns were also highly key for the News Report register, but the effect size for proper nouns in Sports Reports is more than two times larger. Clearly, proper nouns are extremely important in Sports Report discourse. The most obvious functional reason for this is related to the topic of Sports Reports, which is nearly always focused on commentary about athletic events and the people who participate in them. Whereas there are a wide range of topics that News Reporters can focus on, many of which do not require a heavy use of proper names, it would be extremely difficult to write most Sports Reports without the use of proper names for athletes, coaching staff, sports teams, among others. This heavy reliance on proper names can be seen in [15].

[15] I know **Brady** thinks he does and all that stuff, but I think there's a little more help from **Belichick** with **Brady** than there is with **Peyton Manning**. I mean, **Tom Moore** has done a great job with him forever, **Jim Caldwell** and **Tony Dungy**, but it's **Peyton Manning**.

> www.boston.com/sports/football/patriots/extra_points/2011/01/
> ryan_on_brady_m.html

Third-person pronouns were also highly key for Sports Reports. While third-person pronouns tend to be highly frequent in narrative registers generally, it is interesting to note that they do not even make the top five list of most key features for News Reports. This is related to the point made above about the heavy use of proper nouns in Sports Reports. It seems that while general News Reports can focus on many topics, there is a heavy focus on human subjects in Sports Report discourse (see [16] below).

[16] "The rowing bug bit me," **she** said. "**She**'s very fearless," said Laura. "Anything anyone can do, **she** can do, too." Claire was only 11 when **she** joined **her** dad at the Head of the Charles in the parent-child double but still fretted that **she** was overtaxing **him**.

> www.bostonglobe.com/sports/2012/10/17/for-campbell-family-connecticut-
> head-charles-regatta-all-family/xIxpWYImMHfyRSwAzXmMuJ/story.html

Activity verbs are also extremely common in Sports Reports. This list includes verbs that denote actions and events (e.g., *try, play, run, win, advance, defend*). Sports Reports often include fast-paced descriptions of sports events, at times written in the style of a play-by-play commentary, similar to the spoken sports reporting one would hear while watching or listening to a live sporting event (see Ferguson, 1983). An example of this can be seen in [17].

[17] Minutes later good work on the right **won** Shetland a long corner which was **taken** quickly by Kristan Robertson. She **ran** at the Aberdeen defence, **beating** the first two players and then slipping the ball back to Stacey Laurenson.

> www.shetlandtimes.co.uk/2012/11/13/impressive-hockey-team-
> see-off-aberdeen-in-district-cup-tie

The negative key features for Sports Reports include nominalizations, common nouns, second-person pronouns, word length, and attributive adjectives (see Figure 5.4). The lower frequency of common nouns and attributive adjectives, along with the generally shorter word length and fewer nominalizations, show that Sports Reports are less focused on information than they are on narration and concrete action. The relatively low frequency of second-person pronouns confirms that Sports Reports are less involved and interactive than other online registers.

The keywords for online Sports Reports offer clear insights into the topics and functions of this register (see Table 5.6). These keywords were classified into six categories, with an additional category for "Other" keywords. The category with the most words was labeled "Gameplay." This category includes words related to sporting events, including activities that occur (e.g., *scoring, playing, coaching*), objects that are used (e.g., *ball, pitch, bench*), and other details associated with gameplay (e.g., *injury, matches, touchdowns*). An example of how some of these words are used can be seen in [18].

Table 5.6. *Keywords for the Sports Report sub-register*

Gameplay	Players/people	Sports, leagues and teams	Outcomes	Seasons/playoffs	Pronouns	Other
ball	alex	arsenal	beat	final	he	against
bench	captain	chelsea	champion	finals	he's	career
coaching	coach	club	champions	playoff	him	fa
defensive	coaches	clubs	championship	playoffs	his	saturday
game	defender	club's	championships	premier		talent
games	fans	everton	cup	season		
goal	goalkeeper	football	fourth	seasons		
goals	manager	league	last	tournament		
injury	midfielder	league's	second			
match	player	liverpool	top			
matches	players	manchester	trophy			
midfield	quarterback	nfl	unbeaten			
offense	rookie	nhl	victory			
penalty	roster	sport	win			
pitch	scorer	sports	winning			
play	striker	spurs	wins			
played	teammates	squad	won			
playing	wenger	team				
points	winger	teams				
score		team's				
scored		tottenham				
scoring						
stadium						
touchdown						
touchdowns						
yards						

[18] I can not imagine Stoke City saying "we are at Arsenal and they have a **pitch** that we are not used to so lets adjust our **game** and match their passing **game**" it doesn't really work the other way round.

> www.arsenalvision.co.uk/my-vision/4015-life-is-a-pitch-away-from-
> the-emirates-mvilla-eyes-arsenal-chamakh.html

The second category deals with players and people. This seems to contradict the finding in the key feature analysis that showed human nouns to be a negative key feature. However, as discussed above, it is clear that these words are specialized animate nouns (e.g., *midfielder*, *striker*, *winger*) that are unlikely to be found in a more general corpus. [19] illustrates the use of some of these terms (Table 5.6).

[19] He was replaced by **midfielder** Augustin Chantrel. The first **goalkeeper** to be sent-off was Gianluca Pagliuca of Italy in a match against Norway during the opening round of the 1994 World Cup. Only three **goalkeepers** have ever captained a World Cup winning side.

> http://goalkeepersaredifferent.com/keeper/facts.htm

The third keyword category was labeled "Sports, leagues and teams." This category includes words related to names for specific sports (e.g., *football*) and for athletic clubs and organizations (e.g., *NFL*, *teams*, *Chelsea*). The use of words in this category can be seen in [20].

[20] [...] including the last couple weeks against the top two **teams** in the TSN.ca **NFL** Power Rankings. Miami's run defence has been among the **league's** best this season [...]

> www.tsn.ca/story/?id=409575

Unsurprisingly, Sports Reports focus heavily on the outcomes of sporting events and tournaments. There were seventeen keywords that were classified as "Outcomes." The bolded words in [21] illustrate how words in this category are used in online Sports Reports. The next category, "Seasons/Playoffs," is closely related to the "Outcomes" category. The difference is that the Seasons/Playoffs words relate to the progression of games and matches during the course of a season, including postseason playoffs and tournaments. The italicized words in [21] fall into this category.

[21] Meanwhile, while Tennessee women's basketball squads have **won** eight NCAA **championships** (1987, 1989, 1991, 1996, 1997, 1998, 2007, 2008), their male counterparts have never reached the NCAA *tournament* **championship**. So, which schools have **won championships** in both the men's and women's *tournaments*?

> www.travelblogs.com.au/articles/1280/1/3-Amazing-NCAA-Schools-With-Mens-
> and-Womens-Basketball-Championships/Page1.html

There were four pronouns in the list of the top hundred keywords (he's, him, his, he) (see [22]). These are all third-person pronouns, which is unsurprising considering the presence of third-person pronouns as the second most key linguistic feature for Sports Reports. One thing we learn from the keyword list that we did not learn from the list of key features is that there is a greater use of male pronouns than female pronouns. It seems that while both males and females participate in sporting events, there is a disproportionate focus on males, at least when Sports Reports are compared with other online registers. This could be because there are simply more male-only sports and male athletes and coaches, or it could be because male athletes are more likely to be covered in online Sports Reports. A detailed analysis of this pattern is beyond the scope of the analysis presented here, but it would be an interesting topic for future research.

[22] Simon plays a north-south game and **he** has to play that style because that's how **he's** effective. Because of **his** injury, **he** couldn't play the way **he** wanted to and **he** was getting apprehensive in practice so I think **he** made the right choice.

> http://thechronicleherald.ca/sports/176275-eagles-darveau-
> shut-down-for-season

Overall, the key features and keywords for online Sports Reports reveal that online Sports Reports are typically focused on narrative and commentary about sporting events. There is also a heavy focus in this register on humans, including athletes, coaching staff, and other athletic administrators. It was found that the people discussed are often male, and referenced in relation to their specific roles. Finally, the discourse of Sports Reports often relies on fast-paced, highly active commentary about gameplay and the progress of athletes and athletic clubs and teams.

5.4.4   Historical Articles

Texts classified as Historical Articles are much less common than the first three register categories covered in this chapter. Like News Reports, Historical Articles describe and narrate past events. Historical articles are typically devoted to noteworthy events from the past, whereas News Reports usually address recent events. Historical Articles are often focused on describing people, resulting in considerable overlap between this register and Descriptions-of-a-person (see Section 7.4.5). The relationship between these two registers can be seen situationally as well as linguistically (see Section 9.1). The five strongest positive key features for Historical Articles are past-tense verbs, prepositions, passive voice, proper nouns, and word length (Figure 5.5).

Past-tense verbs are more than twice as frequent in Historical Articles as the rest of CORE. The use of past tense is expected, considering the past orientation

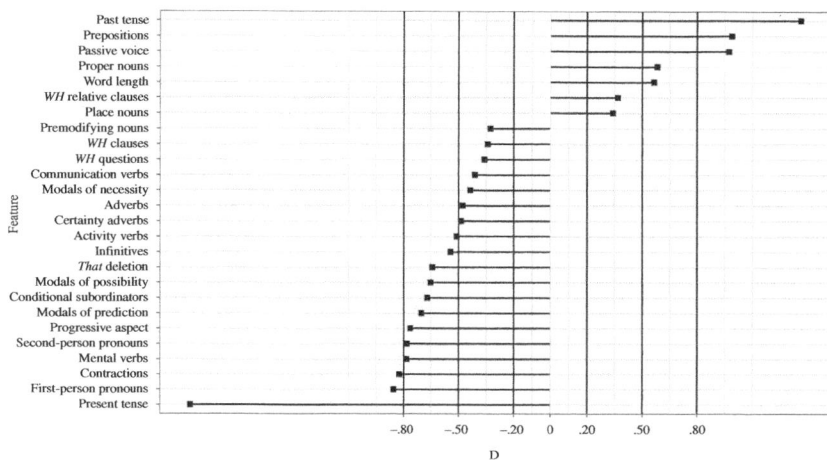

Figure 5.5. Key grammatical features for the Historical Articles sub-register

of these texts. However, it is impressive to observe just how marked Historical Articles are for this feature. The bolded words in [23] illustrate the heavy focus on past orientation in this register.

[23] Despite *the* deaths of four young girls, and *the* many that **were injured**, no-one **was** initially **arrested** for this crime even though *the* authorities **suspected** four men within days of *the* outrage.

                www.historylearningsite.co.uk/1963_birmingham_church_bombing.htm

Prepositions are the second positive key feature for Historical Articles. Prepositions are typically frequent in informational writing. More specifically, they are often used for the purpose of compressing information into noun phrases rather than elaborating it using clause structures. The frequent use of prepositions in Historical Articles allows authors to describe relationships between nouns (people, places, events, etc.) and to provide additional information about them, often expressing a sense of what, where, and when. This function is illustrated in [24] below.

[24] The Civil War spurred the growth **of** print advertising **for** many reasons. The conflict created a need **for** hundreds **of** thousands **of** uniforms, underwear and shoes and ready-made food which triggered mass production **of** clothing and canned goods. **In** addition, when men went off **to** war, women went **to** work **in** the factories to earn money.

                http://content.lib.washington.edu/advertweb/index.html

Passive voice is another linguistic feature that is much more frequent in Historical Articles than other online registers. The passive construction functions to increase emphasis on the person or object that experiences an action by fronting it and making it the grammatical subject. This allows an author to either completely exclude the logical subject of the sentence (i.e., short passive) or to deemphasize the logical subject by moving it into a "by phrase" (i.e., long passive). The short passive is often used when the logical subject is either unknown or deemed to be irrelevant. The passives in [23] illustrate a case where the people who committed the crime are not known. [25] contains two long passives. It is clear that the agent is known in both cases, but the author has chosen to use a passive construction to place increased emphasis on the logical objects.

[25] The stadium **was designed** by architect Myron Hunt in *1921*. His design **was influenced** by the Yale Bowl in New Haven, Connecticut, which was built in *1914*.

Like News Reports and Sports Reports, Historical Articles contain many more proper nouns, on average, than the rest of the CORE. In Historical Articles, proper nouns are used to refer to important events ([24]: Civil War), people ([25]: Myron Hunt), and locations ([25]: New Haven, Connecticut).

A large number of key features on the negative end met our inclusion cut-off. Logically, present tense verbs are, to some degree, in complementary distribution with past-tense verbs, which was the strongest positive key feature. Functionally, there is little discussion of present events in Historical Articles. Historical Articles are also characterized by the lack of features related to interaction and involvement (first- and second-person pronouns) and other features associated with oral discourse (contractions, modals, *that* deletion, activity verbs).

The keyword list for Historical Articles has (Table 5.7) five major semantic categories. The most common category was "Past verbs," which contains twenty-five verbs in the past tense. This list of verbs confirms the finding from the key feature analysis that past tense is extremely common in this register. Additionally, this list clearly shows this register's heavy emphasis on past actions, events, and experiences. Finally, this list also provides insights into some of the major topics of Historical Articles. [26] shows the use of two of these past verbs (Table 5.7).

[26] By the end of the 18th *century* Manchester had **established** itself as the centre of the cotton industry in Lancashire. The merchants **brought** the raw cotton from Liverpool [...]

www.spartacus.schoolnet.co.uk/ITmanchester.htm

Table 5.7. *Keywords for the Historical Articles sub-register*

Past time verbs	Time reference	Governments/people	War/military	Geography	Other
appointed	1914	Britain	allied	east	famous
arrived	1915	British	armies	land	hundred
became	1916	Charles	army	lands	museum
began	1917	colonial	battle	near	royal
believed	1918	colonies	civil	north	
brought	1922	colony	conquest	railway	
came	1939	empire	death	river	
carried	1940	England	died	ships	
continued	1941	France	force	south	
declared	1942	German	forces	southern	
destroyed	1943	Germans	fought	west	
established	1944	Henry	infantry		
followed	1945	historian	march		
formed	century	John	military		
had	during	king	naval		
held	early	men	soldiers		
joined	history	settlement	treaty		
killed	July	settlers	troops		
led	later	Spartacus	war		
named	were	tribes			
proved		William			
remained					
returned					
sent					
took					

Time reference words are also strongly associated with Historical Articles. Examples of time reference words or numbers are italicized in [25] (1914, 1921) and [26] (century).

"Government/people" is the third semantic category. This category includes references to governments and political bodies (see [27]), as well as groups of people and individuals (see [28]).

[27] Russia had broken her chains and stands as the greatest free nation in Europe with republican **France** and liberal **England**.

www.spartacus.schoolnet.co.uk/RUSmarchR.htm

[28] Another source is the book "Tragedy and Hope" by Carroll Quigley, a brilliant **historian** who had access to Illuminati secrets. **John** Coleman worked for MI6, resigned in disgust and got a doctoral degree in History.

http://inquiringminds.cc/
fw-books-the-dark-history-of-the-new-world-order-and-the-eu-annette-r-s

War and military references are a major theme in online Historical Articles. The recurring nature of this theme is intuitive when we consider that few events have as profound an impact on humanity as war and conflict. [29] contains a narrative account of a battle fought in the early history of the United States.

[29] Although only a handful of the **soldiers** had had previous **battle** experience, the army bloodily **fought** off the reckless, determined Indian attack. Two hours later, thirty-seven **soldiers** were dead, twenty-five others were to die of injuries, and over 126 were wounded.

www.warof1812.ca/tipcanoe.html

The final semantic category was assigned the label of "Geography." References to place and location are prevalent in Historical Articles. This corroborates the finding that prepositions are frequently used in this register since prepositions are often used to describe locations (see [24]).

In sum, the register of online Historical Articles can be characterized by a narrative focus with a strong tendency toward past orientation. This past orientation goes beyond the summary of recent events covered in News Reports. The primary focus in Historical Articles is on events and people in the relatively distant past that have had the strongest influence on humanity. The narrative discourse style in Historical Articles is coupled with informational prose that functions to provide contextual detail. The major themes of the online Historical Articles in CORE seem to be people, government, and war, but there are also many other themes that recur.

5.4.5   Travel Blogs

Compared with the other registers in the Narrative category, Travel Blogs are relatively infrequent on the web. Travel Blogs share many of the situational characteristics of Personal Blogs. The most important difference between these two registers is the topic: Personal Blogs are typically focused on the author's life and Travel Blogs are focused on travel experiences and destinations. The strongest positive key grammatical features for Travel Blogs are place nouns, place adverbs, and first-person pronouns (see Figure 5.6).

The heavy use of place nouns (e.g., desert, stream, country) and place adverbs (e.g., above, there, far) are closely related to the topic of Travel Blogs. These words are used to reference locations and describe distances and positions relative to those locations. [30] illustrates how both place nouns (bolded) and place adverbs (underlined) are used in a text.

[30] I studied there and lived two blocks *from* the Acropolis, so it's a **city** very near *to* my heart. The people who claim they don't like it normally are the ones who don't give it a chance and are there *for* a night *before* heading north or out *to* the **islands**.

www.runawayjane.com/why-does-nobody-like-athens/

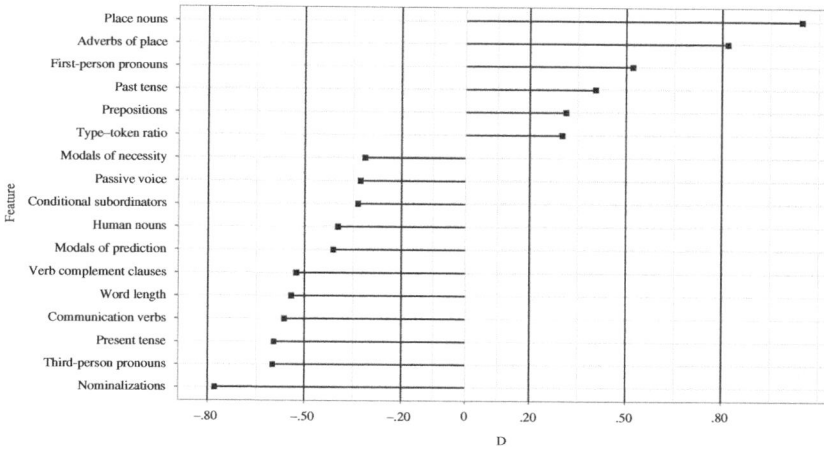

Figure 5.6. Key grammatical features for the Travel Blogs sub-register

Like Personal Blogs, Travel Blogs are often written from the perspective of the writer about their travel experiences. Thus, first-person pronouns serve an important function in this register. [30] contains two first-person pronouns. [31] is an example of a text that relies heavily on this feature to express the author's point of view.

[31] **My** visit *to* Portofino was completely ruined *by* this person and was to have been a highlight *of* **my** 10 day trip *to* the Italian Riviera. However Monterosso and Nervi were beautiful and **I** shall always remember **my** visit *for* that reason.

www.cntraveller.com/guides/europe/italy/portofino/what-to-do

The negative key features are nominalizations, third-person pronouns, present tense verbs, communication verbs, word length, and *that* verb complement clauses. As mentioned above, Travel Blogs tend to focus on the perspectives and experiences of the author (first-person pronouns) rather than those of others (third-person pronouns). The typical past orientation of Travel Blogs leads to low frequencies of present tense verbs. The relatively low frequency of communication verbs reveals that reference to speaking and writing is not a major function in Travel Blogs. Travel Blogs also tend to use shorter words and fewer verb complement clauses.

We classified all of the top hundred keywords for Travel Blogs into one of six categories (Table 5.8). The first two categories, "Transportation/Lodging" and "Tourism" contain the same number of words. Both of these categories relate to the logistical details of travel and tourism, including places to stay

Table 5.8. *Keywords for the Travel Blogs sub-register*

Transportation/ lodging	Tourism	Narrative/ description	Physical features	Places/attractions	Food/drink
airport	adventure	afternoon	beach	city	beer
biking	arrived	amazing	beaches	gardens	delicious
boat	attractions	around	cliffs	museum	dinner
booked	destination	beautiful	hills	park	lunch
bus	explore	day	island	places	restaurant
ferry	exploring	enjoyed	islands	shops	restaurants
flight	guide	famous	mountain	town	
flights	holiday	hour	mountains	village	
headed	locals	located	river	villages	
hike	photo	lovely	rocks		
hiking	photos	nearby	sea		
hostel	sights	night	trees		
hostels	tour	north	water		
hotel	tourist	scenery			
hotels	tourists	scenic			
journey	tours	south			
ride	travel	spectacular			
road	travellers	steep			
streets	travelling	stunning			
trail	trip	sun			
trails	visit	sunny			
walk	visited	sunset			
walked	visiting	swimming			
walking	visitors	weather			

(e.g., *hotel*, *hostel*), modes of transportation (e.g., *bus*, *ferry*), and tourism (e.g., *sights*, *tourist*).

[32] The main centre for nightlife and **tourist** shopping on Phuket is the town of Patong and, not surprisingly, its also where the majority of **hotels** are located. However, as Patong is a reasonable size in itself and local transport fees are hugely inflated for **tourists** it would pay to know where in Patong your **hotel** is located relative to where you intend spending most of your time

www.phuket-holiday-guide.com/where_to_stay_in_phuket.html

The third keyword category was labeled "Narrative/Description." The words in this category share a focus on providing detail and description to narrative accounts of travel experiences. Words in this category have been bolded in [33] below.

[33] High class resort located on a *hill* allowing **stunning** views of Kamala Bay and a great place to watch the often **spectacular sunsets**. Highly praised by guests! Kamala *Beach* Resort – Very reasonably priced for a hotel right on the *beach* and with two nice **swimming** pools.

www.phuket-holiday-guide.com/where_to_stay_in_phuket.html

References to physical features of nature make up the fourth category of keywords. These words include geological features (e.g., *mountains, rocks*) and bodies of water (e.g., *river, sea*). Examples of these words are italicized in [33].

The fifth category of keywords is composed of words about places (e.g., *villages, town*) or tourist attractions (e.g., *museum, gardens*). The last category contains words related to eating and drinking. Narrative descriptions about places to go and things to eat are both common themes in Travel Blogs. These descriptions are often expressed in the form of a review of services and the overall experience of the author/traveler. Examples of both of these semantic categories can be seen in [34], with places/attraction words bolded and food/drink words italicized.

[34] You've found a perfect place to stay in a small **village** and you've managed to book a room at a bargain price. If there is not a *restaurant* in the hotel, you need to make sure there is a place in that small **town** to eat *dinner*.

http://experiencefrancebybike.com/best-itinerary-for-bicycling-in-france-in-2013/

The key feature and keyword analyses reveal that Travel Blogs are generally narrative descriptions of past travel locations and experiences, shared in the First-person through the perspective of the traveler. Authors of Travel Blogs typically provide detailed information about the physical characteristics of the locales they visit, as well as review-style descriptions of the lodging, transportation, and food of those places.

5.4.6   Short Stories

Online Short Stories are unique in that this is the only fictional written register in the Narrative category. Fiction has been a major component of several popular corpora (e.g., *BNC, COCA, COHA*), but our sample reveals that fictional prose texts are relatively rare on the searchable web.

There is a large number of positive key features for the short stories subregister (Figure 5.7). As we have seen already, past-tense verbs are an important feature in several of the Narrative registers. However, none of these registers rely on past-tense verbs to the same extent as Short Stories, which use nearly three times as many past-tense verbs as the average text in the CORE. Examples of past-tense verbs in an online Short Story can be seen in [39].

[35] *He* **muttered** something about not finding any open at first, and **went** into *his* room. *He* **closed** and **locked** the door behind *him*, and although Peter **whined** and **scratched**, *he* **did** not let *him* in. *He* **looked** so agitated that I **thought** I **had been** harsh, and that perhaps *she* **was** really ill.

http://digital.library.upenn.edu/women/rinehart/brice/brice.html

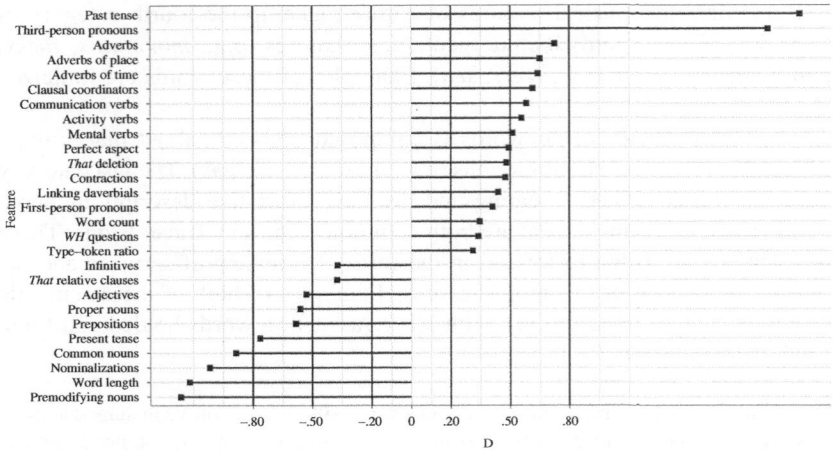

Figure 5.7. Key grammatical features for the Short Stories sub-register

The second most key linguistic feature was third-person pronouns, which have traditionally been associated with narrative writing. Interestingly, third-person pronouns only emerged on the lists of the top five key features for Sports Reports and Short Stories. Personal Blogs and Travel Blogs, on the other hand, are most often written in the first-person. Most Short Stories use past orientation to present fictional narrative, and this register uses them more than the overall mean for texts in the CORE. This heavy use of third-person pronouns is illustrated in [35].

Adverbs are also frequent in online Short Stories, primarily used to add descriptive detail about the time, place, and manner of events in the narrative.

[36] [...] but he no longer radiated the **aggressively** antisocial vibes he had before. He was **a lot less** unpleasant to look at (the **outrageously** seedy clown description had been replaced by that of a **mildly** creepy but **actually rather** natty young man [...])
www.juliandibbell.com/articles/a-rape-in-cyberspace/

Clausal coordinating conjunctions are used in Short Stories to make explicit connections between descriptions of events. These coordinators also function to keep the action moving without unnecessary syntactic interruptions. Several examples of this feature have been underlined in [35] above.

The final key feature for online Short Stories that we discuss here is communication verbs. These verbs emerged as the most key feature for News Reports. They are used for a similar function in Short Stories – to report direct speech. The major difference, of course, is that the reported speech in Short Stories is dialogue from fictional characters rather than statements and quotes from sources and public figures. Four cases of three different communication verbs are bolded in the dialogue in [37].

[37] [...] she weighed that against the prospect of having her quiet day disturbed, and **replied**, "Yes. Yes, of course. Come right in. What is your name?" "Jason," he **replied**. "Ah," **said** Mia, mysteriously. "You look like a Jason. Pisces?" "What?" **asked** the confused boy. "Never mind."

www.littletree.com.au/jigsaw1.htm

There were also several negative key features for short stories. The relatively low frequency of present tense verbs in Short Stories reflects the past orientation discussed above. The relatively low frequency of proper nouns was somewhat surprising because fiction writing does use proper nouns for character names. However, it seems that this does not result in frequencies for proper nouns that are as high as some of the other registers in the CORE. The remaining eight negative features are all related in some way to informationally dense writing, which is not characteristic of Short Stories.

The top hundred keywords for Short Stories were classified into six semantic categories, with an additional category for "Other" words (see Table 5.9). The first category is related to action, including both activity verbs (e.g., *shook, walked*) and adverbs that describe action (e.g., *slowly, softly*). Examples of the high activity narrative typical of Short Stories can be seen in [38] below.

[38] I was just bracing myself to smack him on the nose when someone rapped on our table. We all looked up. "It would have been nice talking to you," said Ziegler. "See you here tomorrow." Then he **turned** and **walked** out. The next day I was sitting at a table on the sidewalk when Ziegler approached.

www.abctales.com/story/chastol/one-dance-too-many

The next most common keyword category was labeled "Body parts." Online Short Stories are focused primarily on fictional accounts of human characters. These accounts typically include detailed descriptions of actions, gestures, and body language of these characters, all of which require the use of words related to body parts. A clear example of this can be seen in [39].

[39] She howled at him, hitting wildly, snapping at his **arm**, pulling at his **face**, his **nose**, his **ears**, anything she could lay **hands** on. Portafack couldn't see. He stopped the car and jerked it in park, snapping Tercepia forward. This caught her by surprise, so he took the opportunity to grab her by the **arm** and smack her **head**. His **face** twisted at her, his **mouth** ugly, his voice harsh as he shouted, "I'll beat the crap out of you if you don't stop!"

www.fantasy-magazine.com/non-fiction/articles/
down-on-the-farm-by-karen-heuler-from-bandersnatch/

Table 5.9. *Keywords for the Short Stories sub-register*

Activity	Body parts	Communication	Seeing/hearing	Thought/emotion	Personal pronouns	Other
came	arm	asked	dark	felt	he'd	bed
fell	arms	chuckled	gaze	grinned	her	beside
gave	cheeks	cried	glanced	knew	herself	breath
gently	chest	exclaimed	heard	seemed	him	chair
grabbed	ear	groaned	looked	smile	himself	door
hurried	eyes	growled	saw	smiled	she	floor
lay	face	laughed	sight	smiling		man
leaned	feet	muttered	silence	thought		room
opened	fingers	nodded	stared	wondered		sleep
paused	forehead	oh	staring			suddenly
pulled	hair	replied	watched			
ran	hand	shrugged				
rolled	hands	sighed				
sat	head	voice				
shaking	legs	waved				
shook	lips	whispered				
slipped	mouth					
slowly	neck					
softly	nose					
stepped	shoulder					
stood	shoulders					
stopped						
threw						
took						
turned						
waited						
walked						

The next category was labeled "Communication," and this category is closely related to the key feature of communication verbs discussed above. The fourth category was assigned the label "Seeing/Hearing." The words in this category are used to describe the sights and sounds that characters are exposed to. The next category, "Thought/Emotion" is related in that these words offer insights into what the characters are thinking and feeling. Examples of both "Seeing/Hearing" keywords (bolded) and "Thought/Emotion" (italicized) keywords can be seen in [40] below.

[40] Joey **looked** up shyly, trying to gauge my reaction. Once our eyes locked, I *smiled*, letting him have my million watt *smile* hoping it would let him *know* just how I *felt*. **Seeing** he still **looked** nervous, I reached out took his hand in mine, and gently squeezed it.

www.screeve.org/Trials_and_Tribulations_04

The final category of keywords was labeled personal pronouns. This category contains only third-person pronouns, which corroborates the key feature of third-person pronouns discussed above. Interestingly, unlike Sports Reports, the list of personal pronouns in the keywords for Short Stories contains the same number of male and female pronouns. Additional examples of third-person pronouns have been underlined in [40].

The key features and keywords in this analysis characterize online Short Stories as a fictional register with past orientation that is heavily focused on third-person accounts of human characters and dialogue between them. Descriptions of these human characters include details about their actions, body language, dialogue, and what they see, hear, think, and feel.

5.5   Summary and Conclusion

The Narrative register represents the most common category of documents found on the searchable web. Regardless of the specific sub-register category, nearly all Narrative texts share the linguistic characteristics of past orientation, a focus on people, and a heavy reliance on descriptive detail.

These are important similarities, but the linguistic analyses in this chapter have revealed that there are also marked differences among the six major Narrative registers that distinguish them situationally, linguistically, and functionally. Having said that, we have also learned that each of these categories has other registers that it is similar to. For example, we found that News Reports and Sports Reports were quite similar, with the major difference being the topical content. Likewise, Personal Blogs and Travel Blogs shared many features in common, despite their topical and style differences. A final, less expected example of registers with shared features is News Reports and Short Stories, which shared features such as past orientation and communication verbs, albeit for very different purposes.

Overall, this chapter has provided insights into the general patterns of online narrative writing, as well as the nuanced differences between its sub-registers. These findings have revealed a complex and interesting picture of register categories that vary greatly in their prevalence, as well as their situational and linguistic attributes. We have shown strong functional connections between the situational and linguistic features of Narrative texts that help explain these differences. There is a great deal more research that needs to be done on the registers introduced in this chapter, but one thing is for certain: narrative registers on the web are a fascinating and important part of online discourse.

6 Opinion, Advice, and Persuasion Registers

6.1 Introduction

Many of the documents found on the web have a primary purpose of expressing personal opinions, offering advice, or persuading the reader. In Chapter 3, we showed that 11 percent of the documents on the searchable web have a primary purpose of expressing opinions, while another 1.6 percent of the documents fall into the specialized category of "informational persuasion" (see Table 3.3). An additional 15 percent of the documents on the web are hybrids with an opinionated purpose combined with other communicative purposes (e.g., Opinion + Information or Opinion + Narration; see Chapter 9.2). Thus, taken together, documents that express opinion, advice, or persuasion are among the most prevalent general registers found on the web.

At the same time, there are many different specific sub-registers that can be grouped under the umbrella of opinion/advice/persuasion. Table 6.1 shows the breakdown of texts in CORE across opinion/advice/persuasion sub-registers.

In Section 6.2, we introduce the range of sub-registers that have opinionated communicative purposes, describing and illustrating the major situational and discourse characteristics of each one. Then, in Sections 6.3 and 6.4, we provide

Table 6.1. *Sub-register categories in the Opinion/Advice/Persuasion category, with text counts*

Sub-register	Text count
Opinion Blog	6,104
Review	1,925
Description-with-intent-to-sell	1,452
Advice	1,146
Religious Blog/Sermon	721
Other Opinion/Persuasion	125
Total	11,473

more detailed descriptions of the lexical and grammatical patterns of register variation within this discourse domain of the web.

6.2   Survey of Opinion, Advice, and Persuasion Sub-registers

There are a diverse set of sub-registers on the web that serve the general communicative purposes of expressing opinions, advice, and persuasion, ranging from Opinion Blogs to Editorials to Product Reviews to Advertisements. Table 6.2 lists the major sub-registers included under these categories that are commonly found on the web, together with a summary of their most important situational characteristics.

In most cases, it is possible to isolate particular situational characteristics that distinguish each of these sub-registers from the others. Opinion Blogs are probably the least well-defined of these categories, because they encompass a wide range of text types: they can range from extended arguments supported by informational facts or narratives, similar to editorials, to shorter expressions of personal opinions offered with little supporting evidence. They are normally written by a single author, who regularly posts his/her opinions and ideas about current affairs or some other topic of interest. In many cases, that author is affiliated with a newspaper, magazine, or other official media outlet. However, reflecting the democratization of information on the web, it is just as common to find blog sites developed by an individual with no institutional backing. Screenshot 6.1 illustrates a blog posting of this type. In both cases, these blogs are clearly opinionated, overtly expressing the thoughts, attitudes, and evaluations of the author. Interestingly, no credentials are required or even necessarily expected for a successful blog writer, apart from the ability to write posts that a group of loyal "followers" find to be interesting.

In some ways, Opinion Blogs on the web are similar to editorials in newspapers. There are key differences, however. Editorials are not commonly found on the web, at least in comparison to the high frequency of Opinion Blogs. Editorials are stand-alone texts written by an expert on a topic, usually associated with the editorial section of a newspaper or magazine. The topics deal with any current events deemed newsworthy by the newspaper and editorial author. In contrast, Opinion Blogs are posted on a blog site, with a series of blogs posted regularly, sometimes daily, usually written by the same author. In many cases, a blog site is restricted to a single narrow topical domain. For example, in our corpus we have blog documents from a very wide range of specialized sites, illustrated in Table 6.3.

Product Reviews will be familiar to most end-users of the web, who regularly use the Internet for commercial purposes. Most Product Reviews are associated with a commercial site that has the ultimate goal of advertising products or services. Reviews are usually written by individual customers, who describe

Table 6.2. *Major situational characteristics of Opinion, Advice, and Persuasion sub-registers*

	Author and venue	Audience	Purposes/goals/intended outcomes
Opinion Blogs	Individual author writing on a personal or institutional website; usually associated with an author who regularly posts documents on the same "blog" website	Anyone interested in the topic, or anyone who "follows" the blogger	To express personal opinions – not necessarily supported by evidence
Reviews	Individual author writing on a personal, institutional, or commercial website. In some cases, the author claims special expertise; in many other cases, the author has simply used the product under review	Anyone interested in the product	To evaluate the quality of a product. Several subtypes are common (reviews of tangible goods, foods, services, movies, hotels, restaurants, etc.)
Description-with-intent-to-sell	Usually no acknowledged author; associated with a commercial site	Anyone interested in the product	Describe a product, with a focus on positive attributes. The text might almost be considered a type of informational description, except that it is associated with a commercial site and thus has the implicit goal of selling
Advice	Authors, usually not identified, and usually writing on an institutional or commercial website. By association with the website, the author claims special expertise	Anyone interested in knowing how to address a particular problem	Personal opinion that leads to suggested actions, intended to solve particular problems
Religious Blogs/ Sermons	Individual author, usually writing on an institutional website (e.g., a church or some other religious organization)	Readers interested in the topic, or readers who regularly read articles on that website	A complex mix of communicative purposes. While the content is based on beliefs and opinion, the discourse is often framed as informational description. The discussion is often supported by narratives or evidential reference to events in society. In some cases, the text can be written-to-be-spoken

The Worm Hole

On Requiring Certain Moods, Seasons, And States In Order To Read Books

Posted 22nd August 2012
Category: *Chit-Chat* Genres: *N/A*

4 Comments

Tweet   Like 2   Share

Jennifer, from *Books Personally*, made a statement in her comment *on my post* about reading a book in a day; it got me thinking. She said:

> Some books need more time or more particular moods...

I have realised that on occasion there have been books that I've not enjoyed and not understood why that was so until I factored in how I was feeling at the time. An example of this, though extreme, is Austen's *Persuasion*. I admit – I dislike the book and find nothing interesting in its contents – but is this a true reflection of how I feel or is it just simply a reflection of the fact that I was ill when I read it? Indeed since reading it I have been conscious to put off reading books when ill, and this was a decision I made long before I realised the possible truth of my feelings towards *Persuasion*.

I love *Pride And Prejudice*, but then I read it during a beautiful summer, and as I'm a summer person I was inevitably happy anyway. It would've taken a really wretched book to knock me down.

Screenshot 6.1. Opinion Blog from a personal site
http://wormhole.carnelianvalley.com/on-requiring-certain-moods-seasons-and-states-in-order-to-read-books/

Table 6.3. *Example topical domains and postings for Opinion Blogs*

Topical domain	Example posting
Top-ten lists (www.toptenz.net)	Top 10 arguments that can't be won
Jungian psychotherapy (www.briancollinson.ca)	A Jungian psychotherapist looks at Hallowe'en as symbol
Climate change (jennifermarohasy.com)	The need for a new theory of climate
Current trends (toptrends.nowandnext.com)	The future of war
Genealogy research (www.geneabloggers.com)	A way to plot cluster genealogy research
Distributed denial of service security (www.securitybistro.com)	Hacking voting machines
Personal opinions (nickpullar.net)	Trust and honesty
Zimbabwe news events (www.newsdzezimbabwe .co.uk)	Do we really have to go with Tsvangirai?
Movies (www.cinemablend.com)	Five more stars we want to see in the expendables 3

their personal experiences with the product and provide their overall evaluation. Reviews are common on the web, related to any type of product or service being marketed (e.g., movies, books, clothing, cooking utensils, restaurants, hotels, software tools, accounting services, lawyers, physicians, plumbers). For example, Screenshot 6.2 shows a screen shot from a review of the British Columbia Ferry, which was posted on the travel website yelp.com.

Descriptions-with-intent-to-sell are presented as if they are simply providing descriptive information about a product or service. The author of the document is not identified, and so any evaluations are simply presented as part of the description, and not directly attributed to the author. However, these documents also have the underlying goal of persuading the reader to purchase the item or service, and so in that sense, they are similar to positive Product Reviews. These documents are quite common on the web; they will be immediately familiar to any reader who uses the web to shop. A common example of this type of online document is a book blurb, such as the text excerpt in [1] below from *Amazon. com*. Book blurbs appear to be simply an informational description summarizing the content of a book. However, that text is framed in ways that reflect the underlying persuasive goals, and it turns out that there are systematic linguistic features reflecting both these informational and persuasive goals.

[1] Book blurb from *Amazon.com*
In God is Not One: The Eight Rival Religions That Run the World, New York Times
   bestselling author of Religious Literacy and religion scholar Stephen Prothero argues
   that persistent attempts to portray all religions as different paths to the same God over-
   look the distinct problem that each tradition seeks to solve. Delving into the different

Katie F.
Vancouver, Canada
246 friends
794 reviews
48 photos
Elite '17

⭐⭐⭐⭐⭐ 4/25/2010

3.5 stars.

Loved the ferry ride itself and the cleanliness... definitely did not like the price!

I haven't taken the ferry to the island since I was a kid, so this was a pretty novel thing for me! That being said, this ferry is fabulous compared to the stench and crowding I've experienced on the ferries in Greece and Mexico. It's reasonably well-organized, lots of seating, TVs, a kid zone, some workstation areas, and food ranging from $10 cafeteria meals to the $22/person dinner buffet.

The views to and from the island are great and the buffet isn't bad - salads, 2 soups, prime rib, salmon, shrimp and canneloni were available when we went. The time flies by if you eat on the ferry.

The wait time sucks if you come when it's busy - we lucked out on the way over but got stuck waiting a couple of hours on the way back to Vancouver.

It's pretty pricey to use - about $46-ish for a car and $14 per person each way. Didn't like the fact that there's a charge to make a reservation but I suppose I'll cough up the money next time if I don't want to risk waiting in line.

Was this review ...?

[👍 Useful 1]   [😄 Funny 1]   [😎 Cool]

Brian W.
Vancouver, Canada
17 friends
63 reviews
5 photos

⭐⭐⭐⭐⭐ 6/14/2012

It's funny that we can review public services, hmm like anyone has a choice to come on a Ferry. Why I love them - well they let me get all over our amazing islands, and happens I will be getting on one in 48 hours for the Sunshine coast. Not many places in the world offer the consistent, classy, working, on time, nice staff, roomy and safe ride our Ferries do. If it wasn't for them, nobody would live on Gambier? etc, lol.... My buddies will be scarfing back whitespot and we can all get some sunshine and wind on the decks. The massive humm of the engines is easy to sleep outside to. I have been on boats on Thailand where we get lost and the captain jumps off and swims to shore, boats in Mexico with waves nearly capsizing us. Most excitement you get on a Ferry is the horn to goto your Car, that's right most these beasts allow you to friggin drive right on and off.

'"And then, we get on the ferry and they made us sit there, for 40 minutes. We had to sit there.' Oh? Really? What happened next? Did you sail through the sea in your car, incredibly, like a whale? Did you partake in the miracle of human sailing, you non-contributing zero?" "People, like, they say there's delays on ferry's. Delays? Really? Vancouver to Victoria in 2 hours. That used to take 30 years. Plus, you would die on the way there."

Was this review ...?

[👍 Useful 1]   [😄 Funny 4]   [😎 Cool 2]

Screenshot 6.2. Product Review from an institutional site
www.yelp.com/biz/bc-ferries-victoria

problems and solutions that Islam, Christianity, Buddhism, Judaism, Confucianism, Yoruba Religion, Daoism and Atheism strive to combat, God is Not One is an indispensable guide to the questions human beings have asked for millennia—and to the disparate paths we are taking to answer them today. Readers of Huston Smith and Karen Armstrong will find much to ponder in God is Not One.

www.amazon.com/God-Not-One-Eight-Religions/dp/0061571288

Descriptions-with-intent-to-sell have not been analyzed in previous studies, suggesting that this register is peculiar to the web but not found in print media. However, more detailed consideration of the texts in this category suggests that they are also quite familiar in print-media contexts, where they usually occur as a flyer describing the attributes of a product or service. In many cases, the text is actually attached to the product that is for sale; for example, book blurbs are often printed on the back cover of a book. Blurbs of this type are also commonly found in print-media catalogs, which adopt the strategy of presenting information about products rather than telling readers outright that they should buy the product. However, as we show below, these informational descriptions are at the same time persuasive, and they differ linguistically from other, more neutral informational documents. The fact that this register has not been described in previous studies of register variation reflects the difficulty of collecting such texts for inclusion in standard written corpora. However, on the web, these documents are quite prevalent and as easy to collect as any other type of document.

Interestingly, the flip-side of this same coin is the relative absence on the web of some opinionated registers that have been well-represented in standard corpora of written published texts. For example, Newspaper Editorials and Letters-to-the-editor are two registers found in most corpora of written texts. These are published registers readily available in all printed newspapers, and thus it is not surprising that they have featured so prominently in standard written corpora. However, our random sample of web documents shows that these registers are not common in the web when compared to the full range of other web documents. In contrast, Opinion Blogs, which are extremely common, have taken over many of the communicative purposes served by these editorial texts in print media. However, there is an interesting difference here. Published newspaper and magazine editorials are written either to give the institutional stance of the editors (in which case no individual author is identified), or they are written by an individual who claims to have special expertise in the topic at hand. In contrast, Opinion Blogs are regular postings written by the same individual but often dealing with a wide range of different topics; in most cases, the blog author feels no obligation to establish credentials or special expertise, apart from the ability to write well and establish a large group of regular readers (the "followers").

It is also surprising that Advertisements are largely absent from our random sample of web documents. Traditional ads often occur in the margins of a webpage, or as auto-playing videos or media that pop up when a user loads a webpage.

These ads are not realized as text documents, and thus they were not part of the population included in our corpus sample of web documents. However, there is another factor that helps to explain the relative absence of advertisements on the searchable web: Descriptions-with-intent-to-sell are often used instead, serving many of the same functions as an advertisement. The text of these documents is usually simply informational, with no direct encouragement to buy the product. However, the immediate context of the webpage is commercial, making it easy for the end-user to purchase the product if they like the informational description. This type of indirect "informational" advertising is effective on the web for two reasons: (1) end-users are directly searching for certain products; and (2) search engines are trained to direct end-users to sites that they might not have been looking for, but are likely to be interested in. For both of these reasons, there is less need to adopt the language of traditional advertising (e.g., trying to convince the end-user that they "need" a given product).

Advice documents are usually associated with an institutional or commercial site. In most cases, there is no identified author. The company or organization hosting the site usually has some kind of expertise on the topic (e.g., healthcare, finding a job, parenting, training for a sport), and thus the advice documents are quite overt about identifying potential problems and offering solutions. Advice documents differ from Opinion documents and Reviews in that they are more directive, not merely giving the personal attitudes and evaluations of the author, but further suggesting actions that the reader should undertake, such as changing one's hairstyle (see Screenshot 6.3). In the case of non-profit organizations, the advice is offered as a way of improving society or individual well-being. In the case of commercial sites, the advice is offered with the possibility that the end-user would actually employ the services of the company or purchase helpful items from the company.

Finally, Religious Blogs/Sermons might be regarded as a special sub-category of Opinion Blogs. In many cases, though, these blogs are focused more on explaining religious "truths," rather than overtly expressing opinions or attempting to persuade readers. As a result, Religious Blogs/Sermons might almost be regarded as more of an "informational" register than an "opinionated" register. [2] presents the opening paragraphs from a religious blog. Unlike most other web registers, the web page in this case presents only the written document; thus, the focus is exclusively on the information being presented, with no distractions in the form of boilerplate information or advertisements in the margins.

[2] The opening paragraphs from a Religious Blog posting.
This article will explain both from the Bible, as well as historical claims and other writers, about the Apostle John. John was a very important apostle for many reasons, and several of those are covered in this article. (Here is a link to a related sermon titled *Apostle John: The Disciple that Jesus Loved*)

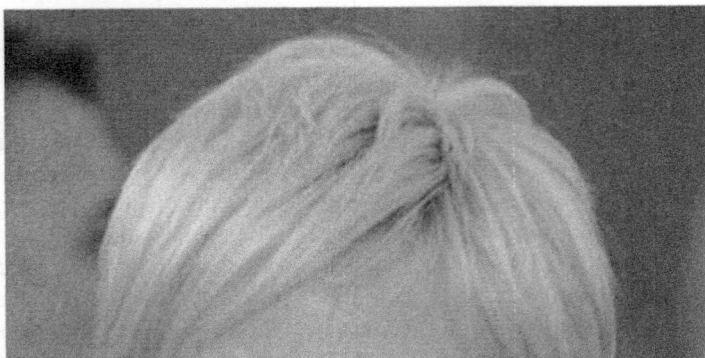

The 4 hair trends to try in 2012.

ZOE FOSTER BLAKE

Does your reading this post mean you're interested in perhaps trying one of them? I'll take your silence as a yes. And then cheer, because I *love* that you're excited to try something new with your hair. Not that it doesn't look marvellous the way it is, obviously. It really suits you. It does! It's a great length and cut for you and it seems almost a shame that we're potentially about to decimate both in one trip to the snip-snips.

Obviously you'll be after some inspiration for this new mop of yours, so I've assembled some of the key cuts for hair in 2012 below. Some of these will seem outrageous (because they are) or ridiculous (again, because they are), or better suited to a small, plastic toy (Barbie), but remember that trends exist to *inspire*, not *dictate*.

1. VERY-SHORT HAIR

The most daring (and potentially exquisite) of all the lady cuts, very short (often pixie) hair will be a strong theme in 2012, especially with the dual emphasis on the '60s and '20s. Keep it modern (and more versatile) by making it a bit less pretty, and a bit more edgy, choppy and androgynous. Also remember that beautiful actresses with travelling hair stylists can pull off this look and the styling nuances that it brings with ease and grace, but us Regular Bombshells need to make sure we are ready for the upkeep (snips every 3 weeks) and intense face focus, and cowlick accentuation such short hair brings. Those with straight-ish hair and oval faces will definitely fare best. For those not as daring, try a (choppy) cut somewhere between the jaw and ears, like Dianna Agron's sensational 2011 cut.

Screenshot 6.3. An online Advice page
www.mamamia.com.au/the-4-hair-trends-to-try-in-2012/

The Bible shows that after Jesus died, Peter and John were shown to be together throughout the New Testament (Acts 3:1-11; 4:13; 8:14; Galatians 2:9) and perhaps even to the time that Peter died (cf. 2 Peter 1:14-15 and 18 with Matthew 17:1-5). John not only assisted Peter, he probably learned how to help guide and lead the true Church from him.

Shortly after Peter apparently died, prior to the destruction of Jerusalem (in 70 A.D.), many Christians fled to Pella, while others moved to Asia Minor. The Apostles John and Philip settled in Asia Minor–some believe this could have happened in the 40s A.D., others later.

www.cogwriter.com/john.htm

Similarly to Opinion Blogs, Religious Blogs can be associated with either an institutional site or a site produced by an individual.

6.3   Summary of MD Analysis Results for Opinion/ Persuasion Registers

Given that Opinion sub-registers differ considerably with respect to their situational characteristics, it should come as no surprise that there is also extensive linguistic variation among these sub-registers. The MD analysis, summarized in Figure 6.1, provides an initial overview of these linguistic differences.

Opinion Blogs are perhaps the most surprising sub-register in terms of their multidimensional profile. Opinion Blogs might be regarded as a quintessential web register: a type of text commonly found on the web but with no direct counterpart in print media. As such, we might expect that Opinion Blogs would be highly distinctive in their linguistic characteristics. However, that expectation is not borne out by the MD analysis. Rather, Opinion Blogs have scores near 0.0 on almost all dimensions. The only exception is Dimension 7 ("literate stance"), where Opinion Blogs have a moderately large positive value, reflecting a relatively frequent use of stance noun phrase features.

There are two major considerations that can help to account for this unmarked characterization of Opinion Blogs. First of all, stance features (including grammatical features marking personal attitudes and evaluations) are for the most part integrated with a range of other lexico-grammatical features, distributed across multiple dimensions in the MD analysis. Apart from Dimension 7, none of these other dimensions is interpreted as having a primary discourse function of conveying stance and evaluation. And second, Opinion Blogs are not especially distinctive with respect to most other situational characteristics. They are not interactive, and they can range from being quite informational (and relatively formal) to being colloquial and informal in tone. That is, the primary distinguishing situational characteristic of Opinion Blogs is that they have the primary communicative purpose of expressing personal opinions, evaluations, and attitudes. Given the absence of dimensions dedicated to the expression of

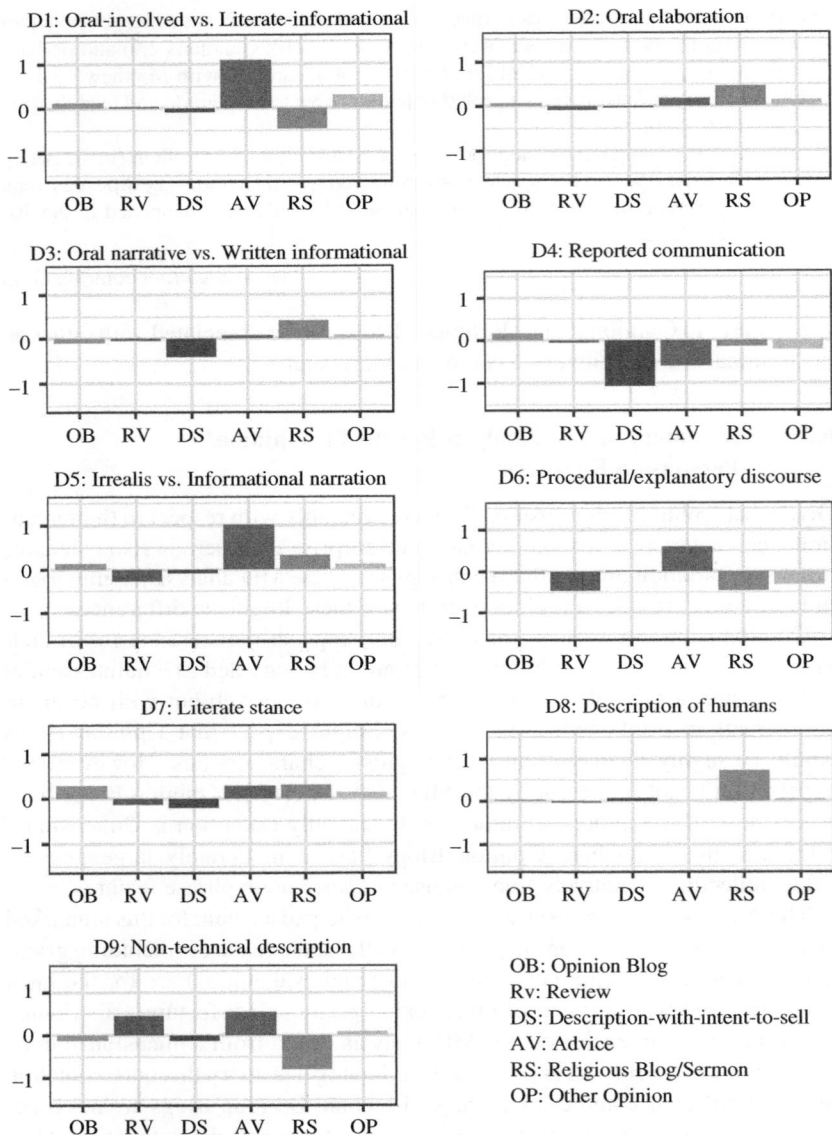

Figure 6.1. MD analysis results for the Opinion sub-registers

stance, it is not surprising that Opinion Blogs are similar to the overall "average" of web documents in their multidimensional linguistic characteristics. However, as we show below, there are a number of more specific lexical and grammatical characteristics that function to distinguish Opinion Blogs from the other registers on the web.

Reviews and Description-with-intent-to-sell are similar to Opinion Blogs in being generally unmarked on the linguistic dimensions, and the functional explanations are also similar. Reviews have a moderate negative score on Dimension 6, reflecting the absence of procedural discourse, and a positive score on Dimension 9, reflecting their informational focus but generally non-technical style. Description-with-intent-to-sell are somewhat more "literate" in their dimension scores than Opinion Blogs or Reviews. Note especially the negative scores for Dimensions 3 and 4, reflecting a frequent use of nominalizations, long words, and phrasal premodifiers in noun phrases (premodifying nouns and attributive adjectives).

In direct contrast to the unmarked MD characteristics of many other opinion sub-registers, Religious Blogs/Sermons are among the most distinctive of the opinionated sub-registers. This linguistic profile in part reflects the fact that Religious Blogs are not overtly opinioned in the same way that Opinion Blogs are. Rather, these texts are often framed as factual information, with little indication that the text portrays the opinions of the author. As a result, Religious Blogs have relatively large "informational" negative scores for Dimensions 1 and 9. At the same time, Religious Blogs can be relatively colloquial, employing clausal elaboration to convey information rather than the dense phrasal embedding found in academic informational registers. This characteristic is reflected in the relatively large positive score on Dimension 2. As noted in Section 6.2, Religious Blogs/Sermons include both narrative recounts as well as informational descriptions and explanations, resulting in the relatively large positive score along Dimension 3. Both narrative and informational descriptions are often biographical, relating to famous religious persons. As a result, Religious Blogs have a large negative score on Dimension 6 and a large positive score on Dimension 8, reflecting the frequent use of proper nouns, human nouns, third-person pronouns, etc. In summary, Religious Blogs are quite distinctive in their multidimensional characteristics, with relatively large positive or negative scores on several of the dimensions.

The Advice sub-register is quite different in many respects from other opinion web registers: advice documents express personal opinions that include overt directives, describing the future actions that readers should undertake to solve their problems. The MD results displayed in Figure 6.1 show that the Advice sub-register is also quite specialized in its linguistic characteristics, reflecting those distinctive communicative purposes. For example, on Dimension 1, Advice documents are among the most marked in the entire corpus for their dense use of "oral-involvement" features, such as progressive activity verbs, first- and second-person pronouns, and various stance features. In contrast, Opinion documents like Opinion Blogs and Religious Blogs are more "informational" in their Dimension 1 characteristics. Advice documents are similarly highly distinctive in their Dimension 5 characteristics, with an extremely dense use of "irrealis" features like modal verbs and conditional adverbial clauses. Along Dimension 6, Advice documents are shown to be highly procedural, with frequent causative/facilitation verbs, progressive aspect verbs, and process nouns. In summary, while Advice documents are similar to other opinion sub-registers in their opinionated/evaluative stance, the MD analysis indicates that they are quite different linguistically, reflecting their specialized directive purposes.

A comparison of Table 6.4 and Table 5.3 shows that Opinion sub-registers are in general less well-defined linguistically than Narrative sub-registers. That is, most Opinion sub-registers have relatively large standard deviations on all dimensions. Reviews are the best defined linguistically, reflecting the fact that Reviews are well-defined in their situational characteristics. However, sub-registers like Opinion Blogs and Advice have relatively large standard deviations, and Descriptions-with-intent-to-sell have quite large standard deviations on most dimensions. These descriptive statistics reflect the fact that there is quite a range of different kinds of documents included in these sub-register categories, and as a result, a relatively wide range of linguistic characteristics. The following sections provide more detailed descriptions of those characteristics.

MD analysis is ideally suited to identifying the basic parameters of linguistic variation in a discourse domain, and identifying the major similarities and differences among registers with respect to those parameters. However, the flip-side of that coin is that MD analysis is not designed for detailed analyses of the distinguishing linguistic characteristics of each individual sub-register. This is especially the case for MD analyses of a large discourse domain that includes many different registers, as in the present study. The results presented here provide a clear illustration of this general pattern. On the one hand, the MD analysis in Chapter 4 uncovers nine underlying parameters of linguistic variation, with distinctive patterns of register variation along each one. At the same time, though, the MD characterizations of Opinion sub-registers are in many cases not highly informative. This is especially the case for Opinion Blogs and Reviews, which have relatively unmarked characterizations on most dimensions. To better understand the distinctive linguistic characteristics of these sub-registers, we need to turn to more detailed lexical and grammatical analyses – descriptions we turn to in the following sections.

Table 6.4. *Dimension score means and standard deviations for Opinion sub-registers*

Register	D_1		D_2		D_3		D_4		D_5		D_6		D_7		D_8		D_9	
	M	SD	M	SD	M	SD	M	SD	M	SD	M	SD	M	SD	M	SD	M	SD
Opinion Blog	0.12	0.80	0.07	0.82	−0.10	0.75	0.17	0.71	0.13	0.76	−0.06	0.83	0.30	0.94	0.03	0.79	−0.13	0.79
Review	0.04	0.70	−0.07	0.84	−0.05	0.74	−0.06	0.58	−0.28	0.69	−0.47	0.69	−0.14	0.82	−0.04	0.90	0.46	0.83
Desc.-to-sell	−0.07	0.88	−0.02	0.87	−0.41	0.92	−1.1	0.89	−0.08	0.93	0.02	1.10	−0.21	0.95	0.07	1.06	−0.12	1.06
Advice	1.08	0.78	0.18	0.88	0.08	0.83	−0.60	0.75	1.02	0.93	0.60	0.89	0.29	0.98	0.00	0.97	0.54	0.93
Religious Blog	−0.46	0.92	0.45	0.85	0.40	0.80	−0.14	0.70	0.33	0.81	−0.48	0.76	0.31	0.97	0.72	0.94	−0.79	0.71

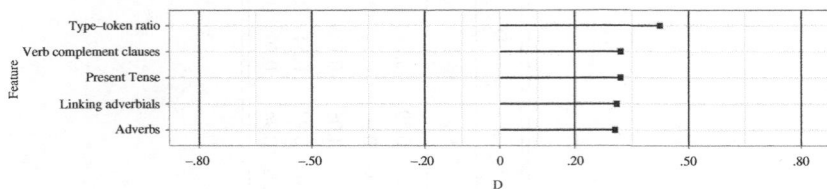

Figure 6.2. Key grammatical features for the Opinion Blogs

6.4   Detailed Grammatical and Lexical Analyses of Opinion/ Persuasion Registers

6.4.1   Opinion Blogs

Figure 6.2 lists the key grammatical features in Opinion Blogs, the features that occur more or less commonly in this register than in CORE overall. The most striking pattern observed from this figure is that there are essentially no grammatical features of this type. Conceptually, Cohen's d is measured on a scale of standard deviation units, so that a d score of +1.0 shows that the mean score in the target register is one standard deviation unit larger than the overall mean score in the rest of the corpus. Conversely, a d score of −1.0 shows that the mean score in the target register is one standard deviation unit smaller than the overall corpus mean.

In the case of Opinion Blogs, no grammatical features meet this standard. In fact, no grammatical feature even has a d value of ±0.5, and there are only five features with d values in the range of +0.29 to +0.42. Thus, the overall grammatical characterization of Opinion Blogs is that they are simply a generic web register, not especially marked for the use of any grammatical features. This characterization confirms the results of the MD analysis, where Opinion Blogs had unmarked dimension scores on nearly all dimensions (except for the small positive score on the "Literate Stance" dimension).

Beyond that overall characterization, Figure 6.2 shows smaller trends for Opinion Blogs to employ a diversified vocabulary (high type–token ratio), present tense verbs modified by adverbs, a discourse style organized by linking adverbials, and some grammatical stance features (stance verb + *that* clause, and stance noun + *that* clause). Overall, the results here, combined with the MD results, show that Opinion Blogs are moderately "informational" in style, with a slightly elevated focus on the expression of stance. Personal Blogs can also be opinionated, shown by their frequent use of some stance features and their stance-related keywords (see Section 5.4.2 in the last chapter). However, while Personal Blogs focus on the first-person narration of past events, Opinion Blogs focus on the present state of affairs, described from a more "detached" perspective. [3] illustrates this focus on the present situation, combined with a

Table 6.5. *Keywords for Opinion Blogs*

Government and politics	Social and political issues	People (political participants)	Status of knowledge	Communicative (argumentative) acts	General evaluations	Other
campaign	economic	Americans	actually	agree	aren't	even
conservative	economy	anyone	believe	argue	bad	let's
democracy	issue	citizens	certainly	argument	doesn't	nothing
democratic	issues	conservatives	doubt	article	don't	rather
election	matter	country	fact	blog	isn't	recent
government	money	democrats	indeed	comments	lack	that's
law	point	majority	maybe	debate	least	thing
liberal	problem	media	obvious	disagree	moral	those
party	public	nation	of course	post	should	yes
policies	social	Obama	opinion	question	simply	yet
policy	tax	Obama's	perhaps	reasons	stupid	
political	taxes	people	real	say	worse	
politics		politicians	reality		wrong	
republican		republicans	seem			
vote		Romney	seems			
voters		society	surely			
voting		state	think			
		themselves	true			
			truth			

relatively sophisticated word choice, and grammatical stance features that are not directly attributed to the author.

[3] Does the Nobel laureate American president think that the victims of the American bombing expeditions deserve drones and cluster bombs? It's high time America understands the fact that terrorism cannot be fought selectively. It's not only the Muslims who are terrorists but if an American soldier runs amok in the bad lands of Iraq and Afghanistan, he must also be treated at par with an Al Qaeda or Taliban terror suspect.

https://muslimvillage.com/2012/07/31/25919/

why-is-a-non-muslim-mass-murderer-not-a-terrorist/

At the lexical level, Opinion Blogs are more clearly distinguished from other web registers. Table 6.5 lists the keywords for this register, grouped into six major semantic domains: government and politics; social and political issues; people, especially political participants; words indicating the status of knowledge; communicative acts, often arguing for a particular perspective; and general evaluations. The first three categories reflect a strong preoccupation with government and politics, especially US government and politics. In this regard, Opinion Blogs are similar to News Reports when one compares the set of keywords here with the keywords listed in Table 5.4. In addition to directly discussing governmental and political issues, these blogs focus on a range of other social issues, with special attention given to the economy and financial issues. However, despite the focus on US politics and society, these blogs are often written by individuals residing in countries other than the United States. For example, [3] above was posted on a blog site in Australia.

The major differences between Opinion Blogs and News Reports are shown by columns 4–6 in Table 6.5. Opinion Blogs rely heavily on words relating to the status of knowledge, communicative acts (often arguing for a particular perspective), and general evaluations, while none of these semantic domains are represented in the most common keywords for News Reports. The evaluations expressed in Opinion Blogs tend to be negative, shown by adjectives and adverbs with negative meanings (e.g., *wrong, worse, bad, stupid*) as well as the frequent use of primary verbs contracted with the negator *n't*. [4] illustrates this combination of semantic domains and discourse functions, with a topical focus on politics and government policies, discussed from a strongly evaluative and argumentative perspective. (Keywords expressing communicative/argumentative acts, status of knowledge, and general evaluations are marked in **bold**.)

[4] That Barack Obama, what a let-down huh? [...] There is a slightly less facetious version of this **argument** constantly trotted out by many who supported Obama when he ran for office in 2008. [...] some still **question** supporting him or **argue** he's only bearable when compared to Mitt **Romney**. [...]
In **fact Obama** was vastly more progressive than Bill Clinton [...]
When reporters write that President Obama ignored climate change, they aren't just **wrong**, they are actively misleading. [...]
The **reason**: **in reality** it has crippled bank profits and hit them really hard [...]
That doesn't mean he can evade responsibility for other parts of his agenda. President Obama's administration has come under heavy criticism for the drones programme [...] **Worse**, the government has a policy of branding all deaths by drones as "militants" – thereby absolving themselves of blame. The Obama administration was also **wrong** in the extra-judicial killing of Anwar al-Awlaki and his son.

www.newyorker.com/online/blogs/culture/2012/11/questioningly-the-inevitable-petraeus-movie.html

In summary, Opinion Blogs are not very distinctive grammatically. Opinion Blogs have a present-time orientation (rather than a strong focus on narrating past events) and a moderately high use of grammatical stance features. Overall, though, their grammatical style approximates the average of other web registers. In contrast, Opinion Blogs are quite marked lexically. Similar to News Reports on the web, Opinion Blogs have a preoccupation with politics, government policies, and other major social issues. However, the discussion of those issues is dramatically different from News Reports, shown by the large number of keywords that make claims about the knowledge status of information, expressing other more general evaluations, or overtly "arguing" for one perspective over another.

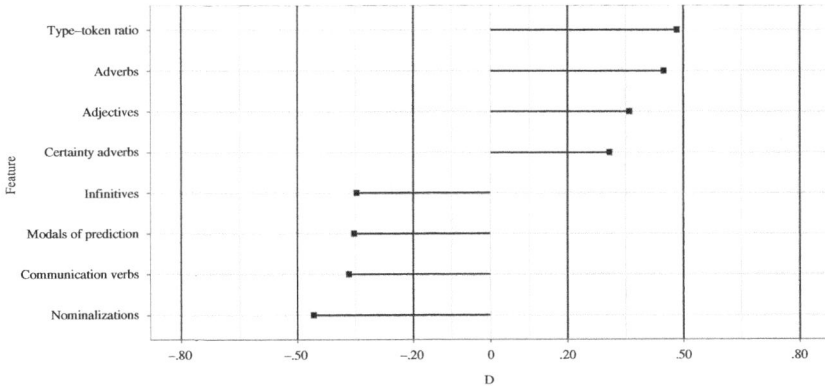

Figure 6.3. Key grammatical features for Reviews

6.4.2   Reviews

Similar to Opinion Blogs, Reviews have few distinctive key grammatical features (see Figure 6.3). They employ a relatively diverse vocabulary as well as slightly more adjectives, adverbs, and stance adverbials than other web documents. But overall, Reviews employ a neutral grammatical style similar to the average web document.

In contrast, Reviews are quite different from other web registers in their keywords (see Table 6.6). Not surprisingly, a large number of these words refer to the products being reviewed (e.g., *album, book, movie*) or to attributes of those products (e.g., *bass, character, climax, drama*). But the largest category of keywords are words that express an evaluation. Many of these words are evaluative adjectives (e.g., *beautiful, brilliant, emotional, enjoyable*), with several adverbs as well (e.g., *beautifully, quite, wonderfully*), in line with the overall higher frequencies of adjectives and adverbs in this register. However, several of these evaluative words are also nouns (e.g., *charm, fun, humour*) or verbs (e.g., *feels, liked, love*). Overall, the lexical characteristics of this register are easy to interpret: discourse focused on the description of consumer products (most commonly music, books, or movies), with evaluative comments relating to the products. Such web documents, illustrated in [5], are familiar to most end-users of the web.

[5] Michael Tumelty at The Herald said: "The music ranges in mood from austere to warm and tender, from the purity of intensity to the almost relaxed expansiveness of a music that knows precisely its purpose, its point and its trajectory. The performance was broad, blazing and stunning." (Full review here)
   Richard Morrison at The Times also gave us four stars, calling it "wonderfully rich in its musical tapestry", and also commenting on the "superb performances all round"

Table 6.6. *Keywords for Reviews*

Evaluations	Attributes	Products	Participants
beautiful	bass	album	actor
beautifully	camera	android	actors
bit	cast	book	audience
brilliant	character	cinema	fan
charm	characters	debut	reviewer
classic	climax	episode	
dark	comedy	film	
emotional	drama	films	
enjoyable	feature	film's	
entertaining	features	movie	
excellent	fiction	movies	
fantastic	gameplay	music	
favourite	gaming	novel	
feels	genre	performances	
finds	guitar	release	
fun	hd	script	
funny	horror	sequel	
humour	moments	series	
impressive	multiplayer	song	
likeable	musical	songs	
liked	narrative	soundtrack	
little	plot	story	
looks	protagonist	tracks	
love	romance	version	
makes	scene		
manages	scenes		
masterpiece	screen		
nice	storyline		
quite	style		
reminiscent	tale		
review	theme		
reviewed	themes		
reviews	tone		
sound	villain		
superb	visuals		
there's	vocals		
wonderfully			

(the review is tucked behind the paywall here). Over in The Scotsman, Ken Walton praised "a supreme clarity of texture, the unbridled simplicity of which heightens the emotional impact," and said "This was an impressive first performance by the Hebrides Ensemble."

http://hebridesensemble.com/?p=811

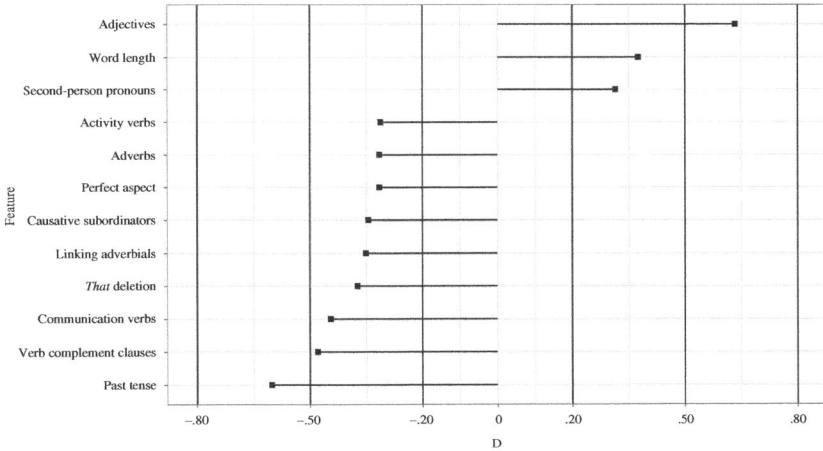

Figure 6.4. Key grammatical features for the Description-with-intent-to-sell sub-register

6.4.3 Description-with-intent-to-sell

As noted in Section 6.2, Descriptions-with-intent-to-sell (DS) are similar in purpose and readership to Product Reviews. The major differences are that Reviews are often written by individuals who are not necessarily promoting a product, while Descriptions-with-intent-to-sell are usually written by unidentified authors associated with a commercial site, having an underlying goal of promoting the product (even if the text itself is portrayed as an informational description).

Reflecting those situational similarities, the results of the MD analysis (see Section 6.3) showed that DS and Review documents are very similar in their dimensional profiles. Thus, it is not surprising that a more detailed analysis of grammatical and lexical characteristics would confirm many of those similarities.

In terms of grammatical characteristics, the most notable characteristic of DS documents (similar to Reviews) is the small number of features that are used with notable frequencies (see Figure 6.4). Adjectives are the only grammatical feature with a moderately large d score, and they are also the most salient feature of DS texts. Two other features with small positive d values – long words and premodifying nouns – reflect the informational purposes of these documents. Finally, second-person pronouns are also somewhat more frequent in DS documents than in the corpus overall, reflecting the focus on the reader. Text excerpt [6] illustrates these grammatical characteristics. The frequent adjectives, which are underlined in this excerpt, tend to express positive evaluations. In general, there are not many grammatical stance constructions in DS documents, but there are frequent evaluative adjectives distributed through-out almost all of these texts.

[6] Ronnie could pull the best out of a simple lyric and melody but more importantly, would allow the best to flow from those talented musicians who he had collected in the band "Slim Chance". He let them shine but all the while knowing exactly what he wanted. Here it is for you to enjoy. Some of the best and beautiful songs Ronnie could cook up... and that band could cook!

Ronnie's solo work is just great. I always appreciated his work with the Steve and Rod versions of Faces. This work is a total shift from Faces/Small Faces feel to a more mellow earthy sound. Very nice in the same way Rod Stewart did on his early solo works

www.amazon.com/Just-Moment-Ronnie-Lane/dp/B000K7UFXK

In several respects, the keywords that are typical of DS documents are also similar to the keywords found in Reviews (compare Table 6.6 to Table 6.7). Both have sets of keywords identifying the products being described, and identifying various attributes of those products. Both registers also employ a large number of evaluative words – mostly adjectives and adverbs, but also including nouns and verbs. Both registers also use words referring to partici-pants. However, the nature of these words differs between the two registers. In Reviews, we find words referring to the actors in movies, and to the audience/fans who enjoy various products (e.g., *movies, music, book*). In DS documents, though, words related to participants usually refer directly to the reader, reflect-ing the overall persuasive purpose of the register. In addition, DS documents employ a number of words that directly relate to the commercial goals of this register (e.g., *customer, delivery, purchase*).

Beyond those differences, the most striking lexical characteristic of DS doc-uments is the extremely large number of evaluative words. Over 50 percent of all keywords in this register are used to express evaluations. The keywords listed in Table 6.7 are just the tip of the iceberg: any DS document illustrates the extremely dense use of evaluative words, including both the words listed in Table 6.7 as well as a large number of additional evaluative words. Text excerpts [7] and [8] below illustrate the dense use of embedded evaluative words typical of DS documents.

[7] The Jordanian town of Aqaba nestles at the top of the Gulf of Aqaba which leads off the Red Sea. Boasting some excellent sandy beaches and one of the world's best-preserved coral reefs, this is a popular resort with divers. But the main attraction of this area is the magnificent fortress city of Petra, buried by sand for more than 2,000 years until it was discovered in the desert near Aqaba in the 19th century and exca-vated in the 1950s.

www.pocruises.com/destinations/world-voyages/

Table 6.7. *Keywords for the Description-with-intent-to-sell sub-register*

Evaluations	Attributes	Commerce	Products	Participants	Other
acclaimed	adventure	customer	album	author's	booklist
award-winning	bedrooms	delivery	albums	reader	excluding
beautifully	biography	promotional	book	reader's	includes
bestseller	chapter	publishers	book's	readers	please
bestsellers	chapters	purchase	collection	you'll	print
bestselling	chronicle	sellers	novel	you're	read
breathtaking	dvd	unavailable	novels	your	reading
charming	essays	warehouses	products		
chronicle	features				
classic	fiction				
compelling	format				
contemporary	gift				
elegance	guide				
engaging	humor				
enjoy	illustrations				
entertaining	literary				
examines	memoir				
excellent	narrative				
explores	nonfiction				
fascinating	prose				
free	secrets				
fulfilment	style				
full	synopsis				
guide	written				
happy					
hassle-free					
highly					
illuminates					
insights					
intimate					
lowest-priced					
must-read					
poignant					
provocative					
readable					
recommend					
review					
riveting					
spacious					
stars					
stylish					
superb					
tale					
thought-provoking					
timeless					
unforgettable					
unique					
weaves					
wish					
witty					
wonderful					

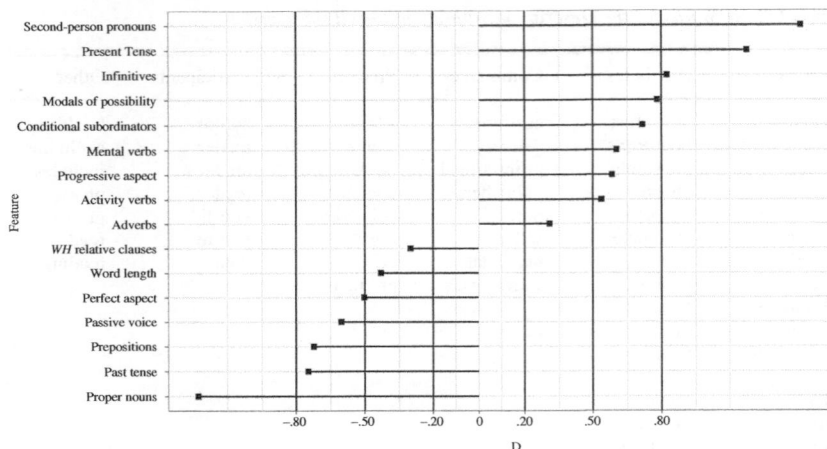

Figure 6.5. Key grammatical features for the Advice sub-register

[8] I have always loved John Garfield, for a number of reasons I suppose, not the least of which he was a great (and I think vastly underrated) actor. He had amazing qualities, and he was tough and at the same time quite vulnerable. He was from a working-class background in New York, and often the roles he played reflected this. He was a tough street-kid. This film to me is classic film noir [...]

www.amazon.co.uk/Ran-All-The-Way-DVD/dp/B001TJKVRI

6.4.4   Advice

In contrast to Opinion Blogs, Reviews, and Descriptions-with-intent-to-sell, which are all relatively unmarked in their grammatical characteristics, Advice documents are quite distinctive grammatically. In fact, Advice documents are more similar linguistically to How-to/Procedural documents (see Section 7.4.1) and FAQs about Information (see Section 7.4.6) than any of the other Opinion registers (see discussion in Section 9.1). Figure 6.5 shows an especially frequent use of second-person pronouns, reflecting the focus on the reader. The grammatical style is focused on the present and dynamic, with present-tense verbs, progressive-aspect verbs, activity verbs, adverbs, and human nouns. At the same time, there is a focus on the thoughts and feelings of the reader (mental verbs) and consideration of multiple possible issues and problems (reflected by the dense use of modal verbs, conditional clauses, and *to-* clauses). [9] illustrates the dense use of this collection of grammatical features.

[9] It's easier to feel brave when you feel good about yourself. See the next tip!

Feel good about you. Nobody's perfect, but what can you do to look and feel your best? Maybe you'd like to be more fit. If so, maybe you'll decide to get more exercise, watch less TV, and eat healthier snacks. Or maybe you feel you look best when you shower in the morning before school. If so, you could decide to get up a little earlier so you can be clean and refreshed for the school day.

Get a buddy (and be a buddy). Two is better than one if you're trying to avoid being bullied. Make a plan to walk with a friend or two on the way to school or recess or lunch or wherever you think you might meet the bully. Offer to do the same if a friend is having bully trouble. Get involved if you see bullying going on

http://kidshealth.org/kid/grow/school_stuff/bullies.html

The keywords common in Advice documents are also quite different from those typical of other Opinion sub-registers (see Table 6.8). Many of these words describe particular problems or issues that are commonly discussed in advice webpages, including *stress, work, foods,* staying *healthy, exercise, happiness,* and even *life* itself! Personal and professional relationships are perhaps the most important of these issues discussed in advice columns, and there are several keywords from that domain. There is also considerable discussion of the mental and emotional states experienced by the reader in relation to these problems and issues: the reader's *feelings* and *thoughts,* or what the readers might *need, feel, want,* or *know.* Text excerpts [9] and [10] are both typical Advice documents with respect to these characteristics.

[10] Sometimes it's difficult to make the time for these things we know are important for our health, but I'm going to hound you until you do.

Larry Lewis, in his blog dedicated to living a healthy lifestyle, argues that eating right and exercising cannot even fully provide for physical well-being. In his list for components of physical health Lewis adds adequate rest as well as stress management, furthering his argument by bringing up some of the things that may result from being too stressed: "Emotional stress plays an important role in many illnesses, both directly and indirectly. People are also more likely to smoke, overeat, drink too much, work too hard, argue with others and so on, when they are feeling stressed" ...

Your dead on Larry, understanding all components helps. Energy, exercise, healthy eating, desire, heart, need and love can move a lot of things in life, but I have a feeling your mind has a big influence.

www.healthylifestylesliving.com/health/healthy-lifestyle/
what-is-a-healthy-lifestyle/

However, judging from these keywords, there is an even greater focus on solutions, rather than problems, in Advice documents. These words include nouns that identify the components of a solution (e.g., *goals, plan, skills, steps, tips*) as well as verbs describing the actions that the reader should take (e.g., *achieve, avoid, choose, spend, try*). Discovery verbs are a special subset of

Table 6.8. *Keywords for the Advice sub-register*

Recommended actions and solutions	Mental and emotional states	Problems	Relationships	Evaluations	Reference to the reader	Discovery verbs	Communication	Frequency adverbs
achieve	emotional	eat	clients	best	you	consider	ask	always
advice	feel	exercise	friends	better	you'll	find	blog	often
avoid	feeling	foods	partner	easier	you're	learn	conversation	sometimes
can	feelings	habit	partner's	easy	you've	learning	talk	usually
choose	focus	happiness	person	good	your	listen	write	
do	know	healthier	professional	important	yours	look		
doing	knowing	healthy	relationship	positive	yourself	remember		
don't	mind	if	relationships	simple				
get	need	job	someone	sure				
getting	personal	life	spouse					
give	self-esteem	stress						
go	thoughts	work						
goals	want							
help								
helps								
how								
keep								
make								
may								
offer								
plan								
prepare								
should								
skills								
something								
spend								
start								
steps								
take								
things								
tips								
try								
way								
ways								

these verbs, promoting ways in which the reader should think through their problem before embarking on a course of action (e.g., *consider, learn, remember*). The communication process, with several nouns and verbs as keywords, is also an important component of these advised plans.

Frequency adverbs (*always, often, sometimes, usually*) modify both the verbs used to identify problems and the verbs used to propose solutions. There are some evaluative keywords in Advice documents, but they are few in comparison to other opinion sub-registers. These words are all positive and extremely general in meaning (e.g., *good, better, best, easy, sure*), providing a general assurance that the prescribed course of action will benefit the reader. Finally, confirming the results of the grammatical analysis above, second-person pronouns with a range of inflections and contractions are also very common in this sub-register.

Almost all Advice documents include both a description of problems and a proposed set of actions that will provide solutions. For example, the paragraph in [10] above includes some discussion of solutions, and other paragraphs in this same advice blog are even more focused on suggesting solutions. Thus, consider [11] below:

[11] Loving yourself is a key to a healthy, happy lifestyle. Self-esteem is all about how much people value themselves; the pride they feel in themselves, and how worthwhile they feel. Self-esteem is important because feeling good about yourself can affect how you act. [...]
If you want to achieve a healthy lifestyle you must take steps to ensure you maintain a certain level of balance ... spiritually, physically, emotionally, socially, mentally and financially. You need to balance work and family, and all the other areas of your life without spreading yourself too thin and having a guilt trip when you do one thing, but think you should be doing another.

www.healthylifestylesliving.com/health/
healthy-lifestyle/what-is-a-healthy-lifestyle/

6.4.5   Religious Blogs

Religious Blogs are for the most part presented as informational documents, rather than overtly opinionated documents. Figure 6.6 shows that Religious Blogs employ an elaborated grammatical style, with frequent coordinated clauses, *WH* relative clauses, *that* complement clauses (especially controlled by communication verbs), and prepositional phrases. At the same time, these texts do not adopt the dense nominal style of modern academic prose. Thus, the density of nouns, adjectives, long words, and premodifying nouns is considerably lower than that found on average across web registers. The result is a discourse style somewhat reminiscent of informational prose from earlier centuries, with a dense reliance on embedded and coordinated clauses but

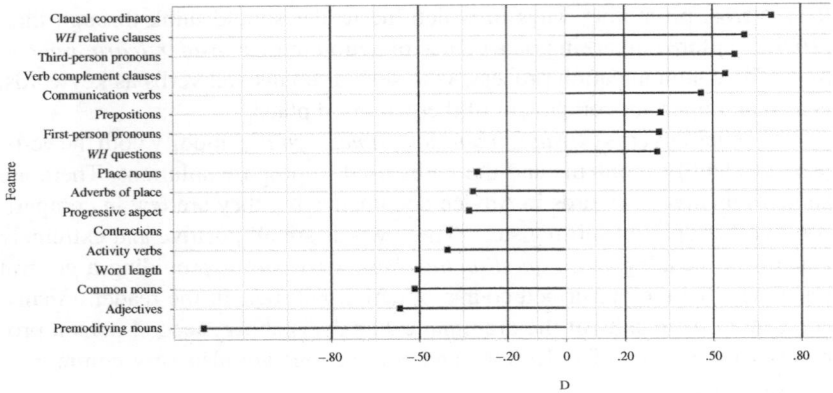

Figure 6.6. Key grammatical features for Religious Blogs

relatively little phrasal elaboration (see Biber and Gray, 2016). [12] illustrates many of these characteristics:

[12] There is that pleasantness **in** the converse **of** servants **of** God, **which** can make those **who** listen to them forget the pain and the weariness **of** labour. Even the sons **of** the prophets must not be unwilling to labour. Let no man think an honest employment a burden or a disgrace. **And** labour **of** the head, is as hard, and very often harder, than labour with the hands. We ought to be careful **of** that **which** is borrowed, as **of** our own, because we must do as we would be done **by**. This man was so respecting the axe-head. **And to** those **who** have an honest mind, the sorest grievance **of** poverty is, not so much their own want and disgrace, as being rendered unable to pay just debts. **But** the Lord cares **for** his people **in** their smallest concerns. **And** God's grace can thus raise the stony iron heart, **which** is sunk **into** the mud **of** this world, and raise up affections, naturally earthly.

http://biblehub.com/2_kings/6-5.htm

Reflecting its very restricted topical domain, the keyword analysis of Religious Blogs uncovered a set of words belonging to only three major semantic domains: religious persons or groups, religious concepts and attributes, and direct biblical references (see Table 6.9). These results indicate that the majority of Religious Blogs posted in the five inner-circle English-speaking countries relate to discussions of Christianity. The keyword analysis for Religious Blogs uncovered a very large set of words that have relatively large keyness values. Almost all of these words belong to the same three major semantic domains. Table 6.9 lists only the hundred words that have the largest keyness values, but there are numerous related words with slightly smaller values (e.g., *heavenly, messiah, temple, death, holiness, sinner, everlasting, sacred, eternity, prophecy*). [12] above illustrates several of these keywords, as does [13] below. [13] also additionally illustrates several of

Table 6.9. *Keywords for Religious Blogs*

Religious concepts and attributes	Religious persons (or groups of people)	Biblical references	Formal (archaic) function words
blessed	apostle	bible	hath
Christianity	apostles	biblical	shall
communion	believers	Corinthians	thou
divine	Christ	Ephesians	unto
doctrine	Christ's	Genesis	upon
eternal	Christians	gospel	whom
evil	church	Hebrews	
faith	churches	Isaiah	
faithful	disciples	Luke	
glory	earth	Matthew	
grace	father	Psalm	
hearts	God	Romans	
heaven	God's	scripture	
holy	him	scriptures	
kingdom	himself	testament	
mercy	Israel	verse	
ministry	Jerusalem	verses	
pray	Jesus	word	
prayer	Jesus'		
religion	Jews		
religious	lord		
repentance	lord's		
resurrection	Moses		
revelation	priest		
righteousness	prophet		
salvation	prophets		
sin	saints		
sins	Satan		
soul	sinners		
souls	son		
spiritual	spirit		
truth			
wisdom			
worship			

the key grammatical features of Religious Blogs, including the dense use of coordinated clauses, relative clauses, and *WH* questions used rhetorically to structure the argument.

[13] The **kingdom** of Messiah supplanting utterly the former will be **eternal** and world-wide [...]

... he moved his earthly headquarters from Pergamos to Rome... There "*the deeds of the nicolaitanes*" were enshrined as "*the **doctrine** of the Nicolaitanes*" ...

Brother Branham said, "Here's the plan of it: the first thing happens, there is an announcement in the **heavens** first. [...] It declares a (natural) war (in judgment upon the Israelites for rejecting the Message of the angel, which is the mystery of **redemption** to that Age). [...]"

www.biblebelievers.org.au/nl638.htm

We noted above that Religious Blogs tend to adopt a structurally elaborated grammatical style, with numerous clauses coordinated and embedded in sentences. This discourse style is typical of informational essays written in the seventeenth and eighteenth centuries, but quite different from the phrasal grammatical styles normally employed in present-day informational texts. A further reflection of this style is the reliance on formal, archaic function words, which were relatively common in earlier historical periods but rare in most present-day registers. For example, see [14] below (Table 6.9).

[14] From the foundation of the world it sealed the full import of the stellar Bible as the Seven Seals bound the Revelation of Jesus Christ **unto** the time of the end.
The twenty-eighth verse promises the glorious second outshining, as it promises, "He **shall** appear." Between these two lights? "he **hath** appeared" and "he **shall** appear"? we **shall** sail safely, if the Holy Spirit will direct our way. [...] Now once in the end of the world **hath** he appeared to put away sin by the sacrifice of himself.
Of old **hast thou** laid the foundation of the earth: and the heavens are the work of thy hands. They **shall** perish, but **thou shalt** endure: yea, all of them **shall** wax old like a garment; as a vesture **shalt thou** change them, and they **shall** be changed.

www.biblebelievers.org.au/nl638.htm

6.5   Summary and Conclusion

In this chapter we have carried out a comprehensive situational and linguistic description of five online registers that share the purpose of expressing opinion. These sub-registers differ in the degree to which, and ways in which, they are focused on expressing opinion. For example, Opinion Blogs tend to be focused entirely on the subjective opinion of the author, whereas Descriptions-with-intent-to-sell are often focused primarily on the transmitting of information while the goal of persuading a potential customer to purchase a product or service is a more subtle, implicit goal. This variation in the situational parameters of these sub-registers was clearly reflected in their linguistic characteristics. While the registers in this chapter are not as well-defined linguistically as the narrative registers described in the previous chapter (see Section 6.3), there were many clear lexical and lexico-grammatical patterns that distinguished them from other registers, both within the general register of Opinion, and with registers in the other general register categories.

7 Informational Descriptions, Explanations, and Procedures

7.1 Introduction

The general category of Informational Descriptions, Explanations, and Procedures is perhaps the most diverse of all the web registers described in the present project. As Table 7.1 shows, we distinguished among seven specific sub-registers within this general register category. Two of these sub-registers were especially common: How-to Documents/blogs, which explain the procedures for accomplishing a task; and Informational Blogs, which provide descriptive or explanatory information about a topic. Several other sub-registers are less common but quite distinctive, including Recipes (a special sub-category of How-to), Academic Research Articles, Encyclopedia Articles, and Informational FAQs. At the other extreme, Descriptions-of-a-person is a relatively general category, with no clear counterpart in previous studies of printed written registers.

However, the most striking characteristic of this general register is the fact that end-users were unable to identify a specific sub-register for many of these

Table 7.1. *Sub-register categories related to informational procedures/descriptions, with text counts*

Sub-register	Text count
How-to/Instructional Documents or Blogs	1,392
Recipes	126
Academic Research Articles/Abstracts	924
Encyclopedia Articles	556
Descriptions-of-a-person	759
Informational FAQs	415
Informational Blogs	1,699
Other information	3,924
TOTAL	9,795

documents. Thus, roughly 40 percent of these documents are grouped into a general category of "other information." This is one of the most important, yet most overlooked, characteristics of the searchable web: the huge amount of "information" available that does not fit tidily into any well-defined register category that has been described in previous research. Similar to the organization of the preceding chapters, we begin this chapter by introducing the range of sub-registers that have informational communicative purposes, describing and illustrating the major situational and discourse characteristics of each one (Section 7.2). Then, in Section 7.3, we provide more detailed descriptions of the lexical and grammatical patterns of register variation within this discourse domain of the web.

Finally, it is important to emphasize what is *not* included here. Given the amazing quantity of information freely available on the web, it is easy to forget about all the information that is not available, including all published texts, as well as all informational reports and documents produced by companies and institutions for their own internal readerships. The first of these is the most noteworthy, because we have always considered the vast amount of information published in books, magazines, newspapers, and academic journals to be "public" information. However, virtually none of that information is freely available on the public searchable web, because it is copyright-protected and available only with a paid subscription. Against that background, it is truly mind-boggling to consider how much information *is* freely available on the web. But, at the same time, it is sobering to consider the fact that this is the information that most of the public relies on, while the huge body of information in published outlets is becoming increasingly less relevant, written by experts and consumed only by other experts who have access to those texts.

7.2   Survey of Informational Sub-registers

Table 7.2 lists the major informational sub-registers that are commonly found on the searchable web, together with a summary of their most important situational characteristics. These are organized into two general categories: informational documents that have a procedural purpose (How-to/Instructions and Recipes) and informational documents that have a descriptive or explanatory purpose.

How-to documents are among the most distinctive of these informational sub-registers, because they normally provide explicit step-by-step instructions for achieving a particular task. These documents can be found on a wide range of websites, including blog sites written by an individual, as well as documents on institutional, governmental, or commercial sites with no acknowledged author. What these documents all have in common, though, is that they provide procedural information explaining how to accomplish a task, such as removing viruses on your computer (e.g., Screenshot 7.1) or using Facebook (e.g., Screenshot 7.2).

Table 7.2. *Major situational characteristics of informational sub-registers*

	Author and venue	Audience	Purposes/goals/ intended outcomes
How-to/ Instructions	Individual or institutional author – can be a blog or institutional website	Anyone trying to learn how to perform certain tasks	Providing step-by-step instructions on how to perform a task. (Note: How-to documents can also take the form of FAQs.)
Recipes	Usually an individual author writing on a personal, institutional, or commercial website	Anyone trying to learn how to cook a particular food dish	Providing a list of ingredients and step-by-step instructions on how to make the food product
Research Articles/ Abstracts	An individual author or group of authors, associated with a publisher or an academic website	Specialist readers interested in the area of research	Describes a research study, including the motivation for the study, the methods used, and the major research findings
Encyclopedia Articles	Usually a collaborative group of coauthors who are not acknowledged, writing on a "wiki" website. Authors are assumed to have special expertise in the topic of the article	Anyone interested in learning information about a specific topic	Descriptive or explanatory information that attempts to synthesize the current state of knowledge from all available studies
Descriptions-of-a-person	Can be an individual author (e.g., associated with a blog site) or an institutional author (e.g., associated with a historical association)	Readers interested in the life of a particular person or group of people	To describe the life of a particular person or group of people. The focus can be either a historical narrative or a description of their current life
Informational FAQs	Usually an unacknowledged author associated with an institutional or commercial site	Anyone trying to learn specific information about a topic	Documents that are structured as questions and answers, to provide highly specific descriptive or explanatory information about particular topics. (Note: Procedural FAQs are discussed under the "How-to" sub-register.)

(cont.)

Table 7.2. (*cont.*)

	Author and venue	Audience	Purposes/goals/ intended outcomes
Informational Blogs	Can be an individual author or an institutional author, writing on a personal, government/NPO, or commercial website; sometimes associated with an author who regularly posts documents on the same "blog" website	Anyone interested in the topic, or anyone who "follows" the blogger	To convey descriptive or explanatory information about a topic, presented as "objective" information rather than personal opinion
Other Information	Usually no acknowledged author. Associated with an institutional, governmental, or commercial site	Anyone trying to learn information about a topic	A huge range of particular goals, all generally associated with providing descriptive or explanatory information about a topic

Recipes are also a type of How-to document, but they are treated as a special sub-register because they are so distinctive and easy to recognize. They are specialized in topic – always giving the procedures for making food – and they typically include description of the ingredients as well as step-by-step information describing how to make the food. This sub-register is widely known and recognized from printed cookbooks, and the Recipes found on the web are often identical in form and content to those found in printed media (see [1]).

[1] Recipe for "creamy chicken pie"
Delicious creamy chicken in a white bechamel sauce in a light puff pastry pocket
Recipe type: Appetiser
Serves: 2
Ingredients

- 1 Pack ready made puff pastry
- 2 Chicken Breasts
- 1 Medium onion
- 1 Cube chicken stock
- 2 Bay leafs
- 3 Cardamon pods

[...]

(Continued on bottom of p. 139)

How-To Geek   WINDOWS   MAC   IPHONE   AND[

How to Remove Viruses and Malware on Your Windows PC
by **Chris Hoffman** on November 2nd, 2016

Malicious program detected
Kaspersky Anti-Virus

8:57 PM
10/20/2016

Whether you saw a message saying a virus was detected, or your computer just seems slow and unreliable, you'll want to scan for malware on your PC and remove any you find.

While many viruses and other types of malware are designed simply to cause chaos, more and more malware is created by organized crime to steal credit card numbers, online banking credentials, and other sensitive data.

Screenshot 7.1. Online How-to document
www.howtogeek.com/126911/what-to-do-if-you-get-a-virus-on-your-computer/

Instructions

1. To cook the chicken, start by filling a medium sized stock pot with boiling water, add the onion, bay leafs, cardamon pods, pepper corns, and chicken stock, then add the chicken breast and cook for 20 mins or until the chicken has cooked fully.
2. When the chicken has cooked, drain from the broth and set a side.
3. To make the creamy béchamel sauce, first heat the milk ready for use. Melt the butter over a medium heat, once the butter has melted add the flour and mix well, then allow the mixture to cook a little for a few minutes.

[...]

http://mongoliankitchen.com/creamy-chicken-pie/

3. How to allow people to follow your Facebook Profile

Facebook only allows you to have 5000 friends, but you can allow an unlimited number of people to follow the *Public* updates you post on your Profile without becoming friends.(Note I'm referring to your Personal Profile here, not a Page, so this is totally different than Likes on a Page.)

This might be nice if you want to let people see a more personal side of you. Simply go to your Follower Settings to enable it. Just set "Who Can Follow Me" to "Everyone."

On the flip side, if you want to follow someone, go to their Profile (here's mine for example) and click the Follow button in the bottom right corner of the cover image.

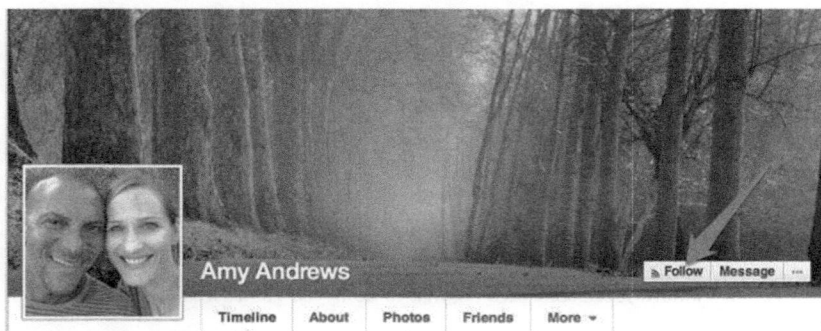

(If you don't see a follow button it's because that person hasn't enabled it. Or you're already following.)

Screenshot 7.2. Online How-to document
https://amylynnandrews.com/facebook-tips/

The other sub-registers discussed in this chapter all have descriptive or explanatory informational communicative purposes, as opposed to the procedural purposes of the two sub-registers above. The first of these, Academic Research Articles (and Abstracts), will be familiar to all readers of this book.

Academic research writing has been one of the most thoroughly investigated registers of English, with numerous books, research articles, and even entire academic journals dedicated to this register. Given that background, it is at first surprising to discover that academic research articles are relatively rare on the public searchable web. But there is a simple reason for this: research articles are normally published in copyright-protected academic journals, and as a result, they are generally not accessible on the publicly searchable web (i.e., without a paid subscription and password to gain access). In recent years, some academic research articles have begun to appear in "open access" online journals, and those are available freely on the publicly searchable web; [2] contains an excerpt from a journal of this type. In general, though, academic research writing does not play a prominent role on the publicly searchable web.

[2] Concurrent validity of the Gyko inertial sensor system for the assessment of vertical jump height in female sub-elite youth soccer players
Melanie Lesinski Email author, Thomas Muehlbauer and Urs Granacher
BMC Sports Science, Medicine and Rehabilitation BMC series – open, inclusive and trusted20168:35
DOI: 10.1186/s13102-016-0061-x© The Author(s). 2016
Received: 24 June 2016 Accepted: 29 October 2016 Published: 11 November 2016
Open Peer Review reports
Abstract
Background
The aim of the present study was to verify concurrent validity of the Gyko inertial sensor system for the assessment of vertical jump height.
Methods
Nineteen female sub-elite youth soccer players (mean age: 14.7 ± 0.6 years) performed three trials of countermovement (CMJ) and squat jumps (SJ), respectively. Maximal vertical jump height was simultaneously quantified with the Gyko system, a Kistler force-plate (i.e., gold standard), and another criterion device that is frequently used in the field, the Optojump system. [...]

> http://bmcsportsscimedrehabil.biomedcentral.com/articles/
> 10.1186/s13102-016-0061-x

Encyclopedia Articles have become one of the most iconic informational registers of the web, especially for college students. The most famous encyclopedia website is Wikipedia, which is a free online site with over five million articles written in English. Reflecting the democratic nature of information on the web, articles on Wikipedia are written collaboratively by individuals who believe they have knowledge about a topic. Articles in Wikipedia, similar to conventional Encyclopedia Articles, attempt to provide a state-of-the-art summary of information relating to a particular subject. Screenshot 7.3 shows a screenshot for the article about the "Arab Spring."

Arab Spring

From Wikipedia, the free encyclopedia

This article is about the demonstrations and revolts in the Arab world in early 2010s. For other Arab revolts, see Arab Revolt (disambiguation).

The **Arab Spring** (Arabic: الربيع العربي *ar-Rabīʻ al-ʻArabī*) also referred to as **Arab revolutions** (Arabic: الثورات العربية *aṯ-'awrāt al-'arabiyyah*) or **Democracy Spring** (Arabic: الربيع الديمقراطي *ar-Rabīʻ ad-Dīmuqrāṭī*) was a revolutionary wave of both violent and non-violent demonstrations, protests, riots, coups and civil wars in North Africa and the Middle East that began on 17 December 2010 in Tunisia with the Tunisian Revolution.

The Tunisian Revolution effect spread strongly to five other countries: Libya, Egypt, Yemen, Syria and Iraq, where either the regime was toppled or major uprisings and social violence occurred, including civil wars or insurgencies. Sustained street demonstrations took place in Morocco, Bahrain, Algeria, Iran, Lebanon, Jordan, Kuwait, Oman and Sudan. Minor protests occurred in Djibouti, Mauritania, the Palestinian National Authority, Saudi Arabia, Somalia and the Moroccan-controlled Western Sahara.[1] A major slogan of the demonstrators in the Arab world is *ash-sha'b yurīd isqāṭ an-niẓām* ("the people want to bring down the regime").[2]

The wave of initial revolutions and protests faded by mid-2012, as many Arab Spring demonstrations were met with violent responses from authorities,[3][4][5] as well as from pro-government militias and counter-demonstrators. These attacks were answered with violence from protestors in some cases.[6][7][8] Large-scale conflicts resulted—the Syrian Civil War,[9][10] Iraqi insurgency and the following civil war,[11] the Egyptian Crisis and coup,[12] the Libyan Civil War, and the Yemeni Crisis and following civil war.[13]

A power struggle continued after the immediate response to the Arab Spring. While leadership changed and regimes were held accountable, power vacuums opened across the Arab world. Ultimately it came down to a contentious battle between a consolidation of power by religious elites and the growing support for democracy in many Muslim-majority states.[14] The early hopes that these popular movements would end corruption, increase political participation, and bring about greater economic equity quickly collapsed in the wake of the counterrevolutionary moves of the deep state in Egypt, the regional and international interventions in Bahrain and Yemen, and the destructive civil wars in Syria and Libya.[15]

Some have referred to the succeeding and still ongoing conflicts as the Arab Winter.[9][10][11][12][13] As of July 2016, only the uprising in Tunisia resulted in a transition to constitutional democratic governance.[1]

Arab Spring

Protesters in Tunis (January 2011)

Date	17 December 2010 – December 2012
Location	North Africa, Middle East (i.e. "Arab world")
Caused by	• Authoritarianism • Capitalism • Demographic structural factors • 2000s energy crisis • Political corruption • Human rights violations • Inflation • Kleptocracy • Sectarianism • Unemployment • Self-immolation of Mohamed Bouazizi
Goals	• Democracy • Free elections • Economic freedom • Human rights • Employment • Regime change • Freedom of religion
Methods	• Civil disobedience • Civil resistance • Defection • Demonstrations • Insurgency • Internet activism • Protest camps • Revolution • Riots • Self-immolation • Silent protests • Sit-ins • Social Media • Strike actions • Urban warfare • Uprising
Resulted in	• **Tunisia:** President Zine El Abidine Ben Ali ousted, charged, exiled and government overthrown. • **Egypt:** President Hosni Mubarak ousted, arrested, charged, and government overthrown. • **Libya:** Leader Muammar Gaddafi killed following a civil war that saw a foreign military intervention, and government overthrown. • **Yemen:** President Ali Abdullah Saleh ousted, and power handed to a national unity government. • **Syria:** President Bashar al-Assad faces civil uprising against his rule that deteriorates into armed rebellion and eventual full-scale civil war. • **Bahrain:** Civil uprising against the government crushed by authorities and Saudi-led intervention. • **Kuwait, Lebanon and Oman:** Government changes implemented in response to protests.

Contents [hide]

Etymology [edit]

The term "Arab Spring" is an allusion to the Revolutions of 1848, which are sometimes referred to as the "Springtime of Nations", and the Prague Spring in 1968. In the aftermath of the Iraq War it was used by various commentators and bloggers who anticipated a major Arab movement towards democratization.[16] The first specific use of the term *Arab Spring* as used to denote these events may have started with the American political journal *Foreign Policy*.[17] Political scientist Marc Lynch described "Arab Spring" as "a term I may have unintentionally coined in a January 6, 2011 article" for *Foreign Policy* magazine.[18][19] Joseph Massad on *Al Jazeera* said the term was "part of a US strategy of controlling [the movement's] aims and goals" and directing it towards western-style liberal democracy.[17] When Arab Spring protests in some countries were followed by electoral success for Islamist parties, some American pundits coined the terms "Islamist Spring"[20] and "Islamist Winter".[21]

Some observers have also drawn comparisons between the Arab Spring movements and the Revolutions of 1989 (also known as the "Autumn of Nations") that swept through Eastern Europe and the Second World, in terms of their scale and significance.[22][23][24] Others, however, have pointed out that there are several key differences between the movements, such as the desired outcomes, the effectiveness of civil resistance, and the organizational role of Internet-based technologies in the Arab revolutions.[25][26][27][28]

Screenshot 7.3. Wikipedia article
https://en.wikipedia.org/wiki/Arab_Spring

Killing Curse

> Editing of this article by newly registered users is currently disabled. Such users may discuss changes, or request unprotection.

Warning!

HARRY POTTER
AND THE CURSED CHILD

Some content in this article is derived from information featured in *Harry Potter and the Cursed Child*, and, as such, **spoilers** will be present.

Keep calm and keep the secrets!

"There was a flash of blinding green light and a rushing sound, as though a vast, invisible something was soaring through the air — instantaneously the spider rolled over onto its back, unmarked, but unmistakably dead"

—Description of the Killing Curse[src]

The **Killing Curse** (*Avada Kedavra*) is a tool of the Dark Arts and one of the three Unforgivable Curses. It is one of the most powerful and sinister spells known to wizardkind. When cast successfully on a living person or creature the curse causes instantaneous and painless death, without any signs of violence on the body.

The only known counter-spell is sacrificial protection, which uses the power of love. However, one may dodge the green bolt, block it with a physical barrier, or by the use of Priori Incantatem. The Killing Curse is an '*unblockable*' curse, thus shield charms won't defend against it. An explosion or green fire may result if the spell hits something other than a living target.

Killing Curse	
Incantation	Avada Kedavra (a-VAH-dah ke-DAH-vra)[1]
Type	Curse
Hand movement	
Light	Green[2]
Effect	Instantaneous death[1]
[Source]	

Screenshot 7.4. Encyclopedia Article
http://harrypotter.wikia.com/wiki/Killing_Curse

However, there are now hundreds of other online encyclopedias, influenced by the "wiki" framework of non-experts working together to create informational documents collaboratively. Reflecting the interests of end-users of the web, any subject area might become the locus for an entire wiki encyclopedia site. For example, Screenshot 7.4 shows a screenshot for an Encyclopedia Article from a wiki devoted to information about Harry Potter books and movies.

Many of the articles posted on wiki sites are biographical, providing informational descriptions of a person's life and accomplishments. In general, the end-users who classified documents in our project grouped these documents into the "encyclopedia" sub-register. However, there are many other biographical web documents that are not found on wiki sites. These are often associated

David Perdue's
Charles Dickens Page
charlesdickenspage.com

Dickens Fast Facts
The Novels
Characters
Dickens Glossary
Illustrations
Timeline
Reading Dickens
Dickens the Journalist
Dickens on Stage
Dickens on Film
Dickens' London
Dickens London Map
Dickens Rochester Map
Dickens & Christmas
Family and Friends
Dickens in America
Dickens on the Web
Shop Dickens
Bibliography
Site Awards/Honors
FAQ & Email

Family and Friends

Parents | Siblings | Wife Catherine | Children | Catherine's Sisters | Friends | Dickens Family Tree

Scenes of family harmony and cozy firesides in many of Dickens' stories seem in stark contrast to his own family life. Growing up, the family situation was often precarious due to his father's trouble with debt, which landed him in debtors' prison in 1824 when Charles was 12.

Later Dickens' own family was marked by strife as his relationship with his wife deteriorated and his sons seemed to have inherited their paternal grandfather's trouble handling finances. Dickens once lamented that he had "brought up the largest family with the smallest disposition for doing anything for themselves." Dickens' extended family's constant drain on his finances, along with his built-in anxiety about money caused by his childhood, resulted in Dickens never feeling comfortable enough about his financial situation.

Dickens' circle of friends consisted of people prominent in the arts, journalism, publishing, politics and public life. A loyal friend who demanded loyalty in return, lines were drawn during Dickens' very public separation from Catherine. Those not sympathetic to Dickens' side soon felt his wrath, in some cases, forever.

Parents

John Dickens (1785-1851) - Dickens' father, was a clerk in the Navy Pay Office. In 1809 he married Elizabeth Barrow with whom he had eight children. John loved to live the good life but was frequently unable to pay for it. He was imprisoned for debt in 1824 in the Marshalsea Debtor's Prison. After his release from prison he returned to the Navy Pay Office, retired, and later worked as a reporter. His money problems continued and when Charles gained fame as a writer he frequently embarrassed his son by seeking loans from Charles' friends and publishers behind his back. Charles retained a warm affection for his father while deploring his inability to manage money. John was the source of Charles' character Mr. Micawber in the autobiographical novel, *David Copperfield*.

Screenshot 7.5. A biographical description of Charles Dickens
http://charlesdickenspage.com/family_friends.html#parents

with non-profit organizations and institutions (e.g., museums, public health organizations, special interest organizations). The biographical descriptions sometimes provide short descriptions of noteworthy people who are currently living, but more often they are historical profiles (see, e.g., Screenshots 7.5 and 7.6).

Screenshot 7.6. An online biography
www.oztorah.com/2010/10/rabbi-danglow-a-40th-yahrzeit-tribute/

Frequently-Asked-Questions, or FAQs, is an informational register that had its origin on the web in the early 1980s. Despite its very short history, this register is now extremely common and will be familiar to any user of the web. Websites that have documents with procedural information are also likely to have special pages with FAQs. Government agencies and organizations are especially likely to have well-developed FAQ pages, anticipating the questions that end-users commonly ask. Text Excerpt [3] shows a set of FAQs posted by the US Department of Labor. Most commercial sites similarly have a page with FAQs, anticipating questions about the products on the site, or questions about policies for purchases, returns, etc.

[3] 1. Does the Office of Foreign Labor Certification expedite applications?
The Office of Foreign Labor Certification (OFLC), as a matter of long standing policy, does not expedite the processing of applications due to the particular circumstances of any individual employer, foreign worker, or a family member.

2. How can an employer file an Application for Permanent Employment Certification, ETA Form 9089?

The employer has the option of filing an application electronically (using web-based forms and instructions) or by mail. However, the Department of Labor recommends that employers file electronically. Not only is electronic filing, by its nature, faster, filing electronically provides prompts that assist in the completion of the ETA Form 9089.

An application for a Schedule A occupation must be filed by mail with the appropriate Department of Homeland Security office and not with a Department of Labor National Processing Center.

NOTE: Employers will not be permitted to submit applications by facsimile.

3. How does the employer file an application electronically?

The employer can access a customer-friendly website (www.plc.doleta.gov) and, after registering and establishing an account, electronically fill out and submit an Application for Permanent Employment Certification, ETA Form 9089.

NOTE: The website also provides an option to permit employers that frequently file permanent applications to set up secure files within the ETA electronic filing system containing information common to any permanent application the employer files. Under this option, each time an employer files an ETA Form 9089, the information common to all of its applications, e.g., employer name, address, etc., will be entered automatically and the employer will only need to enter the data specific to the application at hand.

www.foreignlaborcert.doleta.gov/faqsanswers.cfm#q!32

Informational Blogs take a variety of different formats. In some cases, these are websites hosted by a university or academic association, where specialists from a particular academic discipline post documents with information of current interest. For example, the Language Log is a blog site hosted by the University of Pennsylvania where linguists recently posted entries about the Aravrit writing system, inflection in Georgian and in English, and Chinese transcriptions of Donald Trump's surname. Similarly, most non-profit organizations host Informational Blogs with posts that provide summaries of recent research findings (e.g., cancer research: www.cancerresearch.org/news-publications/our-blog; animal health: www.animalhealthfoundation.net/blog/).

However, it is also common to find Informational Blogs associated with commercial sites. These are offered as a kind of public service, with informational postings on a range of topics which are somehow related to the products offered elsewhere on the commercial site. For example, Screenshot 7.7 shows an Informational Blog posting relating to dietary health. The post does not directly describe a commercial product, and thus was not classified as informational Description-with-intent-to-sell. However, there is an underlying commercial motivation for blog sites of this type, with the hope that they will provide information that will lead readers to explore other goods or services available for purchase on the same site.

SWANSON Health Products | **Blog**

Vitamins & Supplements   ≡   Food & Nutrition   ≡   Health & Be

Tuesday, October 9, 2012   Print Me 🖶

Sweet Potato Power: How Alkalizing Sweet Potatoes Fight Inflammation

By **Raena M.**

When we think of sweet potatoes, very often we are reminded of Thanksgiving and a sweet potato casserole with brown sugar, marshmallows and cinnamon that looks something like the picture at right (credit: myrecipes.com). While cinnamon is gaining a good reputation these days for helping control blood sugar, marshmallows and brown sugar continue to remain high-carb villains! Furthermore, the acidity of the two takes away from the natural alkalinity of sweet potatoes. They are also rich in potassium —342 mgs in just one! Indeed, there are much better ways to serve up this delicious tuber and preserve its nutritional value at the same time.

In **Sweet Potato Power**, author Ashley Tudor gives a thorough account of what she refers to in chapter 2 as "The Story of the Lowly Sweet Potato". It's an informative and entertaining read. She explains the difference between yams and sweet potatoes—there really isn't much—as well as touting its smart carb value. After all, in these days of Paleo, low-carb and low-glycemic load diets, potatoes are on the do-not-ingest list, though we now have an exception.

As it turns out, sweet potatoes do not have the high starch content of regular potatoes. **What they do have is fiber—more than a serving of oatmeal. They also have anti-inflammatory properties.** Chapter 5 is devoted to the very common health condition known as "chronic inflammation," including the many ways that sweet potatoes can remedy the situation, due to their high amounts of the powerful antioxidant, vitamin E and of bioavailable beta carotene. Not only that, but they actually rank higher in nutritional value than either spinach or broccoli! This book has some wonderful recipes too, like Sweet Potato Frittata, Sweet Potato Slaw, Sweet Potato Bars, and Sweet Potato Gratin Stackers, just to name a few.

Screenshot 7.7. Informational Blog from a commercial website
www.swansonvitamins.com/blog/raena-morgan/the-issue-of-acidity-everything-true-is-new-again

Some documents that users classified as Informational Blogs are not overtly identified as Blogs on the host website. In many cases, these documents are found on commercial, governmental, or organizational sites with no named author. Thus, these documents are essentially indistinguishable from the sub-register of Other Informational, the largest informational sub-register (discussed below). The only constant defining characteristic for both Informational Blogs and Other Informational is the general communicative goal of providing information about some topic. Beyond that, there is an extremely wide range of situational characteristics associated with both sub-registers.

It will probably be clear at this point that some of the informational sub-registers found on the web are relatively easy to distinguish because they have clearly distinct purposes, such as procedural versus explanatory sub-registers. Others are easy to distinguish because they have distinctive textual formatting, as in the case of FAQs. At the other extreme, though, Informational Blogs are not well defined: Many of these documents are overtly identified as a "blog" written by an individual author, but other documents grouped into this category are simply informational documents on an institutional website with no identified author.

It turns out that there is a much larger category of informational documents that were problematic for raters, who were unable to identify any specific sub-register for nearly half of the web documents that had been classified as generally informational. That is, there is a vast amount of information available on the web that simply does not fit tidily into any named sub-register category. These documents occur on all types of websites, including organizations, associations, institutions, agencies, and commercial sites. In many cases, these pages simply describe the organization itself. For example, think of the website associated with a university. The site consists of hundreds of informational documents, with each one providing a description of a department, academic unit, degree program and requirements, research interests of faculty, etc. And this is just the tiniest tip of the iceberg, as every non-profit or governmental organization with a website likely includes numerous pages with similar descriptive content.

However, the web has also spawned a mind-boggling number of informational, or "niche" websites that have been created for commercial purposes. These are created by individuals interested in a topic, with the goal of providing free information to the public. Such websites have been created for almost any conceivable topic, such as information about academic engineering programs in the United States (http://educatingengineers.com/), information about the states in the United States (www.netstate.com), informational study guides for virtually all school topics at any grade level (www.softschools.com/), information about training to become a security guard (www.securityguardtraininghq.com/), and even information about how to create an informational website (www.2createawebsite.com/). These informational websites include some of the most visited sites on the web, such as the WebMD site (www.webmd.com/), which provides detailed information about an extensive range of health-related topics.

In nearly all cases, these informational sites have been created with a dual purpose: to provide free information to the reading public and to make money for the website developers. The business model employed by these websites differs dramatically from information distributed by print media. In both cases, authors and publishers seek financial profit by distributing information. In the case of printed books and magazines, end-users pay for the information, providing the primary source of income for the authors and publishers. In addition, there is sometimes additional advertising, with additional income from the companies paying for those ads. In contrast, informational websites are free to the public; end-users pay no fees to obtain the information on these sites. The companies and individuals creating these sites hope to generate profit entirely through advertising associated with the website. Anybody can create such a commercial site, with no need to obtain approval from a publisher. As a result, informational websites currently exist on virtually any imaginable topic, providing yet another dramatic reflection of the democratization of information on the web. For our purposes here, these sites are especially interesting because they represent a new linguistic register with no direct counterpart in print media.

7.3   Summary of MD Analysis Results for Informational Sub-registers

Given that all sub-registers discussed in this chapter have a primary communicative purpose of conveying information, it might be expected that they would exhibit similar linguistic profiles with respect to the MD analysis. However, even a quick glance at Figure 7.1 shows that this is not consistently the case.

With respect to three of the dimensions – Dimension 2 (oral elaboration), Dimension 4 (reported communication), and Dimension 6 (procedural/ explanatory discourse) – most informational sub-registers tend to pattern in a similar way. But even along those dimensions, Descriptions-of-a-person and Recipes are outliers with different MD profiles. The differences among sub-registers are considerably more noticeable along the other six linguistic dimensions, with some informational sub-registers having large positive scores, and other sub-registers having large negative scores. These linguistic differences reflect the wide range of specific communicative purposes among these sub-registers, described in Section 7.2.

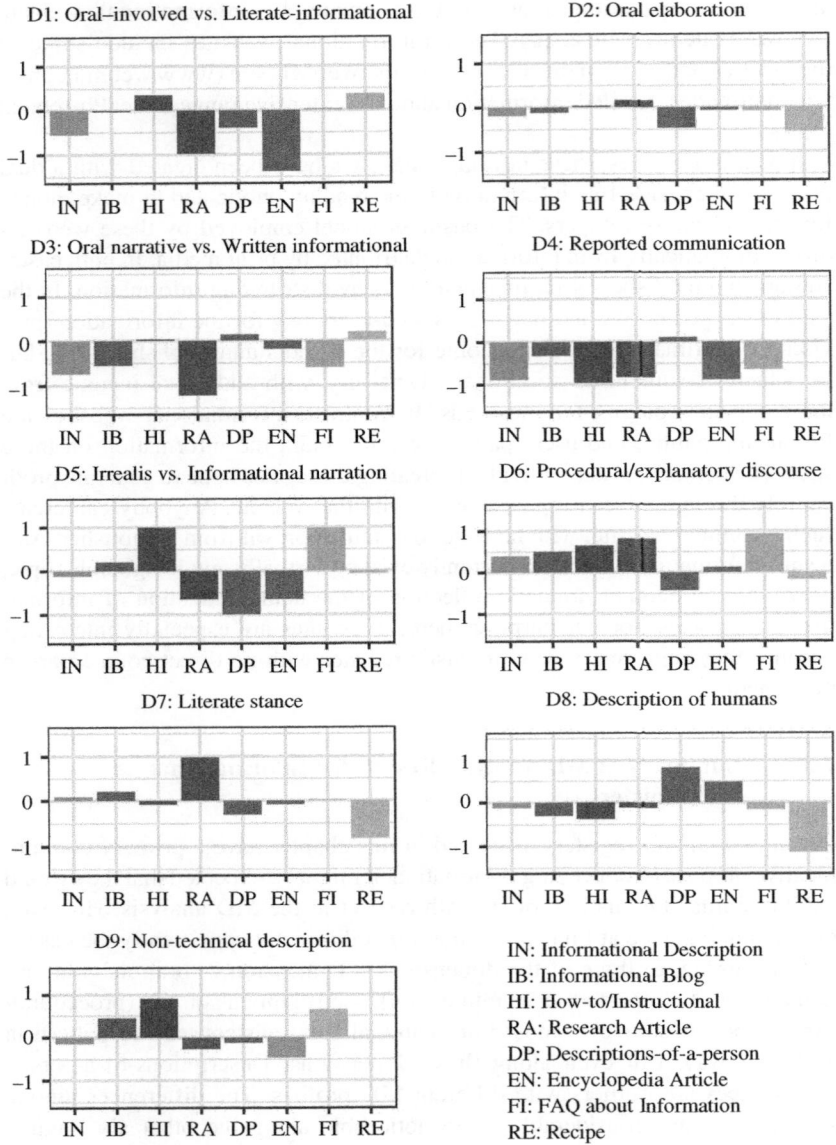

Figure 7.1. MD analysis results for the Informational sub-registers

The How-to/Instructional sub-register has distinctive linguistic characterizations along six dimensions:

- Dimension 4, where it is marked for the strong absence of reported communication features
- Dimension 5, where it is marked for a heavy reliance on irrealis features
- Dimension 6, where it is marked for a heavy reliance on procedural/explanatory features
- Dimension 9, where it is marked for a heavy reliance on noun phrase features associated with non-technical description
- Dimension 1, where it has a slight tendency to rely on oral/involved features
- Dimension 8, where it is marked by the absence of linguistic features referring to humans

In sum, the MD analysis shows that this is a sub-register with a heavy reliance on nouns (especially concrete nouns and process nouns), activity verbs, causative verbs, modal verbs, conditional adverbial clauses, and second-person pronouns.

Although Recipes can be regarded as a stereotypical procedural register, they are quite different in their MD profile from other How-To/Instructional documents. Recipes have unmarked characterizations on most dimensions, indicating that they have "average" scores on those dimensions. They have large negative scores on Dimension 7 – reflecting the absence of features marking "literate stance" – and on Dimension 8 – reflecting the absence of features relating to the description of humans. Recipes do have moderately positive scores on Dimension 9, reflecting a relatively frequent use of nouns (especially concrete nouns) and indefinite articles. Overall, though, Recipes are not highly distinguished from other sub-registers by the MD analysis, probably reflecting the general absence of prose discussion in this register.

In contrast, the sub-register of Research Articles has large dimension scores on several of the dimensions:

- Dimensions 1 and 3, where it is marked for the frequent use of literate-informational features (e.g., nouns, long words, premodifying nouns, prepositional phrases)
- Dimension 4, where it is marked for the strong absence of reported communication features
- Dimension 6, where it is marked for a heavy reliance on procedural/explanatory features
- Dimension 7, where it is marked for a heavy reliance on literate stance features

For the most part, these are features associated with complex noun phrases used to express both propositional information as well as various kinds of stance and evaluation.

Although Encyclopedia Articles generally have similar communicative purposes to Research Articles, their MD profile is less marked. This difference probably reflects the more popular audience of Encyclopedia Articles, with more of a focus on simple description rather than explaining or empirically defending informational research. The overall discourse style for Encyclopedia Articles on Dimension 1 is literate rather than oral/involved, reflecting a frequent use of definite articles and prepositional phrases (and the relative rarity of verbs as well as first- and second-person pronouns). The negative score on Dimension 5 reflects their "informational-narrative" focus, with a frequent use of past tense verbs, prepositional phrases, and a diversified vocabulary (high type: token ratio). The positive score on Dimension 8 – related to the frequent use of human nouns, third-person pronouns, and relative clauses – reflects the large number of biographical articles found on encyclopedia sites. However, the large negative Dimension 4 score shows that this sub-register is marked for the absence of reported communication features. Beyond those dimensions, Encyclopedia Articles are generally unmarked, indicating that they are overall much more similar to average web documents than Research Articles. Descriptions-of-a-person are relatively similar to Encyclopedia Articles, but with less "informational" marked scores on Dimension 1 and Dimension 4. However, Descriptions-of-a-person are more extreme than Encyclopedia Articles in their use of linguistic features that describe humans (Dimension 8) and their use of informational narrative features (Dimension 5).

Informational Blogs are also surprisingly similar to "generic" or "average" web documents on most dimensions, with moderately "informational" characterizations on Dimensions 3, 6, and 9, but otherwise having dimension scores close to 0.0. FAQs similarly have moderately "informational" characterizations on Dimensions 3 and 9, and are marked for the lack of reported communication features on Dimension 4. However, FAQs have even more distinctive linguistic characterizations with respect to the irrealis features of Dimension 5 (modal verbs, *if* adverbial clauses, second-person pronouns) and the procedural/explanatory (causative verbs, activity verbs, progressive aspect, verb + *to* clause, process nouns).

Finally, we noted in the last section that the Other Informational sub-register is large and encompasses a wide range of document types that do not fit tidily into any of the other informational categories. In terms of their situational characteristics, Informational Blogs is the most similar of these specific sub-registers to the general category of Other Informational. It turns out that the two are also relatively similar in their MD characterization. Thus, Other Informational documents are moderately "informational" and "explanatory" (frequent use of noun-phrase features, causative verbs, etc.), as well as strongly marked for the absence of reported communication features along Dimension 4 and the absence of human-descriptive features along Dimension 8.

Whereas Table 5.3 in Chapter 5 showed that narrative sub-registers tended to be relatively well-defined linguistically, Table 7.3 shows that Informational/ Procedural sub-registers tend to include a wide range of linguistic styles,

Table 7.3. *Dimension score means and standard deviations for Informational sub-registers*

Register	D1		D2		D3		D4		D5		D6		D7		D8		D9	
	M	SD	M	SD	M	SD	M	SD	M	SD	M	SD	M	SD	M	SD	M	SD
How-to	0.35	0.94	0.04	0.85	0.04	0.83	−0.96	0.83	1.00	0.94	0.66	0.97	−0.09	0.96	−0.39	0.99	0.91	1.18
Recipes	0.36	0.77	−0.54	0.75	0.19	0.59	0.02	0.49	−0.07	0.63	−0.18	0.69	−0.83	0.49	−1.1	0.54	1.57	1.08
Res. Articles	−0.97	0.76	0.17	0.88	−1.2	0.96	−0.83	1.07	−0.66	0.76	0.82	1.00	0.98	1.58	−0.13	0.97	−0.28	1.14
Enc. Articles	−1.4	0.69	−0.06	0.69	−0.19	0.88	−0.89	0.76	−0.65	0.76	0.12	0.86	−0.08	1.00	0.49	1.01	−0.47	1.20
Desc.-of-person	−0.39	0.93	−0.46	0.84	0.14	1.05	0.11	0.63	−0.99	0.74	−0.43	0.76	−0.31	0.82	0.83	0.97	−0.31	0.76
Info. FAQs	0.05	0.86	−0.08	0.79	−0.60	0.91	−0.65	0.79	0.98	1.13	0.92	0.88	0.01	1.00	−0.16	1.00	0.66	1.05
Info. Blogs	−0.03	0.93	−0.12	0.85	−0.54	0.85	−0.33	0.82	0.20	0.99	0.51	1.01	0.20	1.06	−0.30	0.89	0.46	1.05

reflecting the fact that most of these informational registers combine multiple communicative purposes. At one extreme, Recipes are the best defined of the informational sub-registers, with small standard deviations for all dimensions except Dimension 9. Other informational sub-registers, like Encyclopedia Articles and FAQs have small standard deviations for some dimensions, but quite large standard deviations for other dimensions. At the other extreme, sub-registers like How-to, Research Articles, and Informational Blogs have relatively large standard deviations for most dimensions. These scores show that there is a considerable range of linguistic styles employed by documents within those sub-register categories, reflecting the fact that these sub-registers include a range of different combinations of particular communicative purposes. We describe several of these patterns in the sections below.

Similar to the descriptions in previous chapters, the MD profiles for these informational sub-registers are very useful for mapping out the overall patterns of linguistic variation, but less useful for providing detailed descriptions of each sub-register. We thus turn to those details in the following sections.

7.4   Detailed Grammatical and Lexical Analyses of Informational Sub-registers

7.4.1   How-to/Instructional Documents

How-to documents have not been included in most previous corpus-based studies of register variation, because they are usually unpublished. That is, in print media, How-to documents are usually instruction pamphlets that come with a product or informational brochures found in a store or at a professional/government office. Because these documents have limited distribution and availability, they have generally been disregarded in previous corpora.

In contrast, How-to documents are quite prevalent and easy to collect on the web. As noted above, these documents can be found on many different types of websites, including Personal Blogs as well as official sites associated with an institution, governmental agency, or business. What these documents all have in common is they provide procedural descriptions that explain the steps required to accomplish a task.

As Figure 7.2 shows, the most distinctive grammatical characteristic of How-to documents is the reliance on second-person pronouns: the focus is on the reader, who is referred to directly as *you*. Conditional clauses and possibility modals are also notably common. These grammatical features are used to anticipate the various issues and problems that might exist and then offer steps to address those issues. Prose of this type relies heavily on present-tense (and non-finite) activity verbs, focusing on actions that will be accomplished in the here-and-now rather than past-time narrative.

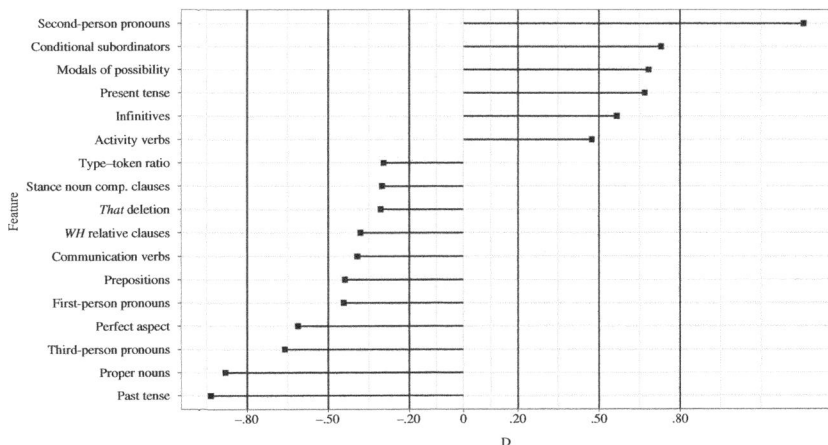

Figure 7.2. Key grammatical features for the How-to/Instructional sub-register

The emphasis on actions is also evident in the list of keywords common in How-to documents (see Table 7.4). However, those keywords further show that How-to documents on the web are quite specialized, in that they focus primarily on procedures used to address technical difficulties on computers. Thus, one of the largest semantic categories of How-to keywords refers to parts of a computer or a software application (e.g., *directory, file, folder, header, settings*). Many of these words have a deictic function, referring to a component that the reader should see directly on their computer screen (e.g., *button, edges, menu, tab, toolbar, width*). In conjunction with these words referring to computer/software components, the "action" keywords in How-to documents also refer mostly to tasks that a user will perform on a computer. Some of these are specialized words, such as *double-click, download,* and *right-click*. However, most of these are general words that have come to be commonly used with technical, specialized meanings in the computer domain (e.g., *apply, click, copy, edit, find, insert, install, paste, save*). Other words, like *add, choose, create, make, try,* and *use,* are even more general in meaning, but still turn out to be especially common in How-to documents giving instructions for technical computational tasks. There are, of course, other How-to documents on the web that give instructions for accomplishing almost any conceivable task, although many of those are presented as videos. The findings here, though, show that the most common sub-category here provides instructions for dealing with technology. [4] illustrates a document of this type.

Table 7.4. *How-to keywords*

Actions	Computers and software	Advice/instruction	Evaluations	*you*	Problems/ conditions
add	application	advice	easier	user	default
adding	below	avoid	easiest	you	depending
adjust	bottom	can	easy	you'll	if
apply	button	ensure	extra	you're	need
automatically	directory	example	handy	you've	option
check	edges	guide	simple	your	want
choose	file	help	sure	yourself	
click	files	helps	useful		
contact	folder	how	usually		
copy	header	information			
create	icon	instruction			
diy	items	method			
double-click	keywords	note			
download	menu	recommend			
edit	options	remember			
find	page	section			
insert	settings	should			
install	software	technique			
keep	tab	tip			
list	template	tips			
make	text	tutorial			
manually	tool	tutorials			
paste	toolbar	wiki-how			
remove	tools				
right-click	web				
save	width				
select	windows				
start					
step					
steps					
try					
type					
use					
using					

[4] The second thing you can do is create a robots.txt file and tell the bots to exclude certain parts of your directory or website. The less you get indexed, the less bandwidth you will use. For example if you have a test web site that you never use, exclude this from indexing so that bots will not waste your time and bandwidth. The robots.txt is pretty easy to create and maintain, but must be done on every major directory level.
Your ISP will also give you access to your Raw Access Log. This file is large, somewhat intimidating, but really useful. Download it and unzip it to a folder of your choice. You will need to rename it *.txt. Open Excel and import it in.

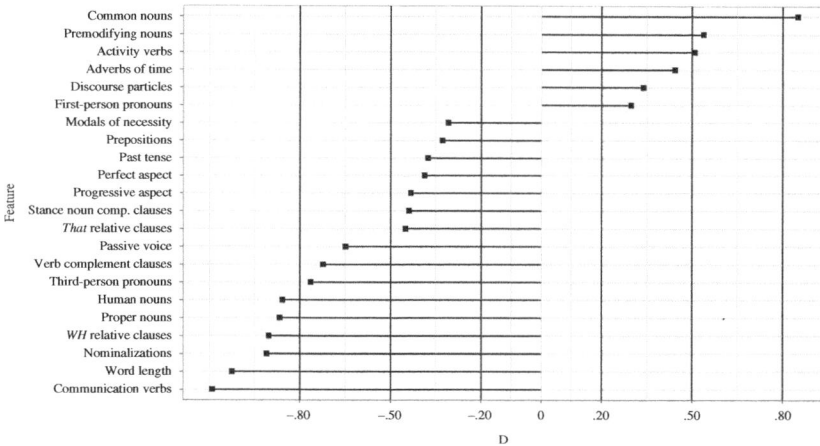

Figure 7.3. Key grammatical features for Recipes

Once you are browsing your raw access log in **Excel**, sort the file by the first column, the IP address. It is from this file that you can determine a lot about how people are accessing your site. [...]

http://dontai.com/wp/2012/09/25/fine-tuning-access-to-your-web-site/

It is interesting to note that one of the largest semantic categories is that of Advice/Instruction. As mentioned previously, there are many situational and linguistic similarities between How-to and Advice documents, despite the fact that we classified them into different general register categories (see Section 6.4.4).

7.4.2   Recipes

Recipes on the web are basically the same as recipes in printed cookbooks. As Figure 7.3 shows, nouns and activity verbs are especially common in these texts. (Imperative clauses are also especially common in this register, but not included in our quantitative analysis.) As the list of keywords shows (Table 7.5), nouns in this register are used primarily to refer to ingredients, utensils, tools, and units of measurement. The activity verbs come from a relatively restricted set, referring to the actions commonly required to prepare and cook various food items. Almost any Recipe illustrates both these grammatical characteristics as well as these classes of keywords (see [1] above, p. 138).

However, the corpus analysis identifies additional linguistic features that rarely occur in the main body of traditional recipes: discourse particles and first-person pronouns (Figure 7.3) along with evaluative keywords (e.g., *delicious, tasty, yummy*). Examination of online Recipes shows that they are often

Table 7.5. *Recipes keywords*

Actions	Ingredients	Tools	Attributes and evaluations	Time/quantity	Other
add	batter	bowl	delicious	cup	recipe
bake	bread	dish	dry	cups	recipes
baking	butter	fridge	flavour	medium	
boil	cheese	lid	flavours	medium-high	
boiling	chicken	oven	golden	minutes	
brown	chilli	pan	large	tablespoon	
browned	chocolate	pot	smooth	tablespoons	
chopped	cinnamon	saucepan	sweet	tbsp	
combine	cloves	skillet	taste	teaspoon	
cook	cream	spatula	tasty	tsp	
cooked	dough	spoon	texture		
cooking	egg	tin	yum		
cool	eggs	tray	yummy		
diced	flour				
fry	garlic				
frying	herbs				
grated	ingredients				
heat	lemon				
melt	milk				
mix	mixture				
peel	oil				
pour	olive				
preheat	onion				
puree	onions				
remove	paprika				
serve	pepper				
simmer	powder				
slice	salad				
sliced	salt				
sprinkle	sauce				
stir	slices				
stirring	soup				
toss	sugar				
until	tomatoes				
whisk	vanilla				
	water				

accompanied by a personal introduction, almost a kind of Personal Blog post. [5] illustrates prose of this type, together with the use of *I*, discourse particles (*anyway*) and evaluative words like *yummy*.

[5] I am always amazed at how much happens, in life, in the span of a year. Things have a way of happening that we never expect or of going in a direction we totally did not see coming.

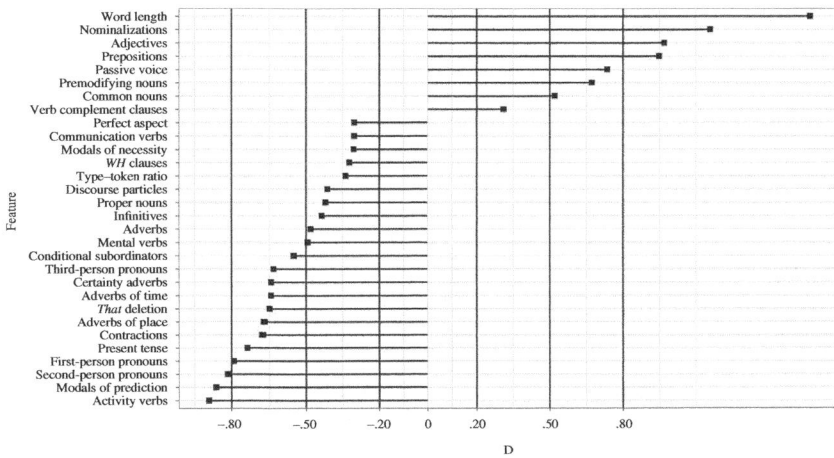

Figure 7.4. Key grammatical features for Research Articles

Anyway, I digress. With Thanksgiving bearing down upon us, I thought I'd share a couple of yummy recipes for dressing. Or stuffing. What name do you call it by? There's always the old joke that the first helping is dressing, the second helping is filling, and the third helping is stuffing! This first recipe came from my Aunt Donna. [...]

www.adelightfulglow.com/2012/11/dressing-or-stuffing-whichever-
it-is-here-are-a-couple-of-recipes/

7.4.3   Academic Research Articles

Similar to Recipes, Academic Research Articles on the web are texts that could have been published in print media. As noted in Section 7.2, the Research Articles that are publicly available on the web are distributed with an open access. Although these articles are sometimes not refereed in the same ways as Research Articles published by major presses, they still have the same communicative purposes, present the same types of information, and are written in the same discourse style.

There have been numerous corpus-based descriptions of Academic Research Articles (see, e.g., Conrad, 1996; Egbert, 2015; Gray, 2015), and so we provide only a brief overview here. Grammatically, academic research writing is distinctive because of its reliance on complex noun phrases, especially phrasal modifiers in noun phrases (see Biber & Gray, 2016). Figure 7.4 shows that these same grammatical features distinguish Academic Research Articles on the web from other web registers. Beyond the use of complex noun-phrase features, passive voice verbs are also common in Academic Research Articles.

It turns out that the Research Articles that are available on the searchable web tend to be quantitative studies in science or medicine, rather than the kinds of qualitative research that will be more familiar to readers from the humanities. As a result, there are numerous keywords (Table 7.6) referring to aspects of the research process or the data considered in the study (e.g., *analysis, calculated, data, evidence, measured*). Keywords relating to statistics and the research design are also prevalent (e.g., *population, sample, variables*). Abstract words relating to theoretical constructs are frequently used (e.g., *component, mechanisms*), together with words identifying the status of a condition or the relations among entities (e.g., *associated, compared, prevalence*). These articles are overt about identifying their conclusions (e.g., *conclusions, effects, findings*) as well as the epistemic status of claims (e.g., *shown* versus *suggests*). Taken together, Academic Research Articles are distinctive in their reliance on abstract constructs and words relating to evidence, data, research methods, claims, and conclusions. As noted above, most serious academic research is published in outlets that require paid subscriptions, thus appearing in documents that are not accessible on the public searchable web. In contrast, many of the documents that coders classified as Research Articles are published by public service organizations. Although these articles could be considered a type of popular science news rather than specialist Research Articles, they still include many of the lexical and grammatical characteristics of academic research writing. [6] illustrates many of these characteristics.

[6] Growing up in countryside "doubles Alzheimer's risk" - Health News
[...] The researchers also included what is known as "grey literature" – data not included in medical journals, but which may still be of value, such as research theses and government reports.
Researchers assessed the quality of the studies by considering study design, methodology, risk of bias, how cases were identified, standardisation of procedures across different study sites, and follow-up (in the case of longitudinal studies). The studies included in the meta-analysis ranged from poor to good quality.
For the meta-analysis, the researchers pooled the prevalence and incidence data from 13 studies to compare the odds of having or developing dementia in rural and urban participants. They conducted multiple sets of analyses [...]
In total, 51 relevant studies were identified, 13 of which were included in the combined statistical analysis on dementia prevalence, and five were used in the dementia incidence meta-analysis.

www.nhs.uk/news/2012/09September/Pages/Growing-up-in-countryside-doubles-Alzheimers-risk.aspx

7.4.4   Encyclopedia Articles

Encyclopedia Articles employ a grammatical style that is very similar to Research Articles. Thus, a comparison of Figure 7.4 and Figure 7.5 shows that many of the same grammatical features are key in both sub-registers, including

Table 7.6. *Research article keywords*

Research process/evidence	Conclusions/claims	Relationships/existence	Statistics/research design	Theoretical constructs	Text/metatext	Participants	Other
algorithm	conclusion	associated	factors	approaches	abstract	authors	cells
analyses	conclusions	compared	levels	characteristics	citation	groups	clinical
analysis	effect	contrast	observations	component	citations	participant	disease
assess	effects	corresponding	outcomes	defined	introduction	patients	molecular
calculated	findings	derived	population	development	journal	researchers	university
conducted	furthermore	differences	proportion	mechanisms	paper		
data	hypothesis	e.g.	sample	models	published		
determine	implication	extent	significant	processes			
evaluate	importance	higher	significantly	source			
evaluation	indicate	increase	statistical	theoretical			
evidence	patterns	increasing	variables				
examine	primary	linked	variation				
examined	relevant	occur					
identified	reported	occurs					
intervention	results	prevalence					
measured	shown	related					
methods	suggest						
observed	suggests						
obtained	therefore						
performed	thus						
questionnaire	understanding						
research	whereas						
retrieved							
selected							
specific							
studies							
study							
survey							
treatment							

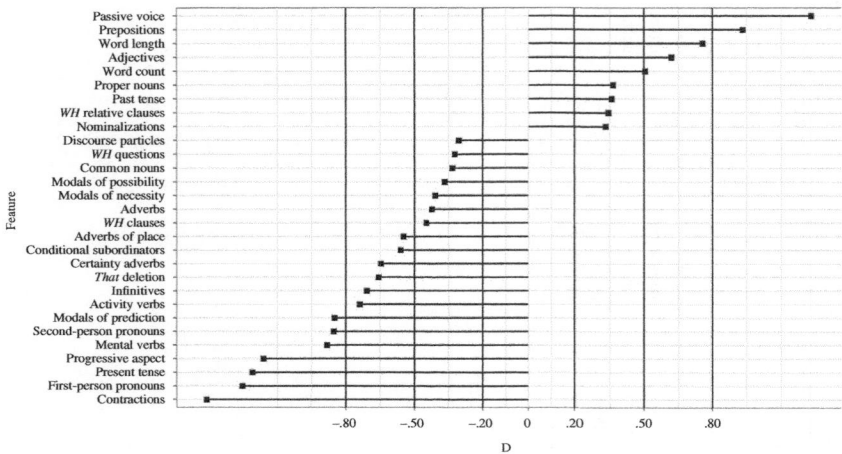

Figure 7.5. Key grammatical features for Encyclopedia Articles

prepositions, adjectives, long words, nominalizations, and passive voice verbs. At the same time, there are some systematic differences. Research Articles tend to use even more nominalizations and other long words than Encyclopedia Articles. In addition, Research Articles rely heavily on simple common nouns and noun-noun sequences. In contrast, Encyclopedia Articles rely heavily on proper nouns, *WH* relative clauses, past-tense verbs, and passive-voice verbs. Overall, these grammatical features reflect a focus on past events and specific persons and places, discussed in an informational style.

[7] Encyclopedia article on the "American Frontier"
Few Southern planters were actually interested in Kansas, but the idea that slavery was illegal there implied they had a second-class status that was intolerable to their sense of honor, and seemed to violate the principle of state's rights. With the passage of the extremely controversial Kansas-Nebraska Act in 1854, Congress left the decision up to the voters on the ground in Kansas. Across the North a new major party was formed to fight slavery: the Republican Party, with numerous westerners in leadership positions, most notably Abraham Lincoln of Illinois. To influence the territorial decision, anti-slavery elements (also called "Jayhawkers" or "Free-soilers") financed the migration of politically determined settlers. But pro-slavery advocates fought back with pro-slavery settlers from Missouri. Violence on both sides was the result; in all 56 men were killed by the time the violence abated in 1859.

http://en.wikipedia.org/wiki/American_Frontier

The keywords typical of Encyclopedia Articles (see Table 7.7) similarly include many past tense verbs that describe past events (e.g., *became, began, continued, developed, established*), including past acts of communication

Table 7.7. *Keywords for Encyclopedia Articles*

Events	Time references	Qualifying or evaluating a description	Characterizing a person/thing	Communication	Other	Linking words
adopted	April	according	associated	argued	American	addition
appeared	August	approximately	believed	claimed	critics	although
became	century	common	called	criticized	eastern	among
began	December	commonly	composed	declared	English	due
continued	during	estimated	considered	introduced	kingdom	however
developed	early	generally	consists	noted	Latin	thus
established	February	large	contains	proposed	second	upon
form	followed	major	derived	recorded	states	
formed	following	notably	described	reported	third	
led	initially	numerous	included	stated	united	
needed	January	official	known	stating		
performed	July	primarily	named	suggested		
produced	June	prominent	referred			
received	later	respectively	refers			
rejected	March	several	regarded			
released	origin	similar	resulting			
remained	original	single	titled			
replaced	originally	various				
resulted	previously	widely				
resulting	prior					
used	shortly					
war	subsequently					

(e.g., *argued, claimed, proposed, suggested*). These words occur together with frequent time references, including references to particular times (e.g., *April, century*) as well as references that position events in a narrative sequence (e.g., *initially, previously, subsequently, following*). Words that hedge or qualify the strength of an assertion are especially common in Encyclopedia Articles (e.g., *approximately, commonly, generally, notably, widely*), as are a set of passive voice verbs used to introduce or frame a characterization of a person or thing (e.g., *believed, called, considered, known*). Nearly any Encyclopedia Article illustrates the co-occurrence of words from these semantic domains; thus consider the following examples:

[8] Encyclopedia article on Stephen Hawking.
Following a conference in Moscow in October 1981, Hawking and Gary Gibbons organized a three-week Nuffield Workshop in the summer of 1982 on the Very Early Universe at Cambridge University, which focused mainly on inflation theory. Hawking also began a new line of quantum theory research into the origin of the universe. In 1981 at a Vatican conference he presented work suggesting that there might be no boundary or beginning or ending to the universe. He subsequently developed the research in collaboration with Jim Hartle, and in 1983 they published a model, known as the HartleHawking state.

http://en.wikipedia.org/wiki/Stephen_Hawking

[9] Encyclopedia article on the Arab Spring.
Due to the electoral success of Islamist parties following the protests in many Arab
    countries, the events have also come to be known as "Islamist Spring" or "Islamist
    Winter". The Arab Spring is widely believed to have been instigated by dissatisfac-
    tion with the rule of local governments, though some have speculated that wide gaps
    in income levels may have had a hand as well.

http://en.wikipedia.org/wiki/Arab_Spring

7.4.5   Descriptions-of-a-person

In many cases, Descriptions-of-a-person (DP) can be considered to be a specialized sub-register of Encyclopedia Articles. For example, many of the articles in Wikipedia are biographical accounts of the life and major contributions
of a person. In other cases, DP documents are found on websites for historical
or governmental organizations, as well as blog sites dedicated to a particular
region, time period, or group of people. In all of these cases, DP documents
are very similar in content and style to biographical Encyclopedia Articles,
with the major difference being whether the article is clearly associated with
an online encyclopedia website (such as Wikipedia) or found on some other
type of website.

However, DP documents are a much more specific category than Encyclopedia
Articles, and as a result, there are clear linguistic differences between the two.
Thus, while Encyclopedia Articles and DP documents both employ frequent
proper nouns, past tense verbs, and prepositions, the two differ in that DP documents have an extremely high frequency of third-person pronouns and high
frequency of human nouns (see Figure 7.6). (In contrast, Encyclopedia Articles
employ frequent passive voice verbs, relative clauses, adjectives, and long
words – features that are not especially prevalent in DP documents.)

One major difference between the two is that DP documents tend to be direct
descriptions of a person's life, while biographical Encyclopedia Articles often
include more discussion of a person's ideas and intellectual contributions (as
in [8] above). DP documents can be descriptions of a contemporary person,
but they are normally historical accounts. Thus, as mentioned in Section 5.4.4,
Descriptions of a Person are often very similar situationally and linguistically
to Historical Articles (see also Section 9.1). In either case, their structure is typically a concrete description of life events. As a result, they tend to incorporate
fewer complex noun phrase features than in Encyclopedia Articles, but they
tend to employ a more straightforward narrative organization.

[10] Description-of-a-Person: The Duke of Edinburgh
After a visit to the Show Jumping Arena at Hickstead, The Duke set up the Windsor Park
    Equestrian Club, also on Smith's Lawn. He was elected President of the International
    Equestrian Federation every four years from 1964 until he retired in 1986. As

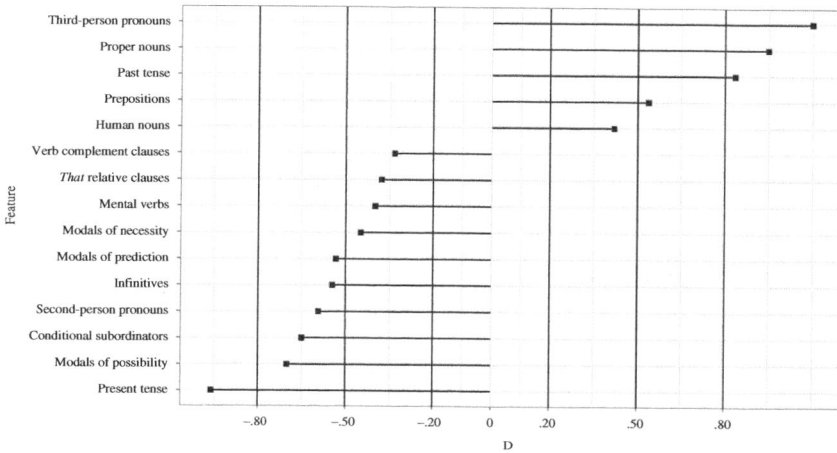

Figure 7.6. Key grammatical features for Descriptions-of-a-person

President, he was instrumental, amongst other things, in establishing a Veterinary Committee and Veterinary Regulations, and in writing the first International Rules for Carriage Driving Events. In his capacity as President of FEI, he attended four Olympic Games in Mexico, Munich, Montreal and Los Angeles. He visited Kiev in 1973 to witness the European three Day Event Championships in which his daughter, Princess Anne, competed. He visited Moscow to inspect the preparations for the 1980 Olympic Games, but he was not able to attend the Games owing to the Soviet invasion of Afghanistan.

www.royal.gov.uk/ThecurrentRoyalFamily/TheDukeofEdinburgh/90facts.aspx

The keywords associated with DP documents are (Table 7.8) among the most constrained of any sub-register analyzed in this book; these are mostly words that describe past states, events, or time references (e.g., *became, began, during, later*), often in relation to a person's life (e.g., *born, awarded, joined, lived*). Most other keywords identify a particular person (proper nouns and third-person pronouns), or relate to a person's occupation, title, status (e.g., *chairman, member, queen; famous, honorary*), or family relationships (e.g., *brother, mother*). The overall characterization is of a sub-register focused exclusively on an individual person, primarily with the goal of recounting important events in that person's life.

7.4.6   FAQs about Information

FAQs are among the most easily recognized sub-registers on the web, because of their highly distinctive rhetorical organization: a series of questions relating

Table 7.8. *Keywords for Descriptions-of-a-person*

Past events, and time references	Occupation/ title/status	Names/third-person pronouns	Places/ institutions	Family/ relationships	Other
age	actress	Charles	academy	brother	artists
appointed	advisory	Edward	American	daughter	arts
April	assistant	he	British	family	autobiography
attended	award	her	Cambridge	father	music
awarded	awards	him	college	father's	musical
became	BA	himself	committee	mother	
began	bachelor	his	England	son	
born	BSC	James	London	wife	
came	chairman	John	school		
career	director	man	Spartacus		
childhood	directors	Mary	university		
death	distinguished	Robert			
debut	fame	she			
died	famous	William			
during	fellow				
elected	honorary				
February	influential				
founding	MBA				
gave	medal				
graduated	member				
graduating	officer				
grew	president				
joined	queen				
joining	royal				
later	scholarship				
led	singer				
life	teacher				
lived					
March					
married					
met					
moved					
named					
played					
recalls					
remained					
retired					
returned					
served					
spent					
stayed					
studied					
took					
went					
worked					
wrote					
young					

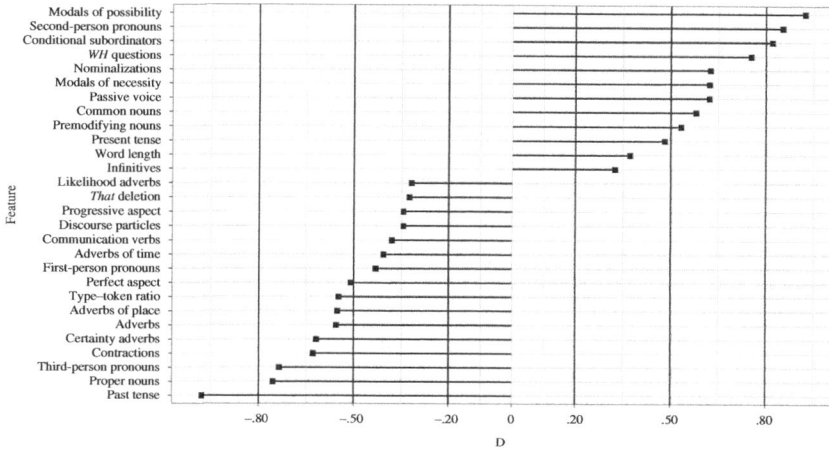

Figure 7.7. Key grammatical features for FAQs

to some topic, with each question followed immediately by an informational response. While there is usually no acknowledged author, FAQs usually address the reader directly, resulting in frequent occurrences of second-person pronouns (*you, your, yourself*). Anticipating questions about things that are possible and permissible, actions that are required, and the range of circumstances and conditions, FAQs also employ frequent possibility modals (especially *can* and *may*), necessity modals (*must, should*), and conditional adverbial clauses (i.e., *if* clauses).

At the same time, FAQs utilize most of the grammatical features that are typical of informational research writing, including nouns, nominalizations, long words, premodifying nouns, and passive-voice verbs (Figure 7.7). This constellation of features reflects the fact that the answers provided to the FAQs are highly informational, employing complex noun phrases in similar ways to other informational sub-registers like Research Articles and Encyclopedia Articles. [11] illustrates this discourse style, combining colloquial/interactive features (e.g., second-person pronouns, conditional clauses, *WH* questions) with complex noun phrase features (Figure 7.7):

[11] FAQs from the University of Texas, relating to "How to Pay for College"
What is the difference between subsidized and unsubsidized loans?
If you are awarded a subsidized loan, the federal government pays the interest charged during periods of at least half-time enrollment, as well as during the six months after you cease to be enrolled at least half-time (graduation, withdrawal).

It is generally recommended that individuals borrow as much as possible from these programs before borrowing from unsubsidized loan programs to save on interest charges. For unsubsidized loans, interest is due and payable as soon as the first disbursement of loan funds is made by your lender.

www.utsystem.edu/students/how-to-pay-for-college#3j

The keywords for FAQs (listed in Table 7.9) reveal an additional important characteristic of this sub-register: although FAQ documents can be employed to provide information on any topic, they are by far most commonly used to tell readers about services offered by an organization or company, and to explain the steps that are required for readers to obtain those services. Thus, there is a large set of keywords listed in Table 7.9 related to these functions (e.g., *applicant, assist, eligibility, procedures, register*), coupled with keywords referring directly to the texts and documents required for those services (e.g., *certificates, forms, information, section*). Although documents of this type are rarely associated with an individual author, they are associated with all types of websites, including governmental agencies (see [3] above, pp. 145–146), organizations and institutions (see [11] above), and commercial sites ([12] below):

[12] FAQs from a commercial site
Why aren't all my accounts displayed when I want to make a transfer?
Only valid linked accounts with appropriate access levels display when you are transferring between your accounts. For example, you cannot transfer funds from most home loans; however you can transfer funds to most home loans. Therefore, your home loan account will only be displayed in the "Select an account to make your transfer to" section.

www.anz.com/internet-banking/help/pay-transfer/between-accounts/#tab_tab03

Coupled with this focus on providing and obtaining services, there are numerous keywords relating more generally to offering "advice" (e.g., *advise, consult, help, recommend*). Interestingly, these documents are also careful to employ language hedging their advice, and thus there are frequent words that indicate the extent to which a statement is true (e.g., *generally, usually, depending*). For example:

[13] How soon can we get our order?
Generally we try to do the purchasing within one day of getting the order.

www.ishop4u.ca/ishop4u_web_site_oct_13th_005.htm

[14] What counts as rent arrears?
Rent usually only covers the amount your landlord charges for living in the property, but sometimes you can also pay your landlord for other things such as bills and service charges.

http://england.shelter.org.uk/get_advice/debt_and_arrears/rent_arrears/
checking_the_amount_of_rent_arrears

Table 7.9. *FAQs keywords*

Offering and obtaining services	Advice	Typicality	Text and information	Other
allow	advice	additional	certificates	date
applicant	advise	alternative	details	does
applicants	affect	and/or	document	following
application	appropriate	cases	documents	however
applies	cannot	circumstances	e.g.	individual
apply	check	depending	fax	number
applying	consult	depends	file	prior
arrange	decide	frequently	forms	telephone
ask	determine	generally	include	use
assist	ensure	maximum	includes	within
automatically	help	may	information	your
available	must	minimum	list	
certificate	necessary	specific	listed	
certified	need	types	section	
choose	note	usually	type	
complete	please	vary	website	
completed	prevent			
contact	recommend			
eligibility	should			
eligible	suitable			
FAQ				
FAQs				
fee				
fees				
form				
issued				
obtain				
payment				
procedures				
processed				
provide				
provided				
provides				
Q				
questions				
receipt				
receive				
refund				
register				
registered				
registration				
request				
require				
required				
requirements				
service				
services				

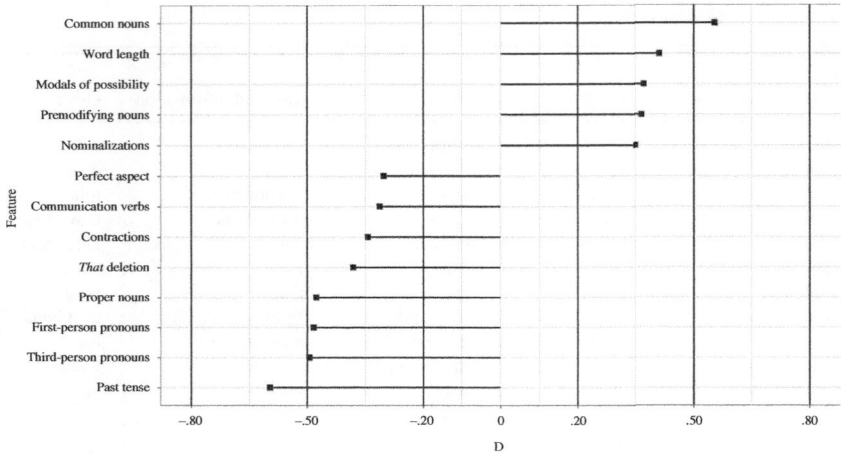

Figure 7.8. Key grammatical features for Informational Blogs

As with How-to documents, many words related to advice-giving and advice-seeking emerged in the FAQ register. There is considerable overlap between these two Informational registers and the Opinion register of Advice (see Section 6.4.4).

7.4.7   Informational Blogs

The grammatical profile for Informational Blogs is quite similar to that of Research Articles, with frequent common nouns, premodifying nouns, nominalizations, and long words (see Figure 7.8). Both of these sub-registers are different in many respects from other informational registers. For example, Informational Blogs are marked by their relative absence of past tense verbs and third-person pronouns, unlike Encyclopedia Articles.

As noted in Section 7.4.3, web Research Articles often have the purpose of reporting science research findings for a relatively generalist audience. Informational Blogs are similar in communicative purpose and audience. Thus, it is not surprising that they turn out to be highly similar grammatically. For example, the following text sample is from a personal blog that was developed to communicate current research about monetary theory. The particular post here reproduces parts of a textbook that the author is working on. After a brief personal introduction, the text shifts to employ the grammatical style of academic research writing, with frequent nouns, nominalizations, long words, etc.

[15] Informational blog on monetary theory

I am now using Friday's blog space to provide draft versions of the Modern Monetary Theory textbook that I am writing with my colleague and friend Randy Wray. We expect to complete the text by the end of this year. Comments are always welcome. [...]

The reason that equilibrium real GDP and national income increases relates to the firms revision of expected expenditure. When the government injects the new autonomous spending in to the economy, aggregate spending at the current equilibrium is greater than real Output. The difference is the line segment AA′.

This distance indicates the excess aggregate demand (relative to current real GDP) and inventories would be becoming depleted. Firms would soon revise their expectations of aggregate demand upwards and start to produce more real output and pay out higher levels of national income.

They would continue to increase production and national income until their aggregate demand expectations were consistent with actual aggregate demand, a state which occurs at Point B (where the new Aggregate Demand Function cuts the 45° aggregate supply line).

http://bilbo.economicoutlook.net/blog/?p=21197

Although Informational Blogs are often attributed to a specific author, first-person pronouns are considerably less frequent than in web registers generally (see Figure 7.8). In Informational Blog postings like [15], there are no first-person references (despite the attribution to a specific author). [15] begins with a brief personal introduction that refers directly to the blogger, but then the entire main body of this posting has no first-person references at all. In many other cases, Informational Blogs do not have an acknowledged author, making it not surprising that they would not use the first-person pronoun. Several of these documents are not even identified as Blogs. Coders classified these as "Informational Blogs" because they could not identify a better category. In many instances, though, documents of this type were simply classified as "other information" (see below).

In contrast to their similarities in grammatical style, the keywords for Informational Blogs are very different from those found in Research Articles (see Table 7.10). Several of the categories that are highly important in Research Articles – conclusions/claims, research process/evidence, and statistics/research design – are virtually nonexistent in Informational Blogs. Instead, we find more general categories of words relating to different types of information, cause-and-effect, and typicality. One unanticipated finding that emerged from this keyword analysis was the large number of keywords relating to health and nutrition, reflecting the fact that many Informational Blogs are from public health organizations, dealing with issues from the health/nutrition domain (see [16]) (Table 7.10).

Table 7.10. *Informational Blogs keywords*

Health/nutrition	Tools and techniques	Cause and effect	Types of information	Typicality	Evaluation	Other
acids	application	affect	content	available	effective	amount
bacteria	check	associated	data	common	higher	below
benefits	help	causes	e.g.	commonly	important	clients
body	need	changes	example	generally	key	companies
cells	process	contain	factors	individual	low	each
diet	provide	contains	information	likely	lower	however
diets	search	depending	keywords	often	significant	may
disease	systems	determine	research	possible	significantly	means
foods	techniques	effects	specific	typically	useful	periods
health	tips	include	summary	usually		products
healthy	tool	increase	type	various		range
medical	tools	increased	types			scientists
nutrients	understand	occur				stored
nutrition	use	occurs				these
nutritional	used	reduce				website
physical	users	results				websites
protein	using					your
risk						
symptoms						
treatments						
vitamin						
vitamins						

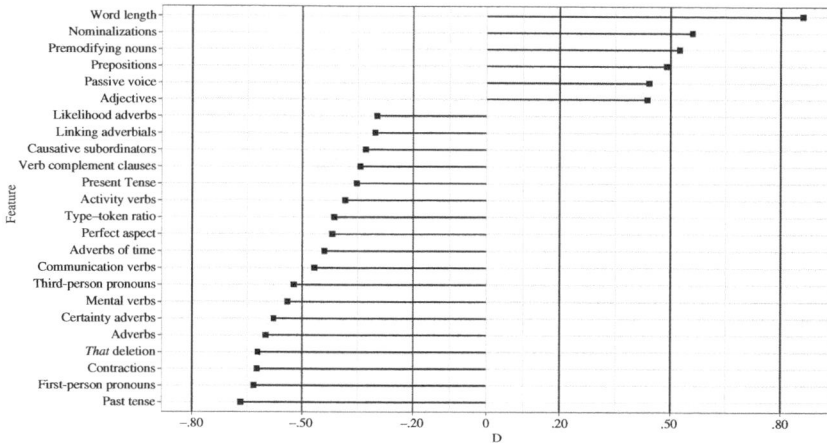

Figure 7.9. Key grammatical features for Other Informational documents

[16] Being depressants, inhalants affect the nervous system by slowing down messages to and from the brain.

Why Is It Taken? (Desired Side Effects):

• Volatile Solvents and Aerosols – the intoxication is similar to that from alcohol except it is achieved faster (between 1 and 5 minutes) and recovery is faster also (usually no longer then 60 minutes).

• Nitrous oxide – Effects are a rapid head rush and euphoria, but they last only for a short moment.

www.ceida.net.au/depressants/inhalants.asp

7.4.8 Other Information

As noted above, there are many informational web documents that do not fit tidily into any named sub-register category. Raters classified some of these as Informational Blogs, but a much larger number of these documents were simply classified as "Other Information."

Other Information documents are very similar in their grammatical style to Informational Blogs (and Research Articles) (see Figure 7.9). Long words, nominalizations, premodifying nouns, prepositions, adjectives, and passive voice are notably common in this sub-register; while features like first-person pronouns, third-person pronouns, past tense, perfect aspect, and verbs and adverbs generally are all notably uncommon (see Figure 7.9).

Because this is such a diverse category, it is not surprising that there is no particular topical domain associated with the Other Information keywords (Table 7.11). It is also not surprising that there are numerous keywords that

Table 7.11. *Other Information keywords*

Offering and obtaining services	Specification of information or services	Text and types of information	Other
applicable	accordance	areas	activities
applicant	addition	courses	administrative
application	amended	documents	assessed
apply	appropriate	e.g.	conditions
assist	arising	forms	date
contact	available	information	develop
eligible	components	introduction	developed
ensure	comprehensive	materials	development
guidance	conjunction	objectives	persons
indemnify	consequential	overview	range
jurisdiction	contain	procedure	students
liability	contains	procedures	vary
liable	designated	processes	
obtain	detailed	provision	
obtained	educational	purposes	
participation	include	resources	
payable	includes	section	
payment	including	statutory	
prescribed	located	subsection	
provide	occur	summary	
provided	practices	warranties	
provides	pursuant	workshops	
providing	referred		
receipt	relating		
registered	relevant		
registration	specific		
required	specified		
requirement	technical		
requirements	variety		
services			
undertake			

refer directly to different types of texts (e.g., *documents, forms, materials*), the parts of those texts (e.g., *introduction, section, subsection, summary*), or the different types of information presented in those texts (e.g., *areas, e.g., objectives, procedures, provision, warranties*). What is surprising, though, is the extremely large number of keywords relating to the ways in which the institutional/commercial author of the website provides services and/or the ways in which the reader can obtain services (e.g., *application, apply, assist, eligible, obtain, payable, provide*). Thus, although these Other Information documents are quite different from FAQs in their grammatical characteristics, it turns out that those two sub-registers are very similar in their keywords (compare Table 7.9 and Table 7.11).

A more detailed survey of Other Information a documents shows that this similarity in keywords reflects an underlying similarity in communicative purpose. Both sub-registers are associated with governmental/institutional/commercial sites that have the primary goal of presenting information that will lead to the reader obtaining some type of product or service. This is the major characteristic that distinguishes between Informational Blogs and other-information. As noted above, Informational Blogs are not necessarily written by an identified author, and are not always marked as a "blog" in the header or URL. Their key defining characteristic is that they simply present information: without any of the procedural goals of How-to documents; without the focus on explaining and justifying current research findings typical of Research Articles; and without the strict organizational structure and focus on past events typical of Encyclopedia Articles and Descriptions-of-a-person. In this respect, other-informational documents are very similar to Informational Blogs, and, as a result, many Informational Blogs could have been grouped into the other-information category.

However, a comparison of the keyword lists (compare Table 7.10 and Table 7.11) suggests one general difference between Other Information and Informational Blogs: there is a strong tendency for Other Informational documents to focus on the information required for providing and obtaining services, while Informational Blogs focus simply on information itself. A concordance search on the word *obtain* in Other Information illustrates the incredibly wide range of services that are described in these documents. Most of these documents are found on governmental or institutional sites, but there are also many similar documents found on commercial sites. Examples of the range of Other Informational documents include:

Government sites, describing:
- Obtaining legal case information
- Using government identity cards
- Methods for paying taxes
- Using fingerprints to obtain a biometric resident permit
- Obtaining information on criminal records
- Warning advice about cash withdrawals
- Visa requirements for Mexico
- Creating a new volunteer agency
- Information about visa extensions
- Obtaining short term travel permits
- Requirements for real-estate licenses
- Travel reimbursements

Sites for public organizations or institutions, describing:
- Requirements for admission to Polish universities
- Preparing for the Cambridge A-level exam
- Obtaining course syllabi
- Scheduling a conference talk
- General university course requirements
- Refugee services
- University course offerings
- Description of a biochemistry course

Commercial sites, describing:
- Visitor assistance services in the Hong Kong Airport
- Tourist and business visa applications
- An aviation continuing education program

7.5   Chapter Summary

This chapter began with a comprehensive description of the situational characteristics of the eight informational sub-registers in the corpus. Each of these sub-registers was then described linguistically through an MD analysis, as well as keyword and key feature analyses. Compared to other general register categories (e.g., Narrative), the sub-registers in this chapter were not well-defined linguistically. As we discussed in Chapter 1, this is a broad and nebulous category that is difficult to tease apart into clearly defined sub-register categories. Despite this general characteristic, we have shown many clear lexical and grammatical differences between the informational sub-registers described in this chapter and the other sub-registers in CORE.

8 Oral Registers

8.1 Introduction

Web documents in the Oral register category are less common online than documents in the Narrative, Opinion/Advice, and Informational register categories. The Oral register contains 4,194 texts and comprises just 8.6 percent of the CORE. Table 8.1 breaks down how these 4,194 texts are distributed across the four sub-register categories: Interactive Discussion; Lyrical; Interview; and Other Spoken. Interactive Discussions are by far the most common, making up over 75 percent of the Oral category and 6.5 percent of the CORE. The Interactive Discussion category contains texts from discussion forums, question/answer forums, and reader/viewer responses. The 636 Lyrical texts in this corpus make up 15 percent of the Oral texts. The Lyrical sub-register comprises primarily song lyrics, with some poems. The 299 texts in the Interview sub-register category comprise just over 7 percent of the Oral register. Finally, there were an additional 103 texts that were classified as Other Spoken texts. This category consists primarily of transcripts, from talk shows, radio shows, and TV shows.

Of the sub-registers in the Oral category, Interactive Discussions are the only register category that is uniquely web-based. The closest traditional print register to Interactive Discussions is probably correspondence through letters. However, letter correspondence is fundamentally different in many ways from the situation in which Interactive Discussions are written. Lyrical texts such as song lyrics and poetry have long been published in written form. However, their presence online has certainly made them available to a much wider potential audience. The Interview sub-register category is composed of transcripts from interviews of celebrities, public figures, or experts. Interview transcripts have a history of publication in venues that include magazines, newspapers, and legal documents.

This chapter begins with a situational analysis and comparison of the three sub-registers of the Oral category (Section 8.2). In Section 8.3 we begin by reviewing the MD analysis dimension scores for the three sub-registers in this category. Each of the next three sub-sections of Section 8.3 focuses on presenting additional linguistic results for one of the sub-register categories, including

Table 8.1. *Sub-register categories in the Oral category with text counts*

Sub-register	Count
Interactive Discussion	3,156
Lyrical	636
Interview	299
Other Spoken	103
TOTAL	4,194

results from key grammatical analysis and keyword analysis. The linguistic patterns reported in Section 8.4 are functionally interpreted with supporting evidence from text excerpts from the corpus. Finally, Section 8.5 summarizes the major findings and conclusions from this chapter.

8.2   Survey of Oral Sub-registers

The three major sub-registers included in the general "oral" category are all quite different from one another. We group them together here because they are all informal and employ colloquial language. At the same time, though, there are important situational differences among the three.

Two of these sub-registers, Lyrics and Interviews, are spoken, while Interactive Discussions are produced in writing. Lyrics are actually intermediate in this respect: performed in speech (singing), but produced in writing. The parameter of Interactivity groups sub-registers in a different way: Interactive Discussions and Interviews are interactive, while Lyrics are never interactive. Interactive Discussions and Interviews are often informational in nature, but they can both be driven by the purposes of opinion and entertainment as well.

In Interactive Discussions, web users interact with each other, sometimes even in real-time, through the mode of writing. Before the invention and widespread use of the Internet and cellular phones, using writing to communicate in real-time was either impossible (when location was not shared) or unnecessary, thus implausible (when location was shared). In addition to their novel situational characteristics, Interactive Discussions also make it possible for interlocutors to simultaneously engage in written dialogue on a much larger scale and in more complex ways than has ever been possible in the history of human language. Participants in Interactive Discussions come from a wide variety of backgrounds, ranging from expert to novice, from desperate seeker of knowledge to casual reader, and from serious, engaged participant to Internet troll.[1] Interactive Discussion

Table 8.2. *Situational characteristics of Oral sub-registers*

Sub-register	Author/ speaker	Audience	Production circumstances	Purpose
Interactive discussion	Discussion participants, readers interested in the topic of discussion		Limited preplanning, not professionally edited, interactive, usually time sensitive	Answer questions, discuss opinions
Lyrical	Songwriters, poets	Fans, listeners (songs), readers (poetry)	Preplanned, edited (at least by composer)	Entertain, express emotion, inspire
Interview	1. Interviewer 2. Celebrity, public figure, expert	Listeners interested in interviewee or the topic of the interview	Varies between fully scripted to fully unscripted, interactive	Entertain, obtain biographical information, explore expert opinions

posts are typically characterized by limited amounts of preplanning and editing. They are interactive, sometimes in real-time and other times with a time lag. Interactive Discussions are typically made available indefinitely online, sometimes long after active posting has stopped. They are also often time-sensitive in that a requester needs information or advice as quickly as possible. Purposes of Interactive Discussions can include answering questions and discussing opinions. Discussion threads are typically initiated by a question or issue that is proposed by a requester. Posts to that thread are then provided by participants and published in the forum (see Screenshot 8.1).

As mentioned above, the Lyrical sub-register is comprised mostly of song lyrics, with some poems (see Screenshot 8.2). Most of the texts in this category are originally written by professional songwriters and poets. However, the vast majority of the song lyrics in this corpus have been posted online by fans and online contributors, rather than the composers or producers of the music. Online poetry can be of two types: published poetry that has been reproduced online or poetry published online by amateur poets. The audience includes fans of the songs or songwriters, and poems or poets who originally wrote the Lyrical text. Lyrical texts are almost always preplanned and edited during the original composition process. However, errors can be introduced during the process of transcription and online posting. The primary purpose of Lyrical texts is to entertain, express emotion, and inspire listeners/readers.

Interviews typically include a single interviewer and a single interviewee, but both groups can include two or more people (see Screenshot 8.3).

Screenshot 8.1. Interactive Discussion
https://au.answers.yahoo.com/question/index?qid=20080117192005AAS39UG

The interviewer is often a TV- or radio-show host, journalist, or other media personality. The interviewee, on the other hand, is usually either a famous person (e.g., celebrity, politician) or an invited expert on a particular issue or topic. Most interviews are staged events in that they are dialogic, but the intended audience is actually a third group of participants or listeners who are interested in the interviewee or the topic of the interview. Interviews can be fully scripted, semi-scripted, or entirely unscripted, but they are always structured around interaction between the interviewer and inter-viewee. Interviews are typically set up in a question-and-answer format

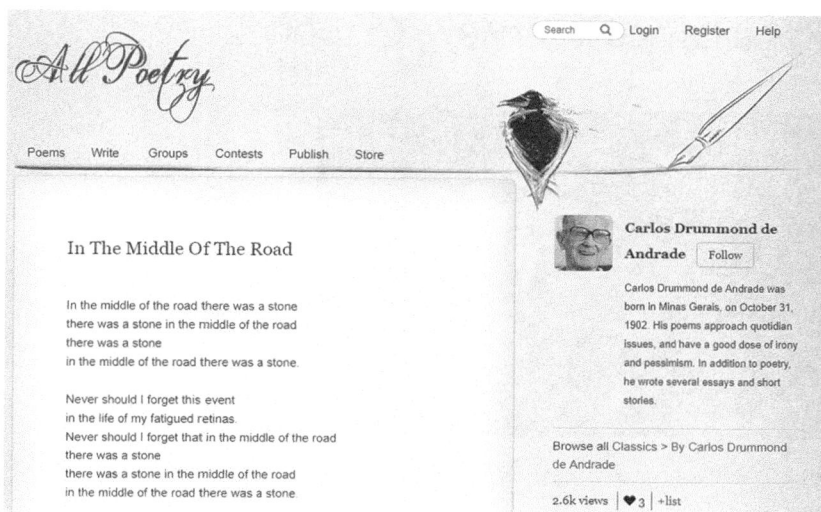

Screenshot 8.2. Online Poem
https://allpoetry.com/In-The-Middle-Of-The-Road

where the interviewer asks a question, sometimes with some background information, and the interviewee answers the question. The purposes of interviews can vary widely, but there seem to be many interviews in the CORE that are primarily driven by the purpose of entertaining the audience and obtaining biographical information about famous people.

8.3   Summary of MD Analysis Results for Oral Sub-registers

This section provides a brief overview of the salient linguistic patterns revealed by the MD analysis we discussed in Chapter 4. Figure 8.1 contains nine bar plots that summarize the mean dimension scores for each of the three major Oral sub-registers, along with the Other Spoken category.

All of the Oral sub-registers received positive scores on Dimension 1 – oral-involved versus literate-informational. The Lyrical sub-register received the highest score, demonstrating that texts in this category, particularly song lyrics, tend to rely heavily on features of involvement (first- and second-person pronouns), as well as other features associated with oral discourse (present tense verbs, mental verbs). Interviews and Interactive Discussions also received relatively high positive scores on this dimension, but it was somewhat surprising to find that Lyrical texts, which are monologic, scored higher on this dimension than the two dialogic categories. One reason for this might be that Interviews and Interactive Discussion focus on a wide array of topics, whereas

Rene LaVice interview, October 2012

BY DAMIAN B · OCTOBER 16, 2012

DB: Hi again Rene, how has 2012 treated you?

RLV: 2012 has been outstanding. My music is being heard by a huge amount of people, I'm getting to travel and have interesting experiences and I've continued to grow creatively. I feel that I'm in a very good place to pursue the goals I've set for the future.

DB: Can I first of all mention the b side of this single, a bulldozer of a tune, have you more like that to populate a set with?

RLV: I hope you have life insurance.

Screenshot 8.3. Interview
www.friedmylittlebrain.com/rene-lavice-interview-october-2012/

song lyrics are focused on humans, with a specific focus on love and relationships between the performer and another person.

The most noticeable pattern on Dimension 2 is that Lyrical texts use far more features associated with oral elaboration than the other Oral sub-registers. The positive-loading features on this dimension included verbs from various semantic categories, *that* complement clauses, and *that* complementizer deletion. Interactive Discussions and Interviews also received positive scores on this dimension that are quite high relative to most of the sub-registers in the CORE.

A similar pattern emerges once again on Dimension 3 – Oral narrative versus Written information, with Lyrical texts receiving the highest positive scores, followed by Interactive Discussions and Interviews. The evidence strongly suggests that on the oral–literate continuum, Lyrical texts are the most oral of all the sub-registers in the CORE. Texts with high scores on Dimension 3 tend to use high frequencies of verbs, adverbs, and pronouns, and low frequencies of nouns and nominal modifiers.

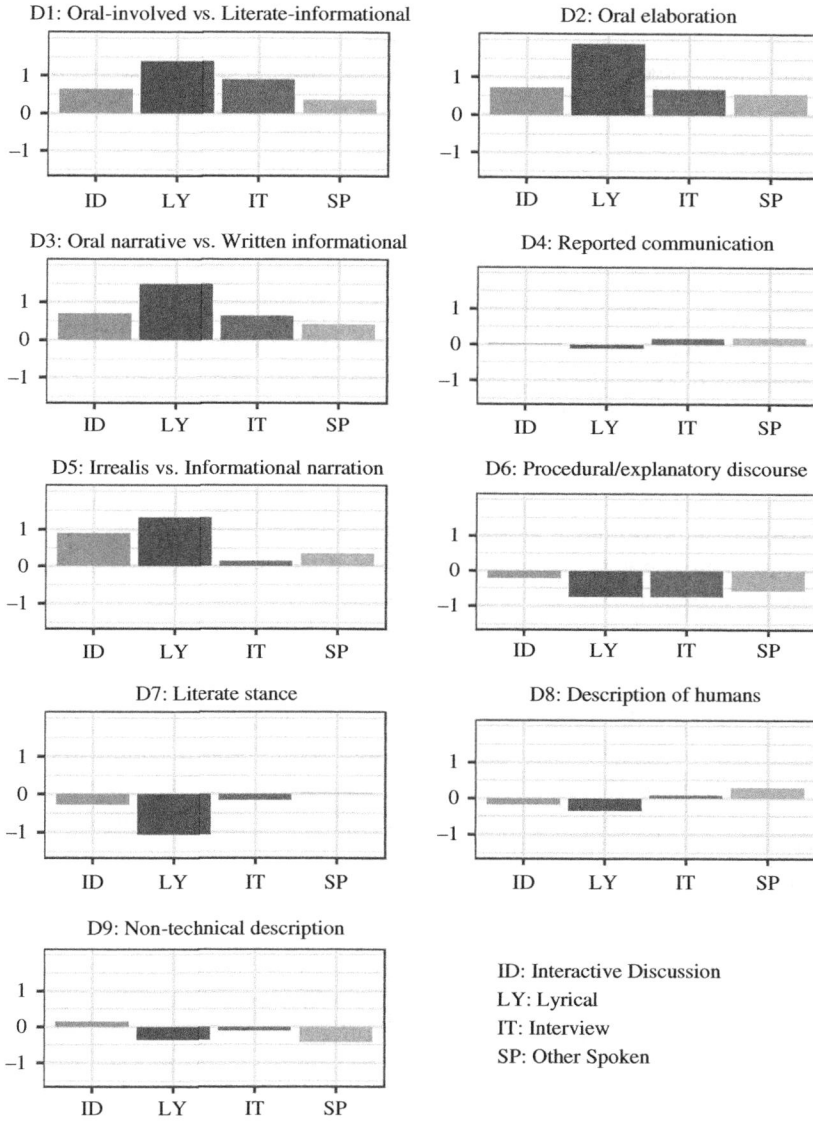

Figure 8.1. Dimension scores across the four Oral sub-register categories

The results for Dimension 4 – Reported communication – show that all four sub-register categories received scores near zero. Clearly, features associated with communication reporting (e.g., communication verbs and likelihood verbs + *that* clauses) and the negative end of this dimension (e.g., nominalizations) are not particularly common in Oral registers.

Lyrical texts and Interactive Discussions tended to receive high positive scores on Dimension 5 – Irrealis versus informational narration – while Interviews and Other Spoken texts received low positive scores. Some of the defining positive features on Dimension 5 are modals, present tense verbs, and second-person pronouns. We will discuss the use of these features in the Lyrical and Interactive Discussion sub-register below.

All the sub-registers in the Oral category received strong negative scores for Dimension 6 – Procedural/explanatory discourse, showing low rates of occurrence for linguistic features such as causative verbs, progressive aspect, and process nouns. It is interesting to note that Interactive Discussions had the highest score on this dimension. This is likely related to the fact that many discussion and question/answer forums are focused on questions about how to do something, resulting in responses that explain steps or procedures. Clearly, however, this is not a defining characteristic of Interactive Discussions as it is for the How-to and FAQ sub-registers.

The Lyrical sub-register was the only one of the four to receive a strong (negative) score on Dimension 7 – Literate stance. Interactive Discussions and Interviews also received negative scores, just to a much lesser degree. This dimension does not have any linguistic features that loaded on the negative end. Thus, the extremely low score for Lyrical texts reflects very low frequencies of the positive features, which include stance nouns, cognitive nouns, and other features related to the explicit expression of personal stance or evaluation.

The results for Dimension 8 – Description of humans – showed that Lyrical and Interactive Discussion texts use the features on the positive end of this dimension with low frequencies. This may be the case for Interactive Discussion because the primary topic of discussion is rarely humans. However, there must be a different interpretation for this pattern in the Lyrical texts since these texts are often, if not typically, focused on people. It seems that Lyrical texts refer to people using first- and second-person pronouns and terms of endearment, rather than through the use of third-person pronouns and human nouns. Interviews and Other Spoken texts received low positive scores on this dimension.

Interactive Discussions were the only register category to receive a positive Dimension 9 score. While this score was quite low, it does show some degree of "non-technical description" in the topics and discussion in that sub-register. Lyrical and Interview texts had relatively low scores on this dimension.

Table 8.3. *Dimension score means and standard deviations for Oral sub-registers*

Register	D1		D2		D3		D4		D5		D6		D7		D8		D9	
	M	SD	M	SD	M	SD	M	SD	M	SD	M	SD	M	SD	M	SD	M	SD
Int. Discussion	0.63	1.02	0.73	1.19	0.71	0.89	0.02	0.94	0.89	1.05	−0.21	1.06	−0.28	0.99	−0.18	1.07	0.15	1.10
Lyrical	1.38	1.57	1.90	2.30	1.49	1.15	−0.12	1.78	1.30	1.79	−0.74	1.49	−1.1	1.12	−0.35	1.28	−0.37	1.37
Interview	0.90	0.74	0.68	0.81	0.64	0.71	0.16	0.52	0.14	0.64	−0.75	0.67	−0.16	0.72	0.08	0.68	−0.11	0.62

A comparison of Table 8.3 with Tables 5.3, 6.4, and 7.3 shows that Oral sub-registers are by far the least well-defined linguistically of any of the sub-registers included in our study. Interviews are the exception here, since they have moderately small standard deviations across all dimensions. However, Interactive Discussions have large standard deviations across the board, while Lyrical texts have extremely large standard deviations for all dimensions. Lyrical texts are among the most marked of all sub-registers in terms of their mean dimension scores. At the same time, though, these standard deviations show that there is an extremely wide range of linguistic variation among Lyrical texts. This range reflects the fact that lyrics can be personal, opinionated, narrative, or informational in purpose, each resulting in different sets of co-occurring linguistic features. We turn to more detailed discussion of those characteristics in the following sections.

8.4   Detailed Grammatical and Lexical Analyses of Oral Sub-registers

8.4.1   Interactive Discussion

The strongest positive key features for Interactive Discussions are present-tense verbs, first-person pronouns, conditional subordinators, and mental verbs (see Figure 8.2). [1] shows the use of several present-tense verbs (italicized) and first-person pronouns (bolded) typical of an online discussion forum. These two features in online discussion forums are used by requestors who seek answers or resolution to a question or problem.

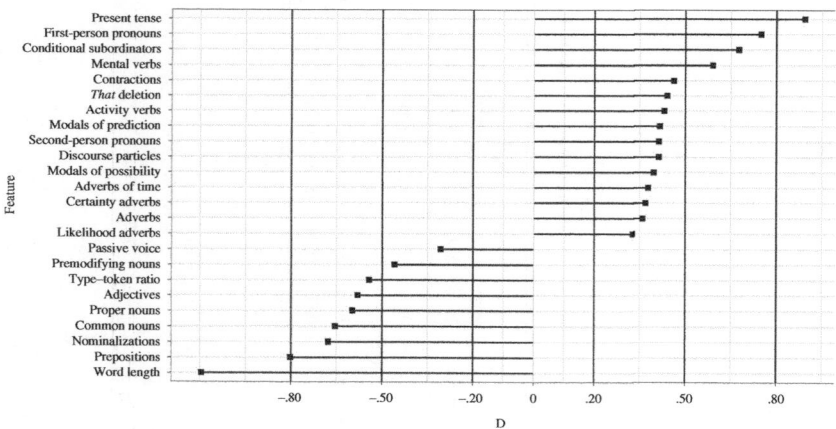

Figure 8.2. Key grammatical features for the Interactive Discussion sub-register

[1] **I** *have* a question that *has* little to do with the thread but **I** will ask anyway. **I** *see* you *are promoting* Madkhalis.com. **I** *am looking* for a tape from Imaam Al-Albaani's Silsilat Al-Hudaa' Wan-Nuur. In it one of Madkhali's students *comes* and *asks* Imaam Al-Albaani to write a few words [...]

> www.ummah.com/forum/archive/index.php/t-262221.html

Conditional subordinators are commonly used in Interactive Discussions because posted questions often lack background knowledge on relevant details, making it difficult for responders to provide a definitive answer. In many cases, this results in the responder providing advice based on more than one possible scenario (see, e.g., [2] below).

[2] **if** he is a acquaintance, buy it, make a profit, **if** he is a mate, go halves in a motor, help him put it an and split the profit (minus 200 for you as thats what he wanted for the car) so you both make a bit of cash, you help your mate out and there can be no disputes.

> http://forums.justcommodores.com.au/just-commodores-polls/141167-
> buy-not-buy-question-point-time.html

Mental verbs (e.g., *think*, *feel*, *know*) are also extremely common in online discussion forums. These verbs are often used to frame responses as subjective opinions and viewpoints from the responder, rather than objective fact. This function can be seen in [3] below.

[3] **I know** some of them are even marked with an arrow as being one direction only. Besides which, drivers and other bikers don't expect bikes to be riding in the opposite direction, so it's hazardous to do so.

I like to **think** of a bike as a hybrid between a walker and a car, which i **think** is reasonable.

> www.omguw.com/2012/07/13340.html

The strongest negative key features for the Interactive Discussion sub-register are features traditionally associated with informational and literate registers (e.g., long words, prepositions, nominalizations, nouns, and adjectives). This is interesting because while it could be argued that online discussion forums have two purposes, interaction and the transmission of information, it appears that these web documents are more likely to draw on linguistic features associated with the former function. This suggests they function first as a forum for discussion and interaction and that their informational focus is a secondary function.

The strongest keywords for this register were divided into six semantic categories, with an additional "Other" category (see Table 8.4). The category with the most words was labeled "Forums" because these words are directly related to the process of posting questions and responses in online forums. It is likely that some of these words are actually boilerplate text that is duplicated on each page of a forum site. However, many of these words are used in discussion forum posts, as can be seen in [4] below.

[4] I have been offline for a while and I have some **questions** that have been bugging me for a while so if anyone could **answer** them for me.

www.roots-archives.com/forum/read.php?2,109517

Two of the semantic categories, Pronouns and Interaction, both demonstrate the highly interactive and interpersonal nature of Interactive Discussions. Examples of these words in context can be seen in [5].

[5] **Hi guys**.. **I** am a 19 year old Girl, living in manchester. **I** am a singer looking for a band that is already established, **i** have both a talent and am enthusiastic.

www.manchester.com/music/wanted.php

Table 8.4. *Keywords for the Interactive Discussion sub-register*

Forums	Pronouns	Contractions	Abbreviations	Stance	Interaction	Other
answer	anyone	can't	alot	basically	guys	am
answerer	anything	didnt	aswell	guess	hi	anyway
answers	his	doesn't	etc	haha	sorry	bit
asker	I	don't	imo	just	sure	check
chosen	I'd	havent	info	know	thanks	fine
click	I'll	isn't	kinda	luck	wondering	get
clicking	I'm	thats	lol	maybe	yeah	got
edit	I've	theres	ok	probably	yes	if
faq	me	wasn't	op	really		stuff
forum	my	whats	tbh	think		try
forums	someone	won't	tho	undecided		
link	you	wouldn't	u	want		
lte-mail	your					
messages						
originally						
post						
posted						
posts						
proceed						
question						
quote						
re						
register						
removed						
replies						
resolved						
select						
thread						
threads						
viewing						

Another two of the keyword lists, Contractions and Abbreviations, are two different types of reduction. Contractions are reduced forms that originated in speech as a means of increasing the fluency of utterances. It should be noted that in many cases the apostrophes are absent from the written contractions, showing an additional level of abbreviation. The words in the Abbreviation category, on the other hand, are orthographic reductions that make written messages more fluent and brief. Despite their differences, both categories are strongly associated with informal language that is produced interactively, often in real time, and with minimal editing. A clear example of this type of online discourse can be seen in [6] and [7] below.

[6] That's what imma be doing this season. I better get that CB place tho, I dnt wanna be running a lot.
http://au.answers.yahoo.com/question/index?qid=20121114185140AAvR932

[7] I find it hard to be a muslim in OZ coz like i cover my face and everytime i go out i get abused.. lol.... even muslims say i wont get educated coz i cover my face.. lol... when will ppl figure out that just coz someone acts religious they wont get educated???
www.aussiemuslims.com/forums/archive/index.php/t-8019.html

8.4.2   Lyrical

There are many similarities between the key feature lists for the Lyrical and Interactive Discussion sub-registers (compare Figure 8.2 and Figure 8.3). This is largely due to the involved and colloquial nature of the registers. The five strongest key features for the Lyrical texts are first-person pronouns, contractions, present tense verbs, second-person pronouns, and mental verbs (see Figure 8.3).

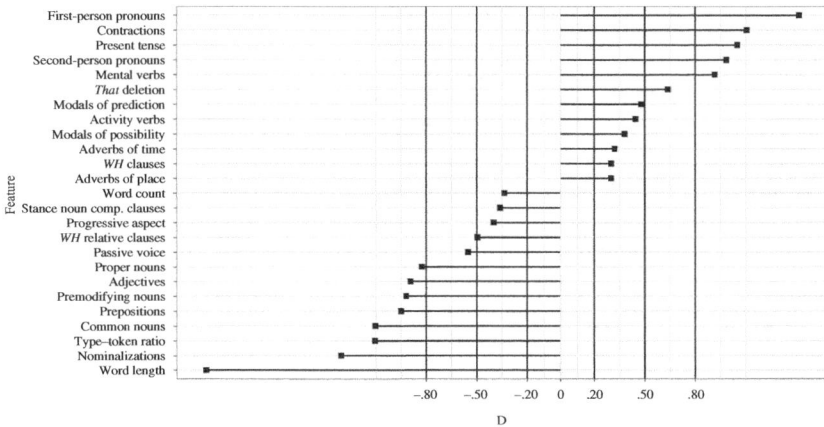

Figure 8.3. Key grammatical features for the Lyrical sub-register

The high frequency of first- and second-person pronouns for song lyrics was interesting since lyrics are not actually interactive, whereas registers like Interactive Discussion are. It seems that while song lyrics are technically monologic (i.e., there is no expectation of a response from the audience), they are written as a direct message from one person to another, usually relating to romance and interpersonal relationships. This type of discourse can be seen in [8].

[8] [...]
But **you** went away,
How dare **you**?
I miss **you**.
They say **I'**ll be okay,
But **I'**m not going to ever get over **you**.
[...]

www.metrolyrics.com/over-you-lyrics-miranda-lambert.html

Contractions are another feature extremely common in Lyrical texts. Contractions are typically used in speech to increase fluency by making utterances easier to articulate. An additional function of contractions in Lyrical texts is to aid the author in creating rhyme and rhythm in verse. Both of these functions can be seen in [9].

[9] You walk in the road, but **you're** going nowhere
You're tryin' to find your way home, but **there's** no one there
[...]
You **wanna** give up, but **it's** worth the fight
You have all the things, that **you've** been dreaming of
[...]

www.lyricsmode.com/lyrics/b/bon_jovi/what_do_you_got.html

The negative key features for Lyrical texts are quite interesting and easy to explain. The relatively short words and lower frequency of nominalizations are due primarily to the difficulty of integrating long words into the rhyming structure of a song. Additionally, nominalizations tend to denote abstract concepts and processes, which are not common themes in song lyrics. The relatively low type–token ratio shows the lack of lexical diversity in song lyrics. This is probably due partly to the lack of topical variability within songs and partly to the repetition of phrases, especially in the chorus.

The keywords for the Lyrical sub-register reveal interesting patterns about both the topics of lyrics and how those topics are presented (see Table 8.5). Somewhat surprisingly, the semantic category with the most keywords comprises reduced forms of words. As with contractions, discussed above, these reduced forms can be used to increase fluency and help with rhyming and rhythm. These reductions are especially common in song lyrics from the Country [10] and Hip Hop [11] genres.

Table 8.5. *Keywords for the Lyrical sub-register*

Reduction	Love/emotion	Lyrics/poems	Metaphor	Pronouns	Interjections	Slang
aint	babe	capo	dream	I	oh	Nigga
ain't	baby	chords	dreaming	I'll	ooh	niggas
an'	cried	chorus	dreams	I'm	yeah	thang
bout	cry	copyrighted	heaven	me		
'bout	eyes	corrections	moon	my		
'cause	feel	enlarge	rain	you're		
'cos	girl	intro	sun			
cryin'	goodbye	lyrics				
em	heart	meaning				
'em	hearts	poem				
feelin'	heart's	poems				
gettin'	kiss	poetry				
goin'	kissed	rhyme				
gonna	lips	sing				
gotta	lonely	singing				
livin'	love	song				
lookin'	love's	songs				
makin'	smile	submit				
mornin'	soul	sung				
nothin'	swear	verse				
puttin'	tears	viewing				
ridin'	tonight	x2				
'round						
runnin'						
sittin'						
somethin'						
takin'						
talkin'						
thinkin'						
'til						
till						
tryin'						
tryna						
waitin'						
wanna						
ya						

[10] You look so **invitin'** ... thought it might be **excitin'**
For a woman with a limousine
To go **bouncin** around ... in a beat up truck
[...]
So don't worry '**bout** your reputation
Cause you can tell all your friends
[...]

www.cowboylyrics.com/lyrics/travis-tritt/country-club-3534.html

[11] Same place I see 'em, same place they chalk 'em out
We speak Guapanese, come see what we talking **bout**
Holla at your homie, **holla** at your dog
Looking for the competition **holla** at the morgue
Once I say hi to her she **gon'** say bye to **ya**
If looks could kill my style might body ya
[...]

www.metrolyrics.com/body-ya-lyrics-fabolous.html

Based on the sample in the CORE, the most common theme in song lyrics is romantic love (see [8], [9], and [10]). This and other themes in song lyrics are often expressed using metaphors and idioms ([9]: "worth the fight," "you've been dreaming of"; [11]: "chalk 'em out," "holla," "if looks could kill"). Slang and interjections (see [12]) are also common in song lyrics.

[12] Oh I, oh I, I'm not even trying
Oh I, oh I but I can't stop smiling
Oh I, oh I, it's sending me flying
Oh I, oh I but I can't stop smiling, yeah
[...]

www.lyricsfreak.com/c/carrie+underwood/do+you+think+about+me_21011760
.html

8.4.3   Interview

Online interviews are not a very frequent register category, but are worth discussing because they are marked for their use of many grammatical features and lexical items. Interviews have more key grammatical features than most of the other registers in CORE (see Figure 8.4). This is due in large part to their colloquial nature, being the only register category in CORE that contains transcriptions of actual spoken interactions. This characteristic of Interviews is evident in the relatively large number of *WH* questions. These are almost always questions posed by the interviewer to the interviewee(s), as in [13].

[13] The song is called "**I** Found You"; *what's* the most important thing *you've* lost?
Tom: "**My** grandma."
Jay: "How are any of **us** supposed to top that?! *I've* lost 21 phones and five bank cards in three years."
Max: "**My** dog Pele."
Siva: "**My** beauty sleep."
Nathan: "**My** dignity!"

www.digitalspy.com/music/interviews/a436927/
the-wanted-interview-were-excited-to-work-with-chris-brown/

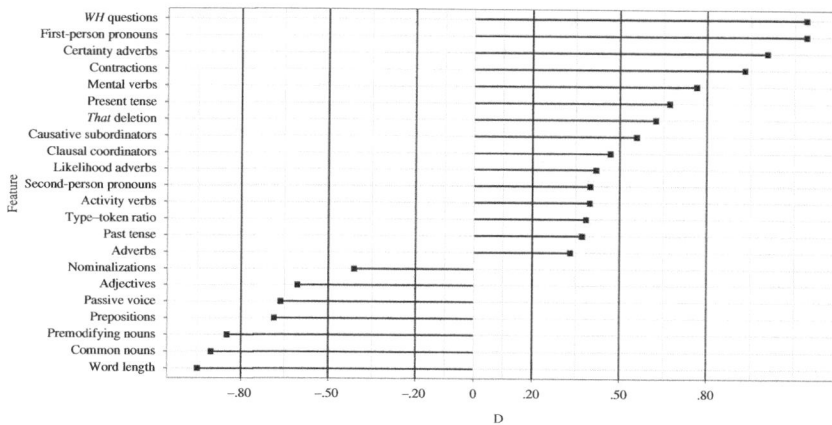

Figure 8.4. Key grammatical features for the Interview sub-register

The use of contractions (italicized) and first-person pronouns (bolded), two other features that are associated with interactive discourse, can also be seen in [13].

The keywords in Table 8.6 offer insights into the common topics and themes of Interviews published online. The most common semantic category is labeled Stance/Emotion. It is common for interviewers to ask questions about how an author, artist, or celebrity feels about a significant work or event in their lives or careers. This results in the interviewee assuming a position in relation to the question or expressing their feelings about it (see [14]). Keywords related to interactive, colloquial discourse (e.g., pronouns, interaction words, and contractions) can also be seen in [14] below.

[14] TrekCore: I still find it **amazing** that you were able to get the original team back together after 25 years. It's such a rare opportunity.
Denise Okuda: We were **very, very excited**. It was a lot of **fun**!
TrekCore: Do you know if they're going to be coming back to help with future seasons?
Denise Okuda: We **really** don't know. If they came back, we would be thrilled again. Both the artists and the folks at CBS Digital and HTV, we have a **great** working relationship. We enjoy the enthusiasm. Mike and I feel so fortunate to be on this project and part of the team.

http://trekcore.com/blog/2012/11/
exclusive-mike-denise-okuda-talk-season-2-interview-part-2/

One set of keywords that surfaced in the Interviews sub-register but no others is the category of Vagueness. These words are traditionally associated with face-to-face conversation in which the speakers have shared context and can afford to use vague references that will be interpretable to their interlocutor. [15] shows examples of this type of language in online Interviews.

Table 8.6. *Keywords for the Interview sub-register*

Stance/ emotion	Music	Pronouns	Activity	Interaction	Vagueness	Contractions
actually	album	anything	came	because	bit	didn't
always	albums	everybody	come	how	couple	don't
amazing	band	he's	coming	say	guys	it's
cool	bands	I'd	did	talk	kind	that's
crazy	creative	I'm	doing	talked	moment	there's
definitely	festival	I've	go	tell	stuff	what's
different	gigs	me	going	yeah	thing	
excited	guitar	my	got	yes	things	
feel	music	something	looking			
felt	play	they're	saw			
fun	played	we'd	started			
funny	playing	we'll	trying			
great	recording	we're	worked			
guess	song	we've	working			
hard	songs	you're				
interesting	studio	you've				
knew	together					
know	touring					
lot	write					
love						
much						
pretty						
quite						
really						
think						
very						
want						
wanted						
whole						

[15] He's got such an insight that a lot of people don't necessarily get. It's been great, personally for me, my achievements have been writing with **guys** like Don. Even the other night I was discussing with a friend that people ask me about Australian Idol and the heights and being a "celebrity" and all that kind of **stuff** and I go cool, yeah yeah but it doesn't really feel like much to me.

http://maytherockbewithyou.com/mtrbwy/2012/09/buffalo/

8.5   Summary and Conclusion

The Oral register category is the smallest of the four general register categories covered in this book, comprising less than 10 percent of the documents on the web. Despite its relatively minor presence, the documents in the Interactive

Discussion, Lyrical, and Interview sub-registers play an important role in the linguistic landscape of online language. All three of these sub-register categories are marked for many key grammatical features and keywords, and each of them exhibits linguistic patterns that are not seen in other web documents. It is due in large part to texts in the Interactive Discussion category that the web is commonly thought of by linguists and end-users alike as being highly colloquial, informal, and conversational. While this stereotype certainly holds true for the registers covered in this chapter, it is not at all true for many of the other registers found on the web (e.g., news reports, encyclopedia articles, product reviews), which are much more similar to highly literate registers that are traditionally found in print form. Overall, the Oral register covered in this chapter demonstrates the wide situational and linguistic diversity that exists on the web.

Note

1. "A person who sows discord on the Internet by starting arguments or upsetting people, by posting inflammatory, extraneous, or off-topic messages in an online community (such as a newsgroup, forum, chat room, or blog) with the deliberate intent of provoking readers into an emotional response or of otherwise disrupting normal on-topic discussion, often for their own amusement" (https://en.wikipedia.org/wiki/Internet_troll).

9 The Web as a Continuous Space of Register Variation

9.1 Comparing Sub-registers across the General Register Categories

In Chapters 1–3, we describe the challenges of working with a random sample of web documents as most documents are not preclassified into a register category. In the present project, we addressed this challenge by asking end-users of the web to code the situational characteristics of each document, resulting in the register classification that we employ for our linguistic analyses. For the sake of efficiency, we employed a hierarchical decision tree for the situational characterizations (see Table 2.1). At the top level, coders decided if a document had its origin in speech or writing. For written documents, coders then decided if language was produced interactively by multiple participants or noninteractively. Then, for noninteractive documents, coders identified the major communicative purpose: narrative; descriptive-information; opinion; informational persuasion; procedural; or, lyrical. These general register distinctions are used to organize the detailed linguistic descriptions in our book: narrative registers in Chapter 5; opinionated and persuasive registers in Chapter 6; informational and procedural registers in Chapter 7; and spoken, interactive, and lyrical registers in Chapter 8.

The primary focus of Chapters 5 through 8 has been on the specific sub-registers under each of these more general categories. One restriction of the analytical approach adopted in the project was that coders were required to treat registers as discrete categories. For example, coders were not permitted to describe a document as having two different communicative purposes (e.g., being both narrative and informational). This restriction in methodology has even more important implications for the classification of sub-registers. As the coding was accomplished through a hierarchical decision tree, coders were constrained in their choice of sub-register based on their previous choices in the decision tree (see Table 2.1). For example, once coders decided that a document was narrative, they were asked to identify the specific narrative sub-register (e.g., News Report, Sports Report, Personal Blog, Historical Article). Similarly, once coders decided that a document was informational, they were asked to identify the specific informational sub-register (e.g., Informational Blog, Research Article, Encyclopedia Article, Descriptions-of-a-Person). As a result, there was no possibility of cross-categorization, eliminating the possibility of registers like informational news reports or narrative encyclopedia articles in our corpus coding.

In hindsight, based on the coding patterns described in Chapter 3 and the detailed situational and linguistic descriptions in Chapters 4 through 8, the situational parameters that characterize registers are clearly not discrete constructs. That is, many web documents share multiple communicative purposes and thus should be treated as documents belonging to hybrid registers. It is also clear that some sub-registers grouped under one general category are quite similar situationally and linguistically to other sub-registers grouped under a different category. For example, Descriptions-of-a-person, one of the informational sub-registers described in Chapter 7, turns out to be highly narrative in purpose and grammatical style. As a result, that sub-register is in many respects similar to Historical Articles, one of the Narrative sub-registers described in Chapter 5.

It is possible to explore the linguistic similarities among sub-registers statistically, cutting across the general register categorizations, by carrying out a cluster analysis of the twenty-seven sub-registers described in Chapters 5 through 8. Cluster analysis is a statistical technique that creates new textual categorization, by grouping together sub-registers that are similar in their linguistic characteristics (see Biber, 1989, 1995, and Staples & Biber, 2015, for more detailed discussion). In the present case, we began with the mean dimension scores (for all nine dimensions from the MD analysis) for each of the twenty-seven sub-registers described in Chapters 5 through 8. We then performed a hierarchical clustering of the sub-registers using Proc CLUSTER in SAS.[1]

For our purposes here, the most important output from this analysis is a hierarchical tree showing the linguistic relations among sub-registers displayed in Figure 9.1. Sub-registers that are listed next to each other in the tree are maximally similar in their multidimensional characteristics. The x-axis plots the linguistic distance between sub-registers, measuring the similarity between the sub-registers. For example, Other Opinion and Opinion Blogs are the two most linguistically similar sub-registers in our analysis because the node connecting them has the smallest "average distance" score of 0.3 on the x-axis. The cluster analysis shows that several other pairs of sub-registers are highly similar, with distance scores less than 0.4 (i.e., How-to and FAQs; Other Information and Description-with-intent-to-sell; Interactive Discussions and Personal Blogs; Spoken Texts and Interviews; Other Narrative and Sports Reports; Reviews and Travel Blogs).

At higher levels in the tree, other sub-registers are added to existing clusters. For example, with a distance of 0.48, we see Advice being added to the How-to + FAQs cluster. With a distance of 0.52, we see Informational Blogs being added to the How-to + FAQs + Advice cluster. Similarly, higher levels of the tree can also combine two lower-level clusters. For example, with a distance of 0.42, we see the Interactive Discussions + Personal Blogs cluster being combined with the Spoken + Interviews cluster.

At the opposite extreme, nodes with large "average distance" scores represent clusters that are maximally different in their multidimensional characteristics. Thus, at the highest level, the Lyrical + TV Dialogue cluster is maximally different from all other sub-registers in the study. These two sub-registers are not actually very similar to each other as they are combined into a cluster with a distance score of 0.62. At the second highest level, Recipes are singled out as a single-register cluster, which is very different from all other sub-registers. Then, at the third level of the tree (with the node having a distance score of 1.0), we see a fundamental split between two major clusters: procedural and informational sub-registers grouped at the top of the tree (e.g., How-to, FAQs, Informational Blogs, Encyclopedia Articles, Research Articles); and personal/opinionated/narrative sub-registers grouped into a large cluster in the middle of the tree (e.g., Personal Blogs, Interviews, Sports Reports, Opinion Blogs, Reviews, Historical Articles).

This cluster analysis provides a useful heuristic device to capture some of the linguistic similarities among sub-registers cutting across general register categories. For example, How-to was initially classified as a Procedural register in our framework, while FAQs was classified as an Informational register (see Table 2.1). But the cluster shown at the top of the tree in Figure 9.1 combines the How-to and FAQs sub-registers, showing that they are highly similar in their MD profiles. We anticipated this finding in Chapter 7, which discusses both Informational and Procedural sub-registers, recognizing that there is extensive overlap between those two general categories. However, the cluster tree identifies a third sub-register that is also highly similar in its MD profile. The Advice sub-register, which was classified as an Opinion register in our framework, turns out to be highly similar to the How-to +FAQs cluster. Thus, the cluster plotted at the top of the tree turns out to comprise three sub-registers which were initially categorized into three different general register categories.

Several other groupings of this type can be observed in Figure 9.1. For example, Descriptions-with-intent-to-sell, which was initially categorized in the Persuasion/Opinion general register, is grouped into a cluster that includes several informational sub-registers (e.g., Other Informational, Encyclopedia Articles, Research Articles), but does not include any other Persuasion/Opinion sub-register. Formal Speeches (from the Spoken general register) is also included in this same cluster.

Similarly, the cluster analysis shows that Reviews (from the Opinion general category) is similar to Travel Blogs (from the Narrative general category). Also, Descriptions-of-a-person (from the Informational general category) is

Name of observation or cluster

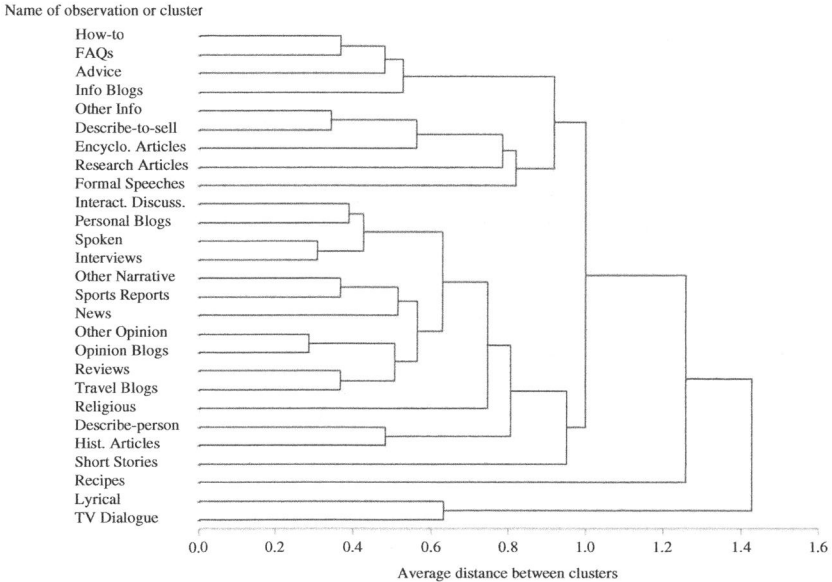

Figure 9.1. Hierarchical cluster tree for the sub-register categories

highly similar to Historical Articles (from the Narrative general category). A careful reading of Chapters 5 through 8 shows that we have anticipated many of these similarities in our detailed situational and linguistic descriptions of sub-registers. However, because those descriptions are split up across different chapters, it would be easy to miss these similarities.

From a situational perspective, many of these sub-registers can be considered as hybrids because they combine multiple communicative purposes. In our initial coding framework, we grouped each sub-register under the general category that seemed to best represent its primary communicative purpose. But it turns out that the hybrid communicative purposes of these sub-registers are more important, resulting in the cross-category groupings seen in Figure 9.1.

In summary, the descriptions in Chapters 5–8, confirmed by the cluster analysis discussed in the present section, highlight multiple cases in which sub-registers are highly similar in both their communicative purposes as well as their associated linguistic characteristics – despite the fact that those sub-registers had been initially placed into different general register categories. These patterns can be accounted for by treating such sub-registers as hybrids, which combine multiple communicative purposes. It turns out that a different type of hybrid register emerged from the coding process itself. We alluded to these hybrid categories in Chapter 3, and turn to a more detailed discussion of these documents in the following section.

9.2　Documents Identified as "Hybrids" during the Coding Process

As noted in Chapter 3, raters achieved majority agreement (at least three of the four raters) on the general register category for almost 70 percent of the web documents in our corpus. These documents thus provided the basis for the detailed register descriptions in Chapters 4–8.

Many of the remaining web documents in the corpus were coded with a 2-2 split. For example, two raters might have coded a given page as a "Narrative" while two other raters classified the same page as "Informational Description/Explanation." One interpretation of these splits is that they simply show a lack of agreement among raters, reflecting a lack of reliability in the register framework. However, the actual distribution of these pairings suggests a different interpretation.

In theory, there are twenty-eight different 2-2 categories that could be formed by combining the eight general register categories in our framework. So, for example, there are seven different 2-2 categories that could have been formed by combining "narrative" with one of the other categories (Narrative + Spoken, Narrative + Interactive Discussion, Narrative + Informational Description, Narrative + Opinion, Narrative + Information-presented-with-the-intent-to-persuade, Narrative + How-to, Narrative + Lyrical). Similarly, there are twenty-one other pairings of general registers that are theoretically possible.

Given this potential, it is surprising that only seven combinations of general registers commonly occurred in 2-2 splits, shown in Table 9.1. This restricted set of recurring register combinations suggests an alternative explanation for the lack of agreement among raters. Rather than reflecting a problem with the coding rubric, these common 2-2 combinations can be interpreted as evidence that these texts belong to "hybrid" registers that combine the communicative purposes and other situational characteristics of two or more general registers.

Two of these hybrid combinations are especially important: Narrative + Informational Description/Explanation, and Narrative + Opinion. Taken together, those two combinations account for 60 percent of all hybrid documents (or 7 percent of the entire corpus). Informational Description/Explanation is also important combining with Opinion (13 percent of 2-2 hybrids), Informational Persuasion (7.5 percent of 2-2 hybrids), and How-to/Instructional documents (6.2 percent of 2-2 hybrids).

Table 9.2 shows that these same three general register categories, Narrative, Informational Description, and Opinion, dominate the 2-1-1 hybrid register categories. Approximately, 37.5 percent of all 2-1-1 hybrids were coded as combinations of these three registers, while most of the other recurrent 2-1-1 categories include two of these three general registers.

Table 9.1. *General register 2+2 hybrid combinations (occurring more than one hundred times in the corpus)*

2-way Hybrid	Frequency	% of 2-way hybrids
Narrative + Informational Description/Explanation	1,786	31.4
Narrative + Opinion	1,623	28.6
Informational Description/Explanation + Opinion	715	12.6
Informational Description/Explanation + Informational Persuasion	427	7.5
Informational Description/Explanation + How-to/Instructional	351	6.2
Opinion + How-to/Instructional	157	2.8
Opinion + Informational Persuasion	153	2.7
Narrative + Other	225	4.0
Opinion + Other	113	2.0
Informational Description/Explanation + Other	91	1.6
All other 2-2 coding splits	41	0.7
TOTAL	5,682	100

Tables 9.1 and 9.2 show that it is especially common to combine narrative and informational purposes in the same document. Some of these documents are biographical recounts that also describe a current social situation. For example, [1] provides a brief biographical history of David and Jackie Segal, while also describing their current lifestyle and specifically their house.

[1] Narrative + Informational Description

Imagine you are rich. Really, seriously rich. So rich that you can afford to build a 90,000 acre dream house, based on an actual French palace – the Palace of Versailles. Then imagine losing everything.

That's what happened to David and Jackie Segal, one of America's richest couples. He made billions from his time-share business, Westgate Resorts, selling (ironically) hundreds of Americans their idea of the American Dream – luxury lifestyles at an affordable rate.

David married former beauty queen Jackie, 31 years his junior, in 2000. Roll on seven years and millions of dollars later, and the couple are intent on re-creating the Palace of Versailles in Florida, thus building America's Biggest House.

With 10 kitchens, 30 bathrooms, two tennis courts, a baseball field, two swimming pools and an ice rink, it was to be twice as big as the Whitehouse. Not too shabby, eh?

http://www.graziadaily.co.uk/conversation/archive/2012/09/04/
the-queen-of-versailles--exclusive-clip.htm

Table 9.2. *General register 2+1+1 hybrid combinations (occurring more than one hundred times in the corpus)*

3-way hybrid	Frequency	% of 3-way hybrids
Narrative + Informational Description/Explanation + Opinion	3,192	37.5
Informational Description/Explanation + Opinion + Informational Persuasion	984	11.6
Narrative + Opinion + Informational Persuasion	934	11.0
Narrative + Info. Description/Explanation + Info. Persuasion	751	8.8
Informational Description/Explanation + Opinion + How-to/Instructional	607	7.1
Narrative + Informational Description/Explanation + Spoken	212	2.5
Narrative + Informational Description/Explanation + How-to/Instructional	210	2.5
Narrative + Opinion + How-to/Instructional	196	2.3
Narrative + Opinion + Discussion	155	1.8
Info. Description/Explanation + How-to/Instructional + Info. Persuasion	144	1.7
Informational Description/Explanation + Opinion + Discussion	138	1.6
Narrative + Opinion + Spoken	116	1.4
All other 2-1-1 coding splits	876	10.3
TOTAL	8,515	100

[2] illustrates a different type of narrative-informational hybrid document, combining a personal travel narrative with an informational description of the "Way of the Roses" biking route in England.

[2] Narrative + Informational Description
"Let me guess," said the stationmaster at Lancaster as he showed me where to stow my bike on the connecting train to Morecambe. "You wouldn't be cycling to Bridlington, by any chance?" When I replied in the affirmative his small audience on the platform were most impressed. At his accuracy, I mean, not my pedalling power. "It's quite simple really," he explained. "Anyone taking a bike to Morecambe must be going to Bridlington. This train never saw any cyclists for donkey's years, now we get dozens of them and they are all doing the same thing."
Beyond a shared desire to turn back the holiday clock by about 70 years, not much would appear to link Morecambe and Bridlington, but now a coast-to-coast cycle route does, and the Way of the Roses is evidently becoming quite popular. [...]

The name is a slight misnomer, since all but the first 20 miles are in the White Rose county and the route only touches the outskirts of Lancaster. A short detour to the city centre would be perfectly possible, but extra mileage is never an appealing prospect for the cyclist looking to fit in 78 miles on the first day.

In order to complete the route in two days I had booked overnight accommodation at Ripon. I was aware most of the hills would come on the first day – and all too painfully aware by the end of it – but I felt I had to aim for something close to halfway to avoid a 100-mile ride on the second. You don't want to be going that far with bags on your bike.

The route is superbly signposted throughout, so much so that you can almost leave the map in your pocket. After following the Lune upstream for a few miles, the flat top of Ingleborough pops into view to give you a chunk of Yorkshire to aim for. [...]

http://www.guardian.co.uk/travel/2012/may/05/british-bike-rides-long-distance

It is perhaps not surprising that opinionated purposes are also commonly combined with narrative or informational purposes. In particular, Personal Blogs commonly combine narrative and opinionated purposes. There are many particular ways in which these general purposes are combined in blogs, for example in a news report presented from a personal perspective, an argumentative editorial illustrated with narratives, or a movie review that also recounts much of the plot (cf. Vásquez's 2012 discussion of involvement and narrativity in opinionated consumer reviews of hotels). Similarly, informational/descriptive texts often incorporate opinionated discussion, such as a business report on a corporation that begins with an explicit disclaimer that the blog represents "personal opinions," even though the text is mostly a simple report of financial information.

Three-way splits, summarized in Table 9.2, suggest that many documents actually combine multiple communicative purposes. The most frequent three-way hybrid is Narrative + Opinion + Description. For example, one document was coded as a News report/blog (two raters), a Description-of-a-person (one rater), and an Opinion blog (one person). The title of this text is enough by itself to suggest this triad of communicative purposes recognized by raters: *On the road: Bradley Wiggins and Team Sky have made Tour de France history – it's been emotional.* This text is a blog post that recounts a recent news story (Narrative), describes a team of athletes (Description), and presents the emotions and attitudes of the author (Opinion).

9.2.1   Hybrid Sub-registers

Raters were also commonly divided in their coding of sub-register categories: 37.6 percent of the documents in our corpus were coded as 2-2 or 2-1-1 combinations at the sub-register level. However, unlike the systematic nature of hybrid combinations at the general register level, these sub-register combinations are

Table 9.3. *Specific sub-register 2+2 hybrid combinations (occurring more than one hundred times in the corpus)*

2-way hybrid	Frequency	% of 2-way hybrids
News Report/Blog + Letter to the editor	411	11.7
Personal Blog + Advice	295	8.4
Description-of-a-thing + Reader/Viewer responses	266	7.5
News Report/Blog + Description-of-a-person	217	6.2
News Report/Blog + Personal Blog	185	5.2
Discussion Forum + Other Forum	145	4.1
Description-of-a-thing + FAQ about Information	103	2.9
All other 2-2 coding splits	1,904	54.0
TOTAL	3,526	100.0

less highly patterned. Thus, Table 9.3 lists the seven 2-2 sub-register combinations that occurred more than a hundred times in our corpus. Taken together, those recurrent combinations account for only 46 percent of all 2-2 sub-register combinations. The remaining 54 percent of these documents belong to more idiosyncratic combinations of sub-registers. Overall, there are 269 different 2-2 sub-register combinations that were assigned by raters in the data, and fifty-three of those combinations occurred ten or more times. For example, there were twenty-four different 2-2 combinations involving Personal Blogs combined with another sub-register (e.g., News Reports, Travel Blogs, Advice, Informational Descriptions, Informational Blogs, Opinion Blogs, Reviews).

The coding is even less systematic for 2-1-1 sub-register combinations. Table 9.4 lists the 12 combinations that occurred in more than one hundred documents in the corpus, but these account for only 13.2 percent of all 2-1-1 sub-register combinations. Overall, there are 2,432 different 2-1-1 sub-register combinations attested in the corpus, and 275 different 2-1-1 combinations that occurred ten or more times.

At the same time, a majority of the raters agreed on the sub-register category of 51 percent of the documents in our corpus (see discussion in Chapter 3). More detailed consideration shows that the sub-registers within some general categories were relatively transparent, while others were highly problematic. Raters usually had no difficulty agreeing on the specific sub-register of documents within the general categories of Spoken, Lyrical, and Interactive Discussion. In addition, raters agreed on the sub-register category of 90 percent of the documents within the general category of Informational Persuasion. Surprisingly, they also agreed on the sub-register of 84 percent of the documents classified

Table 9.4. *Specific sub-register 2+1+1 hybrid combinations (occurring more than one hundred times in the corpus)*

3-way hybrid	Frequency	% of 3-way hybrids
News Report/Blog + Informational Blog + Advice	233	1.6
News Report/Blog + Opinion Blog + Description-with-intent-to-sell	222	1.5
News Report/Blog + Description-of-a-thing + FAQ about Information	214	1.5
Description-of-a-thing + FAQ about Information + News Report/Blog	188	1.3
News Report/Blog + Opinion Blog + Other Informational Persuasion	157	1.1
News Report/Blog + Description-of-a-thing + Advice	152	1.0
Personal Blog + Informational Blog + Advice	137	0.9
News Report/Blog + Description-of-a-thing + Opinion Blog	136	0.9
News Report/Blog + Description-of-a-thing + Religious Blog/Sermon	132	0.9
Description-of-a-thing + Informational Blog + Legal Terms and Conditions	132	0.9
News Report/Blog + Other Narrative + Opinion Blog	127	0.9
Description-of-a-thing + Informational Blog + Other How-to/Informational	108	0.7
All other 2-1-1 coding splits	12,638	86.7
TOTAL	14,576	100.0

as Narrative. At the other extreme, raters found it difficult to agree on the specific sub-register of Informational Description/Explanation documents. Only 43 percent of those documents had majority agreement on a specific sub-register category. As a result, the Other Informational sub-register was the most frequent of all sub-registers discussed in Chapter 7 (on informational and procedural sub-registers).

The existence of hybrid register categories that emerged from the coding process itself is consistent with the research findings presented in Section 9.1. When they are subjected to a detailed situational and linguistic analysis, most web sub-registers turn out to be hybrids to some extent, combining multiple communicative purposes and integrating multiple sets of linguistic features as a result. The descriptions in Chapters 5 through 8 describe these characteristics, which are highlighted by the cluster analysis in Section 9.1.

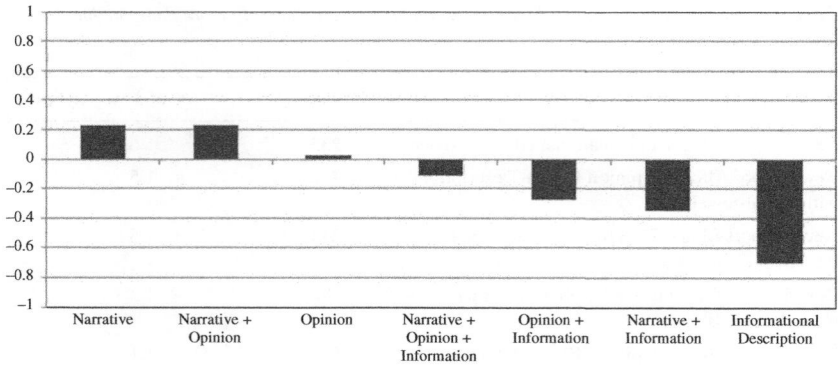

Figure 9.2. Dimension 3 scores for selected registers and hybrids: oral narrative versus written information

Thus, both sets of analyses lead to the same general conclusion that many registers are hybrid combinations of situational and linguistic characteristics, rather than being discrete categories with sharply defined boundaries as assumed in most previous treatments.

9.2.2   The MD Analysis of Hybrid Registers

The linguistic dimensions that emerged from the MD analysis (discussed in Chapter 4) can also be used to characterize hybrid registers, enabling a linguistic comparison of these registers with their related single-category "parent" registers. This analysis turns out to provide additional evidence that hybrid registers employ a blending of linguistic characteristics associated with their multiple communicative purposes.

Several of the major hybrid registers have dimension scores that are intermediate between the "parent" general register categories. For example, Figure 9.2 shows the Dimension 3 scores ("Oral Narrative versus Written Information") for three general registers (Opinion, Narrative, Informational Description), compared to the scores for four hybrid registers that represent combinations of those general categories. Linguistically, this dimension is interpreted as opposing "narrative" features (e.g., past-tense verbs, perfect-aspect verbs, time and place adverbs) versus "informational" features (e.g., long words, nouns, and nominal modifiers). The hybrid registers Opinion + Information and Narrative + Information are intermediate in their Dimension 3 scores, showing that these documents employ both positive and negative linguistic features. In contrast, Narrative + Opinion has essentially the same Dimension 3 score as

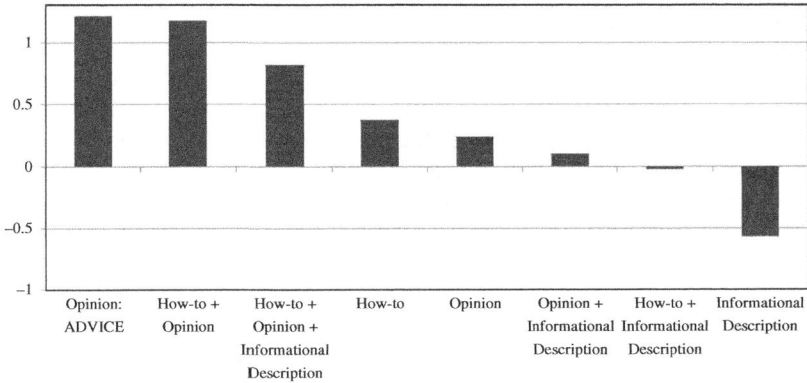

Figure 9.3. Dimension 1 scores for selected registers and hybrids: oral-involved versus literate-informational

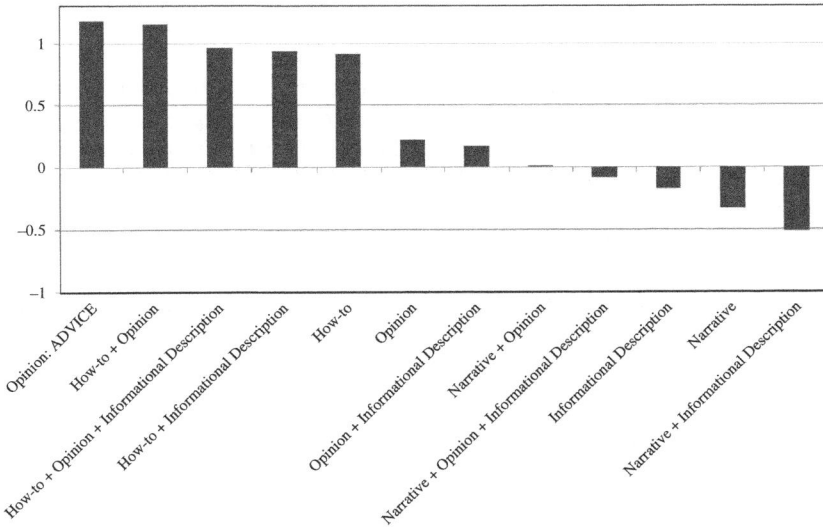

Figure 9.4. Dimension 5 scores for selected registers and hybrids: irrealis versus informational narration

simple Narrative, indicating that narrative communicative purposes have a much stronger influence on the use of Dimension 3 features than opinionated purposes.

Dimensions 1 and 5 show similar patterns for hybrids that combine Narrative/Opinion/Information. Figures 9.3 and 9.4 show that those hybrids are usually intermediate between the simple "parent" registers. However, there are some interesting exceptions. For example, on Dimension 1, hybrids with Opinion + How-to have extremely large positive scores ("oral-involved"), in comparison to the more moderate scores for the general How-To and general Opinion registers.

Figure 9.4 shows similar patterns for Dimension 5. In this case, the simple register How-to is extremely marked for positive ("irrealis") Dimension 5 features, and the hybrid registers with How-to are even more marked. At the other extreme, the hybrid register Narrative + Information has a larger negative score than either of the two parent registers (Narrative or Informational Description).

In the preceding chapters, we have noted repeatedly that specific sub-registers within a general category are often better defined linguistically than the higher level general registers. The Advice sub-register within the general category of Opinion is an example of this type. While general Opinion has intermediate scores on Dimensions 1 and 5, the Advice sub-register is among the most marked text categories, with extremely large positive scores on both dimensions (see Figure 6.1 and Table 6.4 in Chapter 6). Figures 9.3 and 9.4 show that the Advice sub-register is nearly identical to How-to + Opinion/ Information hybrids in their scores on Dimensions 1 and 5.

Thus, the results of the MD analysis indicate that hybrids can often be regarded as register categories with readily interpretable linguistic characteristics. In many cases, hybrid registers have dimension scores that are intermediate between the parent registers, indicating a blending of linguistic characteristics that reflects the blending of communicative purposes identified by coders. In other cases, though, hybrid registers have more extreme linguistic characterizations than either of the parent registers, indicating that coders were identifying a particular kind of sub-register that goes beyond a simple integration of general communicative purposes. How-to + Opinion hybrids are an example of this type, which turn out to be highly similar to the Advice sub-register.

9.3   Register Variation on the Web in a Continuous Linguistic Space: The Text-Type Perspective

Previous MD studies have recognized two competing perspectives on linguistic variation among registers: on the one hand, registers can be compared quantitatively for their central tendencies (their mean scores) on the linguistic dimensions, similar to the results presented in Chapters 5 through 8 (Figures 5.1, 6.1, 7.1, and 8.1). However, at the same time, it is important to recognize that there is considerable linguistic variation among the texts grouped within a register category. That is, because registers are defined on the basis of situational criteria rather than linguistic criteria, there will always be some degree of linguistic variation among the texts within a register category. It turns out that the texts within a register category tend to be similar linguistically, reflecting the functional associations between linguistic use and situational context. But, to the extent that there is situational variation in the communicative purposes of texts within a register, there will also likely be linguistic variation among those texts.

This second perspective on linguistic variation, attempting to account for the variation within register categories, has always been a key component of MD analyses. For example, Chapter 8 in Biber (1988) – the first book-length MD study – specifically takes up the topic of linguistic variation within register categories, describing how a register can be described for the extent to which it is linguistically well-defined (or not), in addition to the comparison of typical linguistic characteristics across registers.

In other early MD studies (see especially Biber, 1989), the finding that there was often an extensive range of linguistic variation within a register led to an alternative type of analysis, associated with a complementary discourse construct: *text types*. In short, a *text type* is a linguistically well-defined grouping of texts. That is, the texts grouped into a text type are all similar linguistically, regardless of any predefined register categories.

Cluster analysis is the statistical technique used to identify text types. However, the research design and research goals are somewhat different from the analysis in Section 9.1. In that case, we used cluster analysis to group together the sub-registers that were most similar linguistically, disregarding the linguistic variation among texts within the sub-register categories. The statistical results identified higher-order categories that were combinations of the existing sub-registers.

In contrast, the analysis presented in the present section begins with each individual document as an observation, with no consideration of the register categories of those documents. The cluster analysis uses the nine dimension scores to group documents into new categories, such that the documents within a grouping are maximally similar in their linguistic characteristics, while the clusters themselves are maximally distinguished; we refer to these new groupings of documents as *text types*.

It would be tangential to the goals of the present book to provide a detailed account of the text type analysis. Rather, our main goals here are to further illustrate some of the ways in which linguistic variation on the web occurs in a continuous multidimensional space. We thus provide only a relatively brief summary of the cluster analysis results here.

Figure 9.5 plots the hierarchical cluster tree (similar to Figure 9.1 in Section 9.1). The difference from Figure 9.1 is that the tree in Figure 9.5 plots clusters for all documents in the corpus, rather than clustering the twenty-seven predefined sub-register categories. Table 9.5 summarizes the results for the two-cluster, three-cluster, and four-cluster solutions in a condensed format. It includes the number of documents that are grouped into each cluster; an indication of the

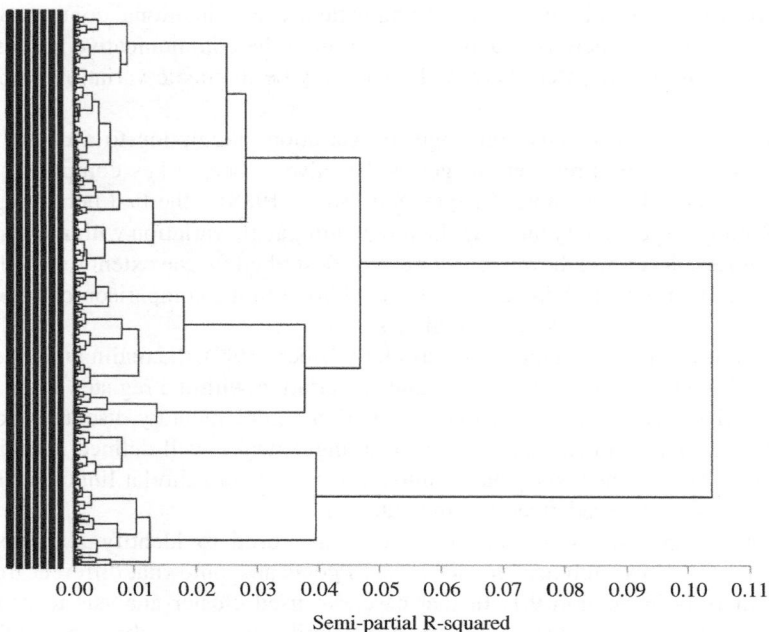

Figure 9.5. Hierarchical cluster tree

overall mean dimension scores for the cluster (simply noting if the cluster is above average or below average for each dimension) as well as a breakdown of the kinds of documents grouped into each cluster in terms of their register categories.

At the top level of Figure 9.5 (the two-cluster solution), the analysis splits all documents in the corpus into two major categories. Based on the average dimension scores for these two clusters, together with consideration of the texts grouped into the clusters, these two categories can be interpreted as an "oral" text type and a "literate" text type. As Table 9.5 shows, the "oral" text type has high positive scores for Dimensions 1, 2, 3, and 5, with most documents from TV Dialogues, Lyrical, and Interactive discussions grouped into this category. In contrast, the "literate" text type has large negative scores for Dimensions 1, 2, 3, and 5, and a high positive score for Dimension 7, with most documents from Historical Articles, Encyclopedia Articles, Research Articles, and News Reports grouped into this category.

At the second level of the hierarchy, the "literate" text type is split into two sub-types: "literate + narrative" and "literate + non-narrative." The "literate + narrative" text type has large scores on the dimensions with narrative linguistic

Table 9.5. *Summary of two-, three-, and four-cluster solutions*

Key (see Table 4.3)
D1: Oral-involved versus Literate
D2: Oral elaboration
D3: Oral clausal narrative versus Literate nominal information
D4: Reported communication
D5: Irrealis versus Informational narration
D6: Procedural/explanatory discourse
D7: Nominal/literate stance
D8: Description of humans
D9: Nontechnical explanation or description

2-cluster solution	**Cluster 1: "Oral"**	**Cluster 2: "Literate"**	
	(10,904 documents)	(32,781 documents)	
	MD profile:	*MD profile:*	
	D1 +	D1 −	
	D2 +	D2 −	
	D3 +	D3 −	
	D4	D4	
	D5 +	D5 −	
	D6	D6	
	D7 −	D7 +	
	D8	D8	
	D9	D9	
	Most important register categories in the cluster:	*Most important register categories in the cluster:*	
	• 93% of TV dialogues	• 99% of Historical Articles	
	• 78% of Lyrical	• 98% of Encyclopedia Articles	
	• 61% of Interactive Discussions	• 98% of Research Articles	
		• 91% of News Reports	

3-cluster solution	**Cluster 1-1: "Oral"**	**Cluster 2-1: "Literate + Narrative"**	**Cluster 2-2: "Literate + Non-narrative"**
	(10,904 documents)	(20,156 documents)	(12,625 documents)
	MD profile:	*MD profile:*	*MD profile:*
	D1 +	D1 −	D1 −
	D2 +	D2	D2 −
	D3 +	D3	D3 −
	D4	D4 +	D4
	D5 +	D5 −	D5 −
	D6	D6 −	D6 +
	D7 −	D7	D7 +
	D8	D8 +	D8 −
	D9	D9 −	D9 +
	Most important register categories in the cluster:	*Most important register categories in the cluster:*	*Most important register categories in the cluster:*
	• 93% of TV Dialogues	• 78% of Historical	• 74% of Research Articles
	• 78% of Lyrical	• 72% of Description-of-a-person	• 52% of Reviews
	• 61% of Interactive Discussions	• 70% of Religious	• 52% of Other-Information
		• 66% Encyclopedia	• 45% of Informational Blogs
		• 65% of Sports	
		• 57% of Travel Blogs	
		• 55% of News	
		• 51% of Short Stories	

(cont.)

Table 9.5. (*cont.*)

4-cluster solution	Cluster 1-1: "Oral + Involved" (7,076 documents) MD profile:	Cluster 1-2: "Oral + Informational/ how-to" (3,828 documents) MD profile:	Cluster 2-1: "Literate + Narrative" (20,156 documents) MD profile:	Cluster 2-2: "Literate + Non-narrative" (12,625 documents) MD profile:
	D1 +	D1 +	D1 −	D1 −
	D2 +	D2	D2	D2 −
	D3 +	D3	D3	D3 −
	D4	D4 −	D4 +	D4
	D5 +	D5 +	D5 −	D5 −
	D6 −	D6 +	D6 −	D6 +
	D7 −	D7	D7	D7 +
	D8	D8	D8 +	D8 −
	D9	D9 +	D9 −	D9 +
	Most important register categories in the cluster:	*Most important register categories in the cluster:*	*Most important register categories in the cluster:*	*Most important register categories in the cluster:*
	• 87% of TV	• 46% of How-to	• 78% of Historical	• 74% of Research Articles
	• 67% of Lyrical	• 45% of Advice	• 72% of Describe-Person	• 52% of Reviews
	• 57% of Interviews	• 37% of FAQs	• 70% of Religious	• 52% of Other-Information
	• 48% of Personal Blogs		• 66% Encyclopedia	• 45% of Informational Blogs
	• 41% of Interactive Discussions		• 65% of Sports	
			• 57% of Travel Blogs	
			• 55% of News	
			• 51% of Short Stories	

features (positive Dimension 4 and negative Dimension 5), and a majority of the documents from the narrative sub-registers are grouped into this category (Historical Articles, Descriptions-of-a-person, Religious Blogs, Encyclopedia Articles, Sports Reports, Travel Blogs, News Reports, and Short Stories). In contrast, the "literate + non-narrative" text type has consistently informational/ literate (i.e., negative) dimension scores on Dimensions 1, 2, and 3, together with positive scores for Dimensions 6, 7, and 9. The texts grouped into this cluster include Research Articles, Other Informational documents, Reviews, and Informational Blogs.

The third level of the hierarchical tree, then, splits the "oral" cluster into two sub-clusters: an "oral + involved" text type and an "oral + informational/ how-to" text type. The "oral + involved" text type has stereotypically "oral" dimension scores (e.g., large positive scores for Dimensions 1, 2, and 3), and includes over half of the documents from TV Dialogues, Lyrical texts, and Interviews, together with a large number of Personal Blogs and Interactive Discussions. In contrast, the "oral + informational/how-to" text type has oral linguistic characteristics on Dimension 1, but has procedural linguistic characteristics associated with positive scores on Dimensions 5 and 6; the texts grouped into this cluster include large numbers of How-To, Advice, and FAQs.

A complete description of the cluster analysis would explore the text types that were identified at deeper levels of the hierarchical tree, and provide much fuller interpretation and illustration of each of these text types. Such a description would also illustrate how documents from a single register category can be grouped into distinct text types (i.e., with different linguistic characteristics), and how these linguistic categorizations reflect the differing communicative purposes of such documents.

Our goals here, though, are simply to illustrate how the analysis of linguistic text types provides yet another analytical perspective on web registers described in a continuous space of variation. The results summarized here are consistent with the descriptions in Chapters 4 through 8, as well as the general patterns described in Section 9.1. For example, the descriptions in Chapters 6 and 7 highlighted a basic level of similarity among the sub-registers of How-To, FAQs, and Advice – all three often have procedural communicative purposes and employ frequent second-person pronouns, possibility modals, conditional clauses, present-tense and infinitives. The hierarchical cluster analysis in Section 9.1 shows that these three sub-registers are highly similar in their MD profile, reflected in the way that they are grouped into a single cluster at the top of the cluster tree (Figure 9.1). Also, Cluster 1–2 in the analysis discussed in the present section includes many of the documents from those same three sub-registers.

Our goal here is not to argue that the text-type perspective is the "correct" perspective. Rather, we would argue that text categories defined in situational terms (i.e., "registers") are equally valid to text categories defined in linguistic terms (i.e., "text types"). The two provide different kinds of information, but neither one is more valid than the other. Rather, the two perspectives reflect different aspects of the realities of situational and linguistic variation found in any discourse domain. In fact, this situation is typical of quantitative discourse research generally, where the integration of multiple analytical perspectives is always more informative than consideration of any single perspective (see Baker & Egbert, 2016). The research perspectives adopted in the preceding sections provide strong evidence for that claim.

9.4   Future Research: Register Variation on the Web in a Continuous Situational Space

The corpus linguistic analyses reported in this book have been primarily quantitative. That is, the analyses have focused on the rates of occurrence for linguistic features in texts, with statistical analyses used to measure the extent to which those rates are meaningful or important. Thus, the key feature analyses reported in Chapters 5 through 8 are based on the mean scores (and standard deviations) for the quantitative rates of occurrence of grammatical features in a sub-register, compared against the baseline of all other sub-registers. The MD analysis and the cluster analyses build on these quantitative results for individual linguistic features, showing how they function together in co-occurrence patterns in a continuous space of linguistic variation, with sub-registers tending to occupy different positions in that space.

However, the situational analysis employed in this study contrasts with those linguistic analyses because it is based on discrete, categorical coding rather than continuous, quantitative parameters. In the first place, each coder made discrete choices regarding situational characteristics (e.g., interactive or not; narrative versus informational versus opinionated). Then, depending on those choices, coders were asked to make a final discrete selection of a specific sub-register.

Because we employed four separate raters for each document, we were able to infer some indication of the extent to which a document clearly manifested the situational characteristics of a register (see Section 9.2 above). If all four raters agreed, we assumed that the situational characteristics were clear-cut. But if there was disagreement among raters, we assumed that the document itself probably manifested multiple communicative purposes. This analysis led to our positing the existence of "hybrid" registers for documents where the coders disagreed in systematic ways.

However, there is no reason why web documents and registers could not be investigated from the outset in a quantitative, continuous situational space (see also Sharoff, 2018). That is, each situational parameter could be operationalized as a continuous variable. For example, coders could be asked to evaluate the *extent* to which a document is interactive, rather than simply making a categorical "yes-no" decision about whether it is interactive or not. Similarly, coders could be asked to evaluate the extent to which a document has a narrative purpose.

In summary, coders could rate the extent to which a document served all of the different communicative purposes. So, for example, a document might be coded as a 5 on a 6-point scale for serving narrative purposes, a 4 for opinionated purposes, a 3 for informational purposes, and a 1 for procedural purposes. The same kind of coding could also be undertaken for coder perceptions of sub-registers. For example, a document could be coded as a 5 for FAQs, a 4 for Advice, a 4 for How-to, and a 2 for Informational blog.

This type of coding would permit analysis of variation among web documents and registers in a continuous situational space. That is, similar to the kinds of linguistic analyses described in the present book, we would be able to describe the extent to which web registers are situationally well-defined, and could systematically analyze the patterns of situational variation within a register category. We would also be able to perform a statistical cluster analysis using the quantitative situational variables, resulting in text type categories that are situationally well-defined (i.e., by definition, the documents grouped into these categories would share the same set of situational characteristics to the same extent).

By combining such an analysis of situational variation in a continuous quantitative space with the current analyses of linguistic variation in a continuous quantitative space, we would be able to better capture the fuzzy and complex patterns of variation among web documents. Our goal here is not to challenge the usefulness of the perspectives adopted in previous chapters. Discourse analyses and register descriptions have always proceeded under the assumption that registers are discrete categories, that there are core exemplars of a register, and that it is useful and informative to provide linguistic descriptions of those typical texts from a register. We have generally adopted this same general approach in Chapters 4 through 8. However, our goal in the present chapter has been to explore the possibility of a complementary perspective that recognizes the ways in which texts and registers pattern in a continuous linguistic *and* situational space. We are not suggesting that one or the other of these two major perspectives are "correct." But the second of these has been largely disregarded in previous research on register variation. It is our belief that these two perspectives provide quite different kinds of information, which complement one another in important ways.

9.5   Conclusion: A Complementary Perspective on Register

So we have come full circle. We began in Chapter 1 by describing how the patterns of variation on the web are fundamentally different from those found for published/printed texts: the register categories of published/printed texts have been regarded as obvious, while there are often no overt indications of register category for web documents. These observations led to the methods for both situational analysis and linguistic analysis employed in the chapters of the present book.

But, is this opposition really as clear as we claimed? That is, have we fully understood the register distinctions used in previous studies of published written texts? Or, would it be useful to complement those descriptions with additional analyses that treat published written registers in a continuous situational space?

Quantitative register studies have repeatedly documented two complementary linguistic patterns: On the one hand, studies show that there are systematic linguistic differences among registers, but at the same time, these same studies show that there can be considerable linguistic variation among the texts within a register category (see, e.g., the linguistic patterns of use reported in Biber, 1988, as well as the patterns described in the preceding chapters of the present book). Such studies leave no doubt that register variation should be studied in a continuous space of linguistic variation.

However, we are suggesting an additional possibility here: that register variation – in all discourse domains – could usefully be investigated from the perspective of a continuous space of *situational* variation, especially with respect to the communicative purposes of a text. Previous analyses of published/printed registers have been based on the methodology of grouping individual texts into discrete register categories based on their format of publication. For example, magazine articles are published in magazines, newspaper articles are published in newspapers, research articles are published in academic research journals. and so on. This perspective has proven to be highly useful for corpus construction and for linguistic descriptions of registers based on analysis of those corpora.

However, we believe that a complementary approach to categorizing register, based on continuous situational parameters, might also prove to be informative. For example, magazine articles could be further classified based on their particular communicative purposes (e.g., informing, persuading, narrating, expressing personal opinions). That classification could also include the possibility that an article might contain all of these purposes to differing extents.

Such an approach could capture the complexities and messiness of variation among published written texts in different ways from traditional approaches. Text-type analysis has been employed to explore the patterns of linguistic variation registers, showing that there are groupings of linguistically-similar texts that cut across traditional register categories (see, e.g., Biber, 1989). In future research, we hope to apply continuous situational parameters to the analysis of registers in the domain of published writing, in addition to their application in the domain of the web. The results of such analyses would lead to descriptions of registers in a continuous situational and linguistic space, providing a useful complementary perspective to traditional analyses based on discrete register categorizations.

Note

1. https://support.sas.com/documentation/cdl/en/statug/63033/HTML/default/cluster_toc.htm.

Appendix A   Linguistic Features Included in the Multidimensional Analysis

Verbs
Copula *BE*
Progressive-aspect verbs
Non-past-tense verbs
Past tense verbs
Perfect aspect verbs
Activity verbs
Existence verbs
Mental verbs
Epistemic verbs (not controlling a complement clause)
Communication verbs (not controlling a complement clause)
Causative/facilitation verbs
Possibility modals
Prediction modals
Necessity modals

Verb complement clauses
Desire verb + *to* clause
Verb + *WH* clause
Likelihood verb + *that* clause
Certainty verb + *that* clause
Verb + *to* clause (excluding desire verbs)
Verb + *WH* clause
That complementizer deletion
Communication verb + *that* clause

Adverbials
Stance adverbs
Time adverbs
Place adverbs
Total other adverbs
Adverbial clauses (excluding conditional)
Conditional adverbial clauses
Linking adverbials

Nouns
Proper nouns
Concrete nouns
Common nouns
Process nouns
Human nouns
Premodifying nouns
Nominalizations
Cognitive nouns

Noun phrase embedded clauses
Stance noun + prepositional phrase
Stance noun + complement clause
Other stance nouns
Finite relative clauses
Passive nonfinite relative clauses

Pronouns
First-person pronouns
Second-person pronouns
Third-person pronouns
Demonstrative pronouns
It

Adjectives
Attributive adjectives
Attitudinal adjectives (not controlling a complement clause)
Epistemic adjectives (not controlling a complement clause)

Other
Type–token ratio
Long words
Contractions
Clausal coordination
Prepositional phrases
Indefinite articles
Definite articles

Appendix B Lexico-grammatical Features Included in the Key Feature Analysis

Verbs
Activity verbs
Communication verbs
Mental verbs
Modals of necessity
Modals of possibility
Modals of prediction
Passive voice
Past tense
Perfect aspect
Present tense
Progressive aspect

Adverbials
Adverbs
Adverbs of place
Adverbs of time
Causative subordinators
Certainty adverbs
Conditional subordinators
Likelihood adverbs
Linking adverbials

Nouns
Common nouns
Nominalizations
Place nouns
Premodifying nouns
Proper nouns
Human nouns

Pronouns
First-person pronouns
Second-person pronouns
Third-person pronouns

Embedded clauses
Stance noun comp. clauses
That deletion
That relative clauses
Verb complement clauses
WH clauses
WH relative clauses

Other
Adjectives
Clausal coordinators
Contractions
Discourse particles
Infinitives
Prepositions
Type–token ratio
WH questions
Word count
Word length

Appendix C   Descriptive Statistics for the Key Feature Analyses

Table C.1. *Key grammatical features for the News Report sub-register*

Variable	Cohen's *d*	News report		Other	
		M	*SD*	*M*	*SD*
Features that are notably common in the target register					
Moderate positive (D > 0.50)					
Communication verbs	0.64	14.16	9.12	8.97	6.95
Proper nouns	0.55	64.91	31.99	46.73	34.12
Word length	0.50	4.70	0.31	4.53	0.39
Small positive (D > 0.30)					
Common nouns	0.46	240.49	39.85	220.52	47.01
Perfect aspect verbs	0.36	8.82	6.12	6.73	5.51
Premodifying nouns	0.34	38.14	18.56	31.59	19.50
Past tense verbs	0.34	32.54	21.22	25.37	20.48
Prepositions	0.30	117.07	19.77	110.68	22.09
Features that are notably rare in the target register					
Small negative (D < −0.30)					
Certainty adverbs	−0.31	2.09	2.84	3.09	3.6
Adverbs	−0.32	31.54	11.54	35.52	13.21
Mental verbs	−0.33	16.17	8.93	19.58	11.38
Modals of possibility	−0.36	5.31	4.55	7.19	5.96
Conditional subordinators	−0.37	2.26	2.88	3.66	4.42
Coordinating conjunction (clausal)	−0.37	7.39	5.34	9.67	6.87
Present tense verbs	−0.47	80.42	25.04	93.47	30.42
Moderate negative (D < −0.50)					
First-person pronouns	−0.54	19.6	14.91	31.07	26.36
Second-person pronouns	−0.68	5.22	7.79	15.25	19.44

Table C.2. *Key grammatical features for the Personal Blogs sub-register*

Variable	Cohen's *d*	Personal blogs		Other	
		M	*SD*	*M*	*SD*
Features that are notably common in the target register					
Large positive (D > 0.80)					
First-person pronouns	1.39	61.53	27.23	26.48	23.08
Moderate positive (D > 0.50)					
Adverbs	0.64	42.21	12.43	34.18	12.86
Mental verbs	0.55	24.44	10.87	18.49	10.90
Small positive (D > 0.30)					
Certainty adverbs	0.49	4.59	4.05	2.76	3.41
Past tense verbs	0.45	36.02	22.46	26.31	20.60
Contractions	0.43	23.97	13.16	18.40	12.91
Time adverbs	0.42	6.83	5.08	4.81	4.50
Activity verbs	0.41	31.81	11.15	27.19	11.48
Discourse particles	0.36	1.28	2.16	0.62	1.51
Progressive aspect verbs	0.35	16.30	8.02	13.61	7.54
Place adverbs	0.33	8.49	5.69	6.62	5.71
Features that are notably rare in the target register					
Small negative (D < −0.30)					
Adjectives	−0.36	60.19	16.14	66.94	20.85
Prepositions	−0.43	103.75	19.36	112.59	21.81
Moderate negative (D < −0.50)					
Passive voice	−0.52	6.99	5.16	10.3	7.29
Premodifying nouns	−0.56	24.32	12.86	33.56	19.71
Proper nouns	−0.57	34.68	23.94	51.66	34.82
Common nouns	−0.63	200.32	35.69	226.39	46.46
Nominalizations	−0.77	11.79	8.65	21.54	15.65
Large negative (D < −0.80)					
Word length	−1.04	4.24	0.27	4.59	0.38

Table C.3. *Key grammatical features for the Sports Report sub-register*

Variable	Cohen's *d*	Sports report		Other	
		M	*SD*	*M*	*SD*
Features that are notably common in the target register					
Large positive (D > 0.80)					
Proper nouns	1.11	86.10	35.11	48.34	33.18
Moderate positive (D > 0.50)					
Third-person pronouns	0.61	30.09	15.21	20.05	17.49
Activity verbs	0.58	33.59	11.06	27.07	11.43
Small positive (D > 0.30)					
Past tense verbs	0.48	35.96	19.53	26.32	20.79
Perfect aspect verbs	0.36	9.21	6.27	7.04	5.65
Contractions	0.35	22.94	12.65	18.47	12.97
Place adverbs	0.34	8.53	5.68	6.62	5.71
Features that are notably rare in the target register					
Small negative (D < −0.30)					
Passive voice	−0.34	8.05	5.48	10.23	7.30
Premodifying nouns	−0.45	25.86	13.81	33.45	19.71
Human nouns	−0.47	6.01	5.26	9.31	8.44
Moderate negative (D < −0.50)					
Attributive adjective	−0.54	57.39	14.64	67.12	20.85
Word length	−0.56	4.4	0.23	4.58	0.39
Second-person pronouns	−0.62	5.09	6.48	13.62	18.47
Common nouns	−0.66	199.98	32.18	226.4	46.61
Large negative (D < −0.80)					
Nominalizations	−0.92	10.51	6.98	21.61	15.65

Table C.4. *Key grammatical features for the Historical Articles sub-register*

Variable	Cohen's *d*	Historical articles		Other	
		M	*SD*	*M*	*SD*
Features that are notably common in the target register					
Large positive (D > 0.80)					
Past tense verbs	1.36	54.23	19.78	26.62	20.67
Prepositions	0.99	130.84	16.20	111.86	21.74
Passive voice	0.97	17.21	7.56	10.02	7.18
Moderate positive (D > 0.50)					
Proper nouns	0.58	69.76	32.02	50.43	34.46
Word length	0.56	4.75	0.28	4.56	0.38
Small positive (D > 0.30)					
WH relative clauses	0.37	5.34	3.72	3.96	3.81
Place nouns	0.34	7.95	6.73	5.69	6.58
Features that are notably rare in the target register					
Small negative (D < −0.30)					
Premodifying nouns	−0.33	27.20	16.03	33.05	19.51
WH clauses	−0.34	0.40	0.92	0.87	1.73
WH questions	−0.36	0.28	0.67	0.76	1.77
Communication verbs	−0.41	7.37	5.30	10.11	7.79
Modals of necessity	−0.44	1.25	1.59	2.35	3.20
Adverbs	−0.48	29.31	9.41	34.72	13.00
Certainty adverbs	−0.49	1.54	1.80	2.89	3.49
Moderate negative (D < −0.50)					
Activity verbs	−0.51	22.34	8.56	27.52	11.52
Infinitives	−0.54	12.38	5.55	16.29	8.5
That deletion	−0.64	1.16	1.64	3.08	3.9
Modals of possibility	−0.65	3.76	3.32	6.82	5.75
Conditional subordinators	−0.67	1.23	1.73	3.38	4.19
Modals of prediction	−0.7	3.92	4.18	7.98	7.04
Progressive aspect verbs	−0.76	8.98	4.75	13.82	7.61
Second-person pronouns	−0.78	2.61	6.08	13.21	18.13
Mental verbs	−0.79	11.82	6.49	18.92	11
Large negative (D < −0.80)					
Contractions	−0.83	10.45	6.03	18.83	13.02
First-person pronouns	−0.86	11.91	12.64	28.79	24.85
Present tense verbs	−1.95	42.2	19.65	91.17	29.51

Table C.5. *Key grammatical features for the Travel Blogs sub-register*

Variable	Cohen's *d*	Travel blogs		Other	
		M	*SD*	*M*	*SD*
Features that are notably common in the target register					
Large positive (D > 0.80)					
Place nouns	1.05	13.35	8.07	5.65	6.53
Place adverbs	0.82	11.99	7.17	6.70	5.69
Moderate positive (D > 0.50)					
First-person pronouns	0.52	41.57	25.34	28.51	24.78
Small positive (D > 0.30)					
Past tense verbs	0.41	35.80	23.37	26.83	20.81
Prepositions	0.31	118.35	18.54	112.00	21.79
Type-token ratio	0.30	31.88	3.64	30.67	4.38
Features that are notably rare in the target register					
Small negative (D < −0.30)					
Modals of necessity	−0.31	1.53	1.80	2.34	3.19
Passive voice	−0.33	8.01	5.47	10.11	7.23
Conditional subordinators	−0.33	2.21	2.51	3.37	4.19
Human nouns	−0.40	6.42	4.90	9.13	8.33
Modals of prediction	−0.41	5.48	4.77	7.96	7.04
Moderate negative (D < −0.50)					
That verb complement clauses	−0.53	1.75	2.32	3.37	3.68
Word length	−0.54	4.39	0.26	4.57	0.38
Communication verbs	−0.56	6.45	4.91	10.11	7.78
Third-person pronouns	−0.60	12.13	10.17	20.72	17.56
Present tense verbs	−0.60	74.59	24.31	90.8	29.84
Nominalizations	−0.78	11.4	8.07	21.02	15.52

Table C.6. *Key grammatical features for the Short Stories sub-register*

Variable	Cohen's *d*	Short stories		Other	
		M	*SD*	*M*	*SD*
Features that are notably common in the target register					
Large positive (D > 0.80)					
Past tense verbs	1.96	74.77	28.04	26.63	20.49
Third-person pronouns	1.80	65.28	30.85	20.41	17.10
Moderate positive (D > 0.50)					
Adverbs	0.72	43.02	10.09	34.62	12.98
Place adverbs	0.65	10.41	5.64	6.72	5.72
Time adverbs	0.64	7.61	3.82	4.92	4.56
Coordinating conjunction (clausal)	0.61	14.02	9.05	9.16	6.61
Communication verbs	0.58	14.63	7.98	10.05	7.76
Activity verbs	0.56	33.58	10.54	27.43	11.51
Mental verbs	0.51	23.76	8.05	18.82	11.00
Small positive (D > 0.30)					
Perfect aspect verbs	0.49	10.09	6.19	7.16	5.70
That deletion	0.48	4.72	3.00	3.06	3.89
Contractions	0.48	24.75	12.45	18.71	12.99
Linking adverbials	0.44	5.22	3.39	3.68	3.60
First-person pronouns	0.41	39.54	28.52	28.55	24.78
Word count	0.35	2530.90	4520.44	1198.81	3025.58
WH questions	0.34	1.31	1.56	0.75	1.77
Type-token ratio	0.31	31.82	2.84	30.67	4.38
Features that are notably rare in the target register					
Small negative (D < −0.30)					
Infinitives	−0.37	13.64	5.21	16.26	8.50
That relatives	−0.37	2.42	2.18	3.52	3.53
Moderate negative (D < −0.50)					
Attributive adjectives	−0.53	57.05	14.8	66.58	20.67
Proper nouns	−0.56	34.78	20.45	50.71	34.54
Prepositions	−0.58	100.75	16.89	112.11	21.78
Present tense verbs	−0.76	69.17	26.66	90.79	29.81
Large negative (D < −0.80)					
Common nouns	−0.89	189.36	33.06	225	46.29
Nominalizations	−1.02	8.9	6.52	21.01	15.5
Word length	−1.12	4.22	0.22	4.57	0.38
Pre-modifying nouns	−1.16	15.24	9.56	33.09	19.48

Table C.7. *Key grammatical features for the Opinion Blogs*

Variable	Cohen's *d*	Opinion Blogs		Other	
		M	*SD*	*M*	*SD*
Features that are notably common in the target register					
Small positive (D > 0.25)					
Type-token ratio	0.42	32.15	3.41	30.46	4.46
Stance verb + *that* clause	0.32	4.37	3.54	3.21	3.67
Present tense verbs	0.32	98.25	22.93	89.58	30.55
Linking adverbials	0.31	4.64	3.40	3.55	3.61
Adverbs	0.31	37.90	10.78	34.20	13.20
Stance noun + *that* clause	0.29	0.73	1.27	0.40	1.05
Features that are notably rare in the target register					
No features with D < −0.30					

Table C.8. *Key grammatical features for Reviews*

Variable	Cohen's *d*	Reviews		Other	
		M	*SD*	*M*	*SD*
Features that are notably common in the target register					
Small positive (D > 0.30)					
Type-token ratio	0.48	32.53	3.55	30.60	4.39
Adverbs	0.45	39.97	11.62	34.45	12.98
Adjectives	0.36	73.27	18.33	66.25	20.70
Certainty stance adverbials	0.31	3.92	3.61	2.83	3.46
Features that are notably rare in the target register					
Small negative (D < −0.25)					
Necessity modals	−0.27	1.64	2.12	2.37	3.22
Passive voice verbs	−0.28	8.43	5.04	10.16	7.29
To-clauses	−0.35	13.68	6.75	16.35	8.53
Prediction modals	−0.35	5.87	4.86	8.02	7.09
Communication verbs	−0.37	7.74	5.16	10.18	7.84
Nominalizations	−0.46	15.27	9.36	21.18	15.65

Table C.9. *Key grammatical features for the Description-with-intent-to-sell sub-register*

Variable	Cohen's *d*	Description-with-intent-to-sell		Other	
		M	*SD*	*M*	*SD*
Features that are notably common in the target register					
Moderate positive (D > 0.50)					
Adjectives	0.63	80.81	25.81	66.09	20.32
Small positive (D > 0.25)					
Long words	0.37	4.70	0.36	4.56	0.38
Second-person pronouns	0.31	18.99	20.54	12.92	17.97
Pre-modifying nouns	0.27	38.69	23.61	32.82	19.32
Features that are notably rare in the target register					
Small negative (D < −0.30)					
Activity verbs	−0.31	23.94	11.78	27.58	11.48
Adverbs	−0.32	30.74	12.72	34.79	12.97
Perfect aspect verbs	−0.32	5.45	5.57	7.23	5.70
Causative adverbial clauses	−0.34	0.57	1.50	1.18	1.99
Linking adverbials	−0.35	2.51	3.34	3.73	3.60
That complementizer deletion	−0.37	1.81	2.96	3.10	3.90
Communication verbs	−0.45	7.04	6.22	10.17	7.79
Verb + *that*-clause	−0.48	1.84	2.77	3.40	3.69
Moderate negative (D < −0.50)					
Past tense verbs	−0.60	16.24	15.17	27.23	20.91

Table C.10. *Key grammatical features for the Advice sub-register*

Variable	Cohen's *d*	Advice		Other	
		M	*SD*	*M*	*SD*
Features that are notably common in the target register					
Large positive (D > 0.80)					
Second-person pronouns	1.41	43.25	25.71	12.38	17.22
Present tense verbs	1.18	120.87	22.51	89.94	29.61
To-clauses	0.82	23.02	8.40	16.08	8.42
Moderate positive (D > 0.50)					
Possibility modals	0.78	11.48	6.60	6.67	5.67
Conditional adverbial clauses	0.72	6.53	4.91	3.28	4.13
Mental verbs	0.60	25.27	10.82	18.69	10.95
Progressive aspect verbs	0.58	18.25	8.14	13.66	7.55
Activity verbs	0.54	33.19	10.31	27.33	11.50
Small positive (D > 0.28)					
Adverbs	0.31	38.34	11.28	34.58	13.00
Necessity modals	0.29	3.23	3.20	2.32	3.18
Human nouns	0.28	11.54	9.36	9.05	8.28
Features that are notably rare in the target register					
Small negative (D < −0.30)					
WH relative clauses	−0.30	2.97	2.95	3.99	3.83
Long words	−0.43	4.42	0.29	4.57	0.38
Moderate negative (D < −0.50)					
Perfect aspect verbs	−0.50	4.75	3.99	7.23	5.73
Passive voice verbs	−0.60	6.46	4.87	10.18	7.25
Prepositional phrases	−0.72	98.67	15.61	112.37	21.80
Past tense verbs	−0.75	14.13	13.27	27.21	20.90
Large negative (D < −0.80)					
Proper nouns	−1.23	18.56	15.56	51.40	34.46

Table C.11. *Key grammatical features for Religious Blogs*

Variable	Cohen's d	Religious Blogs		Other	
		M	SD	M	SD
Features that are notably common in the target register					
Moderate positive (D > 0.50)					
Coordinated clauses	0.70	14.85	9.57	9.10	6.55
WH relative clauses	0.61	6.40	4.30	3.93	3.79
Third-person pronouns	0.58	31.47	20.55	20.49	17.43
Verb + *that* clause	0.54	5.45	4.15	3.32	3.66
Small positive (D > 0.30)					
Communication verbs	0.46	13.56	7.55	10.03	7.76
Prepositional phrases	0.32	118.57	19.09	111.95	21.80
First-person pronouns	0.32	36.04	22.63	28.50	24.83
WH questions	0.31	1.40	2.45	0.74	1.75
Features that are notably rare in the target register					
Small negative (D < −0.30)					
Place nouns	−0.30	4.02	4.61	5.74	6.60
Place adverbials	−0.32	5.16	4.26	6.76	5.74
Progressive aspect verbs	−0.33	11.51	6.22	13.81	7.61
Contractions	−0.40	14.24	9.69	18.81	13.02
Activity verbs	−0.40	23.31	9.28	27.53	11.53
Moderate negative (D < −0.50)					
Long words	−0.51	4.40	0.27	4.57	0.38
Nouns	−0.52	204.12	33.82	225.11	46.39
Adjectives	−0.57	55.74	17.83	66.69	20.66
Large negative (D < −0.80)					
Pre-modifying nouns	−1.24	14.01	10.42	33.28	19.45

Table C.12. *Key grammatical features for the How-To/Instructional sub-register*

Variable	Cohen's *d*	How-to		Other	
		M	*SD*	*M*	*SD*
Features that are notably common in the target register					
Large positive (D > 0.80)					
Second-person pronouns	1.26	39.82	25.77	12.32	17.19
Moderate positive (D > 0.50)					
Conditional adverbial clauses	0.73	6.80	5.53	3.26	4.09
Possibility modals	0.68	10.86	6.58	6.67	5.67
Present tense verbs	0.67	108.14	23.52	90.16	29.85
To-clauses	0.57	20.95	8.67	16.11	8.44
Small positive (D > 0.30)					
Activity verbs	0.47	32.93	12.23	27.31	11.45
Features that are notably rare in the target register					
Small negative (D < −0.30)					
Type-token ratio	−0.30	29.44	4.22	30.71	4.37
Stance noun + *that* clause	−0.30	0.19	0.55	0.45	1.09
Complementizer *that* deletion	−0.31	2.08	2.53	3.09	3.91
WH relative clauses	−0.38	2.67	3.14	4.01	3.82
Communication verbs	−0.39	7.33	6.57	10.16	7.79
Prepositional phrases	−0.44	103.27	19.36	112.31	21.79
First-person pronouns	−0.44	19.17	18.45	28.89	24.92
Moderate negative (D < −0.50)					
Perfect aspect verbs	−0.61	4.26	3.90	7.26	5.73
Third-person pronouns	−0.66	11.22	11.07	20.94	17.60
Large negative (D < −0.80)					
Proper nouns	−0.88	25.62	22.77	51.36	34.51
Past tense verbs	−0.93	11.95	10.29	27.34	20.92

Table C.13. *Key grammatical features for Recipes*

Variable	Cohen's *d*	Recipes		Other	
		M	*SD*	*M*	*SD*
Features that are notably common in the target register					
Large positive (D > 0.80)					
Nouns	0.85	264.40	47.21	224.69	46.26
Moderate positive (D > 0.50)					
Nouns as NP pre-modifiers	0.54	42.88	17.26	32.97	19.48
Activity verbs	0.51	33.07	10.55	27.45	11.51
Small positive (D > 0.30)					
Time adverbials	0.44	7.08	5.16	4.93	4.56
Discourse particles	0.34	1.30	2.17	0.66	1.56
First-person pronouns	0.30	35.51	21.60	28.59	24.82
Features that are notably rare in the target register					
Small negative (D < −0.30)					
Necessity modals	−0.31	1.55	1.74	2.34	3.19
Prepositional phrases	−0.33	105.53	17.95	112.07	21.78
Past tense verbs	−0.38	20.33	13.42	26.92	20.86
Perfect aspect verbs	−0.39	5.26	4.09	7.18	5.71
Progressive aspect verbs	−0.43	10.85	5.81	13.78	7.60
Stance noun + *that*-clause	−0.44	0.09	0.37	0.44	1.08
That relative clauses	−0.45	2.11	2.68	3.52	3.52
Moderate negative (D < −0.50)					
Passive voice verbs	−0.65	6.20	4.51	10.11	7.23
Verb + *that*-clause	−0.72	1.29	1.70	3.36	3.68
Third-person pronouns	−0.76	10.17	8.45	20.69	17.54
Large negative (D < −0.80)					
Human nouns	−0.86	3.59	3.75	9.12	8.32
Proper nouns	−0.87	26.03	20.73	50.69	34.50
WH relative clauses	−0.90	1.31	1.72	3.98	3.81
Nominalizations	−0.91	8.88	10.62	20.97	15.49
Long words	−1.02	4.27	0.16	4.57	0.38
Communication verbs	−1.09	3.62	3.19	10.10	7.77

Table C.14. *Key grammatical features for Research Articles*

Variable	Cohen's *d*	Research articles		Other	
		M	*SD*	*M*	*SD*
Features that are notably common in the target register					
Large positive (D > 0.80)					
Long words	1.57	5.16	0.40	4.55	0.37
Nominalizations	1.16	40.81	19.53	20.56	15.15
Adjectives	0.97	88.47	25.56	66.10	20.32
Prepositional phrases	0.95	132.45	22.34	111.65	21.57
Moderate positive (D > 0.50)					
Passive voice verbs	0.74	16.21	9.63	9.98	7.12
Nouns as NP pre-modifiers	0.67	47.81	25.28	32.71	19.24
Nouns	0.52	253.49	64.96	224.24	45.69
Small positive (D > 0.30)					
Verb + *that*-clause	0.31	4.59	4.43	3.33	3.66
Features that are notably rare in the target register					
Small negative (D < −0.30)					
Perfect aspect verbs	−0.30	5.56	5.13	7.21	5.71
Communication verbs	−0.30	7.94	6.53	10.12	7.78
Necessity modals	−0.31	1.48	2.48	2.35	3.19
WH complement clauses	−0.32	0.41	1.05	0.88	1.73
Type-token ratio	−0.34	29.22	4.42	30.70	4.37
Discourse particles	−0.41	0.17	0.70	0.67	1.57
Proper nouns	−0.42	37.88	26.72	50.87	34.58
To-clauses	−0.44	12.75	7.87	16.31	8.48
Adverbs	−0.48	28.74	12.15	34.78	12.97
Mental verbs	−0.49	14.05	8.72	18.94	11.01
Moderate negative (D < −0.50)					
if adverbial clauses	−0.55	1.52	2.35	3.39	4.20
Third-person pronouns	−0.63	11.52	11.13	20.84	17.58
Certainty adverbials	−0.64	1.06	2.09	2.91	3.49
Time adverbials	−0.64	2.44	3.23	4.98	4.57
Complementizer *that* deletion	−0.65	1.07	2.12	3.10	3.90
Place adverbials	−0.67	3.44	4.18	6.80	5.73
Contractions	−0.68	11.47	8.42	18.88	13.02
Present tense verbs	−0.74	70.46	26.15	91.07	29.77
First-person pronouns	−0.79	13.54	11.63	28.91	24.91
Large negative (D < −0.80)					
Second-person pronouns	−0.82	2.26	6.09	13.31	18.17
Prediction modals	−0.86	3.12	3.89	8.03	7.04
Activity verbs	−0.89	18.48	8.87	27.64	11.49

Table C.15. *Key grammatical features for Encyclopedia Articles*

Variable	Cohen's *d*	Encyclopedia articles		Other	
		M	*SD*	*M*	*SD*
Features that are notably common in the target register					
Large positive (D > 0.80)					
Passive voice verbs	1.23	19.28	7.92	9.99	7.15
Prepositional phrases	0.93	130.21	17.41	111.84	21.73
Moderate positive (D > 0.50)					
Long words	0.76	4.82	0.30	4.56	0.38
Adjectives	0.62	79.48	21.64	66.38	20.60
Word count	0.51	2713.34	2997.97	1188.82	3033.66
Small positive (D > 0.30)					
Proper nouns	0.37	63.28	35.65	50.48	34.45
Past tense verbs	0.36	34.11	19.80	26.82	20.84
WH relative clauses	0.34	5.19	3.36	3.95	3.81
Nominalizations	0.33	25.95	14.97	20.88	15.49
Features that are notably rare in the target register					
Small negative (D < −0.30)					
Discourse particles	−0.31	0.21	1.38	0.66	1.56
WH questions	−0.32	0.29	1.05	0.76	1.77
Nouns	−0.33	209.62	46.13	224.97	46.27
Possibility modals	−0.37	4.85	4.96	6.81	5.74
Necessity modals	−0.41	1.26	1.99	2.35	3.19
Adverbs	−0.42	29.14	13.51	34.73	12.96
WH clauses	−0.45	0.28	0.67	0.87	1.73
Moderate negative (D < −0.50)					
Place adverbials	−0.55	4.07	3.96	6.77	5.74
if adverbial clauses	−0.56	1.47	2.39	3.38	4.19
Certainty adverbials	−0.65	1.12	1.71	2.90	3.49
Complementizer *that* deletion	−0.66	1.13	1.64	3.09	3.90
To-clauses	−0.71	10.74	7.20	16.31	8.48
Activity verbs	−0.74	20.12	8.37	27.55	11.51
Large negative (D < −0.80)					
Prediction modals	−0.85	3.18	3.85	7.99	7.04
Second-person pronouns	−0.85	1.96	4.47	13.23	18.14
Mental verbs	−0.88	11.03	6.29	18.94	11.00
Progressive aspect verbs	−1.16	6.69	4.30	13.85	7.59
Present tense verbs	−1.21	57.51	25.64	91.06	29.67
First-person pronouns	−1.25	5.58	8.67	28.88	24.81
Contractions	−1.41	4.50	6.40	18.90	12.96

Table C.16. *Key grammatical features for Descriptions-of-a-Person*

		Descriptions-of-a-Person		Other	
Variable	Cohen's *d*	*M*	*SD*	*M*	*SD*
Features that are notably common in the target register					
Large positive (D > 0.80)					
Third-person pronouns	1.10	41.08	20.34	20.33	17.28
Proper nouns	0.95	84.24	37.69	50.09	34.18
Past tense verbs	0.83	45.54	24.56	26.61	20.65
Moderate positive (D > 0.50)					
Prepositional phrases	0.54	123.67	22.22	111.87	21.72
Human nouns	0.42	12.46	7.91	9.05	8.31
Features that are notably rare in the target register					
Small negative (D < −0.30)					
Adverbs	−0.30	30.96	12.23	34.72	12.98
Verb + *that*-clause	−0.33	2.30	2.68	3.37	3.69
that relative clauses	−0.38	2.36	2.59	3.53	3.53
Mental verbs	−0.40	14.82	9.43	18.91	11.00
Necessity modals	−0.45	1.19	1.82	2.36	3.20
Moderate negative (D < −0.50)					
Prediction modals	−0.53	4.64	5.44	7.99	7.04
To-clauses	−0.54	12.00	7.31	16.31	8.48
Second-person pronouns	−0.59	4.85	8.40	13.24	18.17
if adverbial clauses	−0.65	1.27	1.94	3.39	4.20
Possibility modals	−0.70	3.53	3.41	6.84	5.75
Large negative (D < −0.80)					
Present tense verbs	−0.96	62.05	30.99	91.13	29.60

Table C.17. *Key grammatical features for FAQs*

Variable	Cohen's *d*	FAQs		Other	
		M	*SD*	*M*	*SD*
Features that are notably common in the target register					
Large positive (D > 0.80)					
Possibility modals	0.92	12.71	7.16	6.74	5.70
Second-person pronouns	0.85	31.97	25.98	12.94	17.91
if adverbial clauses	0.82	7.83	6.58	3.32	4.13
Moderate positive (D > 0.50)					
WH questions	0.75	2.75	3.36	0.73	1.74
Nominalizations	0.63	31.38	18.10	20.85	15.44
Necessity modals	0.62	4.71	4.41	2.32	3.16
Passive voice verbs	0.62	14.67	7.62	10.06	7.21
Nouns	0.58	252.04	48.47	224.56	46.21
Nouns as NP pre-modifiers	0.53	44.01	22.20	32.90	19.43
Small positive (D > 0.30)					
Present tense verbs	0.48	103.23	22.28	90.57	29.87
Long words	0.37	4.70	0.36	4.56	0.38
to-clauses	0.32	19.00	8.66	16.22	8.48
Features that are notably rare in the target register					
Small negative (D < −0.30)					
Likelihood adverbs	−0.32	0.37	1.16	0.84	1.74
Complementizer *that* deletion	−0.32	1.98	2.76	3.07	3.89
Progressive aspect verbs	−0.34	11.42	6.15	13.79	7.61
Discourse particles	−0.34	0.22	0.93	0.66	1.56
Communication verbs	−0.38	7.51	5.68	10.10	7.78
Time adverbials	−0.41	3.30	3.48	4.95	4.56
First-person pronouns	−0.43	19.49	17.14	28.69	24.85
Moderate negative (D < −0.50)					
Perfect aspect verbs	−0.51	4.69	3.99	7.20	5.72
Type-token ratio	−0.55	28.42	3.93	30.70	4.37
Place adverbials	−0.55	4.11	3.65	6.76	5.74
Adverbs	−0.55	28.03	11.05	34.72	12.98
Certainty adverbials	−0.62	1.13	2.02	2.89	3.48
Contractions	−0.63	11.72	9.25	18.80	13.00
Third-person pronouns	−0.73	10.39	9.46	20.75	17.55
Proper nouns	−0.75	29.05	21.76	50.81	34.52
Large negative (D < −0.80)					
Past tense verbs	−0.98	10.92	10.33	27.04	20.86

Table C.18. *Key grammatical features for Informational Blogs*

Variable	Cohen's *d*	Informational Blogs		Other	
		M	*SD*	*M*	*SD*
Features that are notably common in the target register					
Moderate positive (D > 0.50)					
Nouns	0.55	249.53	46.31	223.90	46.05
Small positive (D > 0.30)					
Long words	0.41	4.71	0.33	4.56	0.38
Possibility modals	0.37	9.05	6.86	6.71	5.68
Nouns as NP pre-modifiers	0.37	40.21	21.46	32.73	19.36
Nominalizations	0.35	26.26	16.07	20.75	15.44
Features that are notably rare in the target register					
Small negative (D < −0.30)					
Perfect aspect verbs	−0.30	5.65	4.67	7.23	5.74
Communication verbs	−0.31	7.96	6.09	10.16	7.81
Contractions	−0.34	14.91	9.80	18.88	13.07
Complementizer *that* deletion	−0.38	1.86	2.45	3.11	3.92
Proper nouns	−0.48	36.22	27.56	51.15	34.61
First-person pronouns	−0.48	18.69	16.71	28.97	24.98
Third-person pronouns	−0.49	13.54	11.55	20.92	17.65
Moderate negative (D < −0.50)					
Past tense verbs	−0.60	16.61	14.07	27.28	20.96

Table C.19. *Key grammatical features for the Other-Informational sub-register*

Variable	Cohen's d	Other-Informational		Other	
		M	SD	M	SD
Features that are notably common in the target register					
Large positive (D > 0.80)					
Long words	0.86	4.87	0.39	4.54	0.37
Moderate positive (D > 0.50)					
Nominalizations	0.56	30.04	20.15	20.14	14.75
Nouns as NP pre-modifiers	0.52	43.43	24.20	32.08	18.74
Small positive (D > 0.30)					
Prepositional phrases	0.49	122.16	23.51	111.16	21.39
Passive voice verbs	0.44	13.41	9.19	9.80	6.95
Adjectives	0.44	75.52	24.43	65.74	20.10
Features that are notably rare in the target register					
Small negative (D < −0.30)					
Likelihood adverbials	−0.30	0.41	1.34	0.87	1.76
Linking adverbials	−0.30	2.72	3.33	3.78	3.61
Causative adverbial clauses	−0.33	0.62	1.51	1.21	2.01
that + verb complement clauses	−0.34	2.26	3.20	3.45	3.70
Present tense verbs	−0.35	81.48	26.65	91.48	29.97
Activity verbs	−0.38	23.44	11.32	27.82	11.46
Type-token ratio	−0.41	28.90	5.02	30.83	4.28
Perfect aspect verbs	−0.42	5.07	5.20	7.36	5.71
Time adverbials	−0.44	3.19	4.02	5.09	4.57
Communication verbs	−0.47	7.01	6.40	10.35	7.82
Moderate negative (D < −0.50)					
Third-person pronouns	−0.52	12.97	14.12	21.33	17.64
Mental verbs	−0.54	13.69	9.78	19.30	10.98
Certainty adverbials	−0.58	1.26	2.45	3.02	3.52
Adverbs	−0.60	27.51	13.17	35.29	12.77
Complementizer *that* deletion	−0.62	1.22	2.28	3.23	3.95
Contractions	−0.62	12.11	9.81	19.32	13.07
First-person pronouns	−0.63	16.16	16.98	29.71	25.09
Past tense verbs	−0.67	15.76	14.70	27.88	21.02

Table C.20. *Key grammatical features for the Interactive Discussion sub-register*

Variable	Cohen's *d*	Interactive Discussion		Other	
		M	*SD*	*M*	*SD*
Features that are notably common in the target register					
Large positive (D > 0.80)					
Present tense verbs	0.89	114.92	28.84	88.99	29.17
Moderate positive (D > 0.50)					
First-person pronouns	0.75	46.79	27.68	27.35	24.10
Conditional subordinating conjunctions	0.68	6.55	5.94	3.14	3.93
Mental verbs	0.59	25.36	12.78	18.40	10.71
Small positive (D > 0.25)					
Contractions	0.46	24.76	15.04	18.32	12.73
THAT deletion	0.44	4.87	4.92	2.94	3.77
Activity verbs	0.43	32.58	14.02	27.11	11.23
Modals of prediction	0.42	10.97	8.65	7.73	6.85
Second-person pronouns	0.41	20.11	18.32	12.62	17.97
Discourse particles	0.41	1.46	2.55	0.60	1.45
Modals of possiblility	0.40	9.12	6.90	6.63	5.61
Adverbs of time	0.38	6.81	6.05	4.81	4.41
Certainty adverbs	0.37	4.27	4.58	2.78	3.36
Adverbs	0.36	39.25	14.39	34.35	12.81
Likelihood adverbs	0.33	1.50	2.62	0.79	1.65
Modals of necessity	0.27	3.28	4.14	2.27	3.10
Causative subordinating conjunctions	0.25	1.73	2.83	1.12	1.90
Features that are notably rare in the target register					
Small negative (D < −0.25)					
Wh relative clauses	−0.29	2.95	3.61	4.04	3.81
Passive voice	−0.31	8.09	6.77	10.23	7.23
Premodifying nouns	−0.46	25.29	16.10	33.53	19.59
Moderate negative (D < −0.50)					
Type-token ratio	−0.54	28.21	5.41	30.85	4.24
Adjectives	−0.58	55.79	18.96	67.27	20.56
Proper nouns	−0.60	33.13	27.59	51.84	34.60
Common nouns	−0.65	197.90	41.76	226.66	46.02
Nominalizations	−0.68	12.67	9.79	21.52	15.65
Type-token ratio	−0.54	28.21	5.41	30.85	4.24
Large negative (D < −0.80)					
Prepositions	−0.80	96.08	21.18	113.16	21.38
Word length	−1.10	4.22	0.29	4.59	0.38

Table C.21.. *Key grammatical features for the Lyrical sub-register.*

Variable	Cohen's d	Lyrical		Other	
		M	SD '	M	SD
Features that are notably common in the target register					
Large positive (D > 0.80)					
First-person pronouns	1.42	79.28	45.44	27.94	23.71
Contractions	1.11	42.45	28.11	18.43	12.37
Present tense verbs	1.05	130.90	46.44	90.14	29.19
Second-person pronouns	0.99	39.95	34.88	12.75	17.48
Mental verbs	0.92	36.12	24.89	18.62	10.50
Moderate positive (D > 0.50)					
THAT deletion	0.64	9.01	12.89	2.99	3.55
Small positive (D > 0.25)					
Modals of prediction	0.48	13.54	15.42	7.86	6.82
Activity verbs	0.44	34.43	19.44	27.37	11.34
Modals of possiblility	0.38	10.29	12.00	6.74	5.59
Adverbs of time	0.32	7.51	10.62	4.90	4.41
Wh clauses	0.30	1.93	4.82	0.85	1.64
Place adverbs	0.30	9.39	11.39	6.70	5.60
Certainty adverbs	0.29	4.27	6.11	2.86	3.42
Features that are notably rare in the target register					
Small negative (D < −0.25)					
Clausal coordinating conjunctions	−0.29	6.88	9.09	9.22	6.60
Word count	−0.33	448.61	1096.37	1216.32	3053.75
Stance noun comp. clauses	−0.36	0.12	0.69	0.45	1.09
Progressive aspect	−0.40	10.06	11.01	13.82	7.53
Moderate negative (D < −0.50)					
Wh relative clauses	−0.50	1.85	4.82	4.00	3.79
Passive voice	−0.55	5.95	8.02	10.15	7.20
Large negative (D < −0.80)					
Proper nouns	−0.83	24.44	29.63	50.97	34.42
Adjectives	−0.89	46.24	25.31	66.80	20.46
Premodifying nouns	−0.92	16.91	15.81	33.21	19.44
Prepositions	−0.95	85.69	33.52	112.40	21.36
Common nouns	−1.10	170.79	53.12	225.51	45.78
Type-token ratio	−1.11	24.91	6.12	30.75	4.29
Nominalizations	−1.31	5.31	7.42	21.15	15.47
Word length	−2.11	3.80	0.36	4.58	0.37

Table C.22. *Key grammatical features for the Interviews sub-register.*

Variable	Cohen's *d*	Interviews		Other	
		M	*SD*	*M*	*SD*
Features that are notably common in the target register					
Large positive (D > 0.80)					
WH questions	1.14	3.02	2.22	0.74	1.75
First-person pronouns	1.14	53.38	18.49	28.46	24.77
Certainty adverbs	1.01	7.12	4.91	2.85	3.45
Contractions	0.93	31.57	14.76	18.66	12.94
Moderate positive (D > 0.50)					
Mental verbs	0.76	26.36	8.64	18.80	10.99
Present tense verbs	0.67	108.02	21.47	90.57	29.85
THAT deletion	0.62	5.23	3.06	3.05	3.88
Causative subordinating conjunctions	0.56	2.23	1.85	1.16	1.98
Small positive (D > 0.25)					
Clausal coordinating conjunctions	0.47	12.23	6.46	9.17	6.64
Likelihood adverbs	0.42	1.62	2.02	0.83	1.73
Second-person pronouns	0.40	18.82	9.25	13.07	18.12
Activity verbs	0.40	31.38	7.92	27.44	11.52
Type-token ratio	0.39	32.05	2.56	30.67	4.38
Past tense verbs	0.37	34.08	17.85	26.86	20.86
Adverbs	0.33	38.35	9.02	34.64	13.00
That relative clauses	0.29	4.48	3.08	3.51	3.52
Place adverbs	0.25	8.01	4.23	6.73	5.73
Wh clauses	0.25	1.24	1.20	0.86	1.73
Progressive aspect	0.25	15.39	5.37	13.76	7.61
Features that are notably rare in the target register					
Small negative (D < −0.25)					
Place nouns	−0.29	4.10	4.18	5.72	6.59
Nominalizations	−0.41	15.38	11.35	20.98	15.51
Moderate negative (D < −0.50)					
Adjectives	−0.61	56.45	11.50	66.59	20.69
Passive voice	−0.66	6.36	3.45	10.12	7.23
Prepositions	−0.69	99.12	15.69	112.13	21.78
Large negative (D < −0.80)					
Premodifying nouns	−0.85	19.98	9.77	33.08	19.50
Common nouns	−0.90	189.16	31.69	225.02	46.29
Word length	−0.95	4.26	0.25	4.57	0.38

References

Baker, P. 2004. Querying keywords: Questions of difference, frequency, and sense in keywords analysis. *Journal of English Linguistics*, 32(4), 346–59.

Baker, P. & Egbert, J. (eds.) 2016. *Triangulating Methodological Approaches in Corpus Linguistic Research*. New York: Routledge.

Baron, N. S. 2010. *Always On: Language in an Online and Mobile World*. Oxford: Oxford University Press.

Baroni, M. & Bernardini, S. 2004. BootCaT: Bootstrapping corpora and terms from the web. In M. T. Lino, M. F. Xavier, F. Ferreira, R. Costa, & R. Silva (eds.) *Proceedings of LREC 2004*. 1313–16. Lisbon: ELDA.

Baroni, M., Bernardini, S., Ferraresi, A., & Zanchetta, E. 2009. The WaCky wide web: A collection of very large linguistically processed web-crawled corpora. *Language Resources and Evaluation* 43(3): 209–26.

Biber, D. 1985. Investigating macroscopic textual variation through multi-feature/multi-dimensional analyses. *Linguistics* 23: 337–60.

    1986. Spoken and written textual dimensions in English: Resolving the contradictory findings. *Language* 62: 384–414.

    1988. *Variation across Speech and Writing*. Cambridge: Cambridge University Press.

    1989. A typology of English texts. *Linguistics* 27: 3–43.

    1995. *Dimensions of Register Variation: A Cross-Linguistic Perspective*. Cambridge: Cambridge University Press.

    2006. *University Language: A Corpus-Based Study of Spoken and Written Registers*. Amsterdam: John Benjamins.

    2014. Using multi-dimensional analysis to explore cross-linguistic universals of register variation. *Languages in Contrast* 14(1): 7–34.

Biber, D. & Conrad, S. 2009. *Register, Genre, and Style*. Cambridge: Cambridge University Press.

Biber, D., Conrad, S., Reppen, R., Byrd, P., Helt, M., Clark, V., Cortes, V., Csomay, E., & Urzua, A. 2004. *Representing Language Use in the University: Analysis of the TOEFL 2000 Spoken and Written Academic Language Corpus* (ETS TOEFL Monograph Series, MS-25). Princeton, NJ: Educational Testing Service.

Biber, D. & Egbert, J. 2015. Using grammatical features for automatic register identification in an unrestricted corpus of documents from the open web. *Journal of Research Design and Statistics in Linguistics and Communication Science* 2(1). 3–36.

    2016. Register variation on the searchable web: A multi-dimensional analysis. *Journal of English Linguistics* 44(2): 95–137.

Biber, D., Egbert, J., & Davies, M. 2015. Exploring the composition of the searchable web: A corpus-based taxonomy of web registers. *Corpora* 10(1): 11–45.

Biber, D. & Gray, B. 2016. *Grammatical Complexity in Academic English: Linguistic Change in Writing*. Cambridge: Cambridge University Press.

Biber, D., Johansson, S., Leech, G., Conrad, S., & Finegan, E. 1999. *Longman Grammar of Spoken and Written English*. Harlow: Pearson Education Limited.

Brown, P., & Fraser, C. 1979. Speech as a marker of situation. In K.R. Scherer & H. Giles (eds.), *Social Markers in Speech* (pp. 33–62). Cambridge: Cambridge University Press.

Cohen, J. 1977. *Statistical Power Analysis for the Behavioral Sciences*. New York: Routledge.

Conrad, S. 1996. *Academic Discourse in Two Disciplines: Professional Writing and Student Development in Biology and History*. Doctoral dissertation, Flagstaff, AZ: Northern Arizona University.

Conrad, S. & Biber, D. (eds.). 2001. *Variation in English: Multi-Dimensional Studies*. Harlow: Longman.

Crowston, K., Kwasnik, B., & Rubleske, J. 2010. Problems in the use-centered development of a taxonomy of web genres. In A. Mehler, S. Sharoff, & M. Santini (eds.), *Genres on the Web: Computational Models and Empirical Studies*. 69–86. New York: Springer.

Crystal, D. 2001. *Language and the Internet*. Cambridge: Cambridge University Press.

Egbert, J. 2015. Sub-register and discipline variation in published academic writing: Investigating statistical interaction in corpus data. *International Journal of Corpus Linguistics*, 20(1): 1–29.

Egbert, J. & Biber, D. 2016. Do all roads lead to Rome?: Modeling register variation with factor analysis and discriminant analysis. *Corpus Linguistics and Linguistic Theory*.

Egbert, J. & Biber, D. (in press). Incorporating text dispersion into keyword analyses. *Corpora*.

Egbert, J., Biber, D., & Davies, M. 2015. Developing a bottom-up, user-based method of web register classification. *Journal of the Association for Information Science and Technology*. 66(9): 1817–31.

Ervin-Tripp, S. 1972. On sociolinguistic rules: Alternation and co-occurrence. In J. Gumperz and D. Hymes (eds.), *Directions in Sociolinguistics*. 213–50. New York: Holt, Rinehart, and Winston.

Ferguson, C. A. 1983. Sports announcer talk: Syntactic aspects of register variation. *Language in Society* 12(2): 153–72.

Fletcher, W. H. 2012. Corpus analysis of the world wide web. In C. Chapelle (ed.), *Encyclopedia of Applied Linguistics*. 1339–47. Oxford: Wiley-Blackwell.

Gray, B. 2015. *Linguistic Variation in Research Articles: When Discipline Tells Only Part of the Story* (Studies in Corpus Linguistics, Vol. 71). Amsterdam: John Benjamins Publishing Company.

Grieve, J., Biber, D., Friginal, E., & Nekrasova, T. 2010. Variation among blog text types: A multi-dimensional analysis. In A. Mehler, S. Sharoff, & M. Santini (eds.), *Genres on the Web: Corpus Studies and Computational Models*. New York: Springer-Verlag.

Guadagno, R. E., Okdie, B. M., & Eno, C. A. 2008. Who blogs? Personality predictors of blogging. *Computers in Human Behavior* 24(5): 1993–2004.

Halliday, M. A. K. 1988. On the language of physical science. In M. Ghadessy (ed.), *Registers of Written English: Situational Factors and Linguistic Features*. London: Pinter: 162–78.

Herring, S. C., Scheidt, L. A., Wright, E., & Bonus, S. 2005. Weblogs as bridging genre. *Information Technology & People* 18: 142–71.

Herring, S. C. & Paolillo, J. C. 2006. Gender and genre variation in weblogs. *Journal of Sociolinguistics* 10: 439–59.

Hymes, D. 1974. *Foundations in Sociolinguistics*. Philadelphia, PA: University of Pennsylvania Press.

Kilgarriff, A. & Grefenstette, G. 2003. Introduction to the special issue on the web as corpus. *Computational Linguistics* 29: 333–47.

Landis, J. & Koch, G. 1977. The measurement of observer agreement for categorical data. *Biometrics*, 33: 159–74.

Paolacci, G., Chandler, J., & Ipeirotis, P. G. 2010. Running experiments on Amazon Mechanical Turk. *Judgment and Decision Making*, 5: 411–19.

Rehm, G., Santini, M., Mehler, A., Braslavski, P., Gleim, R., Stubbe, A., Symonenko, S., Tavosanis, M., & Vidulin, V. 2008. Towards a reference corpus of web genres for the evaluation of genre identification systems. In N. Calzolari, K. Choukri, B. Maegaard, J. Mariani, J. Odijk, S. Piperidis, M. Rosner, & D. Tapias (eds.), *Proceedings of the 6th Language Resources and Evaluation Conference*. 351–58. Marrakech.

Rosso, M. A. 2008. User-based identification of web genres. *Journal of the American Society for Information Science and Technology* 59(7): 1053–72.

Rosso, M. A. & Haas, S. W. 2010. Identification of web genres by user warrant. In A. Mehler, S. Sharoff, & M. Santini (eds.), *Genres on the Web: Computational Models and Empirical Studies*. 47–68. New York: Springer.

Santini, M. 2007. Characterizing genres of web pages: genre hybridism and individualization. In R. H. Sprague (ed.), *Proceedings of the 40th Hawaii International Conference on System Sciences (HICSS-40)*. 1–10. Hawaii.

  2008. Zero, single, or multi? Genre of web pages through the users' perspective. *Information Processing and Management* 44: 702–37.

Santini, M. & Sharoff, S. 2009. Web genre benchmark under construction. *Journal for Language Technology and Computational Linguistics* 25(1): 125–41.

Scott, M. 1997. PC analysis of key words – and key key words. *System*, 25(2): 233–45.

Sharoff, S. 2005. Creating general-purpose corpora using automated search engine queries. In M. Baroni & S. Bernardini (eds.), *WaCky! Working Papers on the Web as Corpus*. 63–98. Bologna: GEDIT.

  2006. Open-source corpora: Using the net to fish for linguistic data. *International Journal of Corpus Linguistics* 11(4): 435–62.

  2018. Functional text dimensions for annotation of web corpora. *Corpora* 31(2).

Sharoff, S., Wu, Z., & Markert, K. 2010. The Web library of Babel: evaluating genre collections. In N. Calzolari, K. Choukri, B. Maegaard, J. Mariani, J. Odijk, S. Piperidis, M. Rosner, & D. Tapias (eds.), *Proceedings of the Seventh Language Resources and Evaluation Conference*. 3063–70. Malta: LREC 2010.

Sindoni, M. G. 2013. *Spoken and Written Discourse in Online Interactions*. New York: Routledge.

Staples, S. & Biber, D. 2015. Cluster analysis. In L. Plonsky (ed.), *Advancing Quantitative Methods in Second Language Research*. New York: Routledge.

Suri, S. & Watts, D. J. 2011. Cooperation and contagion in web-based, networked public goods experiments. *PLoS One*, 6(3): e16836.

Titak, A. & Roberson, A. 2013. Dimensions of web registers: An exploratory multi-dimensional comparison. *Corpora* 8(2): 239–71.

Vásquez, C. 2012. Narrativity and involvement in online consumer reviews: The case of TripAdvisor. *Narrative Inquiry*, 22(1): 105–21.

Vidulin, V., Luštrek, M., & Gams, M. 2009. Multi-label approaches to web genre identification. *Journal for Language Technology and Computational Linguistics* 24(1): 97–114.

Index